Refiguring the Sacred

Studies in the Thought of Paul Ricoeur

Series Editors: Greg S. Johnson, University of Providence, and Dan R. Stiver, Hardin-Simmons University

Studies in the Thought of Paul Ricoeur, a series in conjunction with the Society for Ricoeur Studies, aims to generate research on Ricoeur, about whom interest is rapidly growing both nationally (United States and Canada) and internationally. Broadly construed, the series has three interrelated themes. First, we develop the historical connections to and in Ricoeur's thought. Second, we extend Ricoeur's dialogue with contemporary thinkers representing a variety of disciplines. Third, we utilize Ricoeur to address future prospects in philosophy and other fields that respond to emerging issues of importance. The series approaches these themes from the belief that Ricoeur's thought is not just suited to theoretical exchanges, but can and does matter for how we actually engage in the many dimensions that constitute lived existence.

Recent Titles in the Series

Refiguring the Sacred

Conversations with Paul Ricoeur

Edited by Joseph A. Edelheit,
James F. Moore, and Mark I. Wallace

LEXINGTON BOOKS

Lanham • Boulder • New York • London

Published by Lexington Books
An imprint of The Rowman & Littlefield Publishing Group, Inc.
4501 Forbes Boulevard, Suite 200, Lanham, Maryland 20706
www.rowman.com

86-90 Paul Street, London EC2A 4NE

British Library Cataloguing in Publication Information Available

Library of Congress Cataloging-in-Publication Data

Names: Edelheit, Joseph A., editor. | Moore, James F., editor.| Wallace, Mark I.,
    1956-editor.
Title: Refiguring the sacred: conversations with Paul Ricoeur / edited by Joseph A.
    Edelheit, James F. Moore, and Mark I. Wallace.
Description: Lanham: Lexington Books, [2024] | Series:Studies in the thought of
    Paul Ricoeur | Includes bibliographical references and index.
Identifiers: LCCN 2024014978 (print) | LCCN 2024014979 (ebook) |
    ISBN 9781666919097 (cloth) | ISBN 9781666919103 (ebook)
Subjects: LCSH: Ricœur, Paul.
Classification: LCC B2430.R554 R44 2024 (print) | LCC B2430.R554 (ebook) |
    DDC 210.92–dc23/eng/20240514
LC record available at https://lccn.loc.gov/2024014978
LC ebook record available at https://lccn.loc.gov/2024014979

We dedicate these conversations about the Sacred to our grandchildren in the hope these ideas might engage you:

To: Arthur, Julia, Rafael, and Ruth; Ashley and Nathaly; Connor and Norah

Contents

Acknowledgments

"Fides quaerens intellectum: Biblical Antecedents," in *The Honeycomb of the World: Interpreting the Primary Testament* with André LaCocque, ed. W. Dow Edgerton (Chicago: Exploration Press, 2001), 179–208. Appearing by permission with the publisher.

"The Self in the Mirror of the Scriptures," in *The Whole and Divided Self: The Bible and Theological Anthropology*, ed. John McCarthy, trans. David Pellauer (New York: Crossroad, 1997), 201–20. Appearing by permission with the publisher.

All biblical references have been taken from:

The Jewish Study Bible. 2nd Edition (Oxford: Oxford University Press, 2014).

The New Revised Standard Version (New York: Harper Collins, 1993).

Acknowledgments

Part I

Introduction to Part I

All You Have Is the Text: Paul Ricoeur's Relationship with the Sacred

Joseph A. Edelheit and James F. Moore

ALWAYS THE TEXT

Paul Ricoeur's relationship with the Sacred is foundational to his lifelong relationship to the *text*! This chapter will introduce the ideas and framework of a book whose purpose is to celebrate Ricoeur's extraordinary legacy as a thinker, teacher, and communal model of dialogue.

Those attributes are the enduring links that we proudly confess as authorial bias; we were his students and have for more than four decades engaged his ideas together and separately in our academic careers and different religious communities. The Sacred is a dynamic that Ricoeur encounters through his multifaceted engagement with thinkers, ideas, and the text.

> I would say that the task of hermeneutics is to explicate the "world of the text."[1]

Ricoeur's legacy of hermeneutics as essential to the contemporary quest for meaning has textual traces already within Scripture; the Hebrew Bible has internal contexts for the text to be opened, explained, translated, and ultimately interpreted. Biblical authors included the need to translate and explain as essential:

בְּעֵבֶר הַיַּרְדֵּן בְּאֶרֶץ מוֹאָב הוֹאִיל מֹשֶׁה בֵּאֵר אֶת־הַתּוֹרָה הַזֹּאת לֵאמֹר:

On the other side of the Jordan, in the land of Moab, Moses undertook to expound this Teaching. He said: (Deuteronomy 1:5)[2]

וַיִּקְרְאוּ בַסֵּפֶר בְּתוֹרַת הָאֱלֹהִים מְפֹרָשׁ וְשׂוֹם שֶׂכֶל וַיָּבִינוּ בַּמִּקְרָא:

They read from the scroll of the Teaching of God, translating it, and giving the sense; so, they understood the reading. (Neh. 8:8)[3]

After 70 CE with the destruction of the Second Temple, the first post-biblical generation created various systems of interpretative schemes. These Rabbinic hermeneutics became the boundaries within which the Torah—the Written Law, would now become the interpreted material, but remain defined as Sacred, and the new content—the Oral Law, determined as equal to the revealed Law of Sinai, the original Torah. Scripture, the source of Rabbinic Judaism, was the source of all validity of the new religion and is never questioned because translation, explanation, and interpretation were all already essential with the scriptural text. Paul Ricoeur understood this critical dynamic when he argued:

> [M]ore important than this development of the content of the Law is the transformation in the relationship between the faithful believer and the Law. Without falling into that old rut of opposing the legalistic and the prophetic, we may discover in the very teaching of the Torah an increasing pulsation that turn by turn sets out the Law in terms of endlessly multiplying prescriptions and then draws it together, in the strong sense of the word, by summing it up in one set of commandments which only retain this being directed toward holiness.[4]

Analogically, there is an ancient precursor to Ricoeur whose unique intellectual and religious values transformed the biblical text. Ricoeur's contributions to hermeneutics are a curious echo of a first-century Rabbinic sage, Akiva ben Joseph. "Rabbi Akiva is this interpreter, the reader for whom the Torah is intended; he is—ontologically—the reader of Torah, since God composed the work with Rabbi Akiva in mind."[5] This comparison between Akiva and Ricoeur illuminates how the Sacred is not merely an ideal sought in ritual observance, but the intention with which that text is read, taught, and interpreted for the purpose of creating and sustaining community.

> "More than an organizer of traditions, Akiva was an interpreter of traditions, and his mode of interpretation set the tone for the approach to reading Jewish texts that influenced all of later Jewish religious history." The legacy of Akiva encompasses not only his specific teachings; perhaps even more influential was his vision of the nature of interpretation, a view that helped define the center of Judaism in general and Jewish learning in particular from his time forward.[6]

Contemporary scholars emphasize that Akiva's unique legacy: "If Rabbi Akiba had not stood up in his time, the Torah would have been forgotten in Israel." "He brought together analytic acuity with systematic farsightedness, methodic virtuosity with ingenious originality, learnedness with profundity, productivity in theory with pedagogical effectiveness, a powerful mind with a holy way of life."[7]

Similarly, Ricoeur, the twentieth -century French Protestant, argues consistently that the text, especially Scripture, requires intentional critical reading:

> This is why I prefer to turn toward some structures of the interpretation of human experience to discern there those traits through which something has always been comprehensible under the idea of revelation understood in a religious sense of the term. "It is this comprehension that may enter into consonance with the non-violent appeal of biblical revelation."[8] "The world of the text designates the reference of the work of discourse, not what is said, but about what it is said. Hence the issue of the text is the object of hermeneutics."[9]

THE "SACRED" IN INTERPRETATION

Though Scriptural interpretation is a classic discipline within Western religious history and thought; Ricoeur transcends the parochial limits of Scripture to argue and model that any and every text be opened, explained, and interpreted with similar critical intention. He models his engagement, "the text is the object of hermeneutics" as he develops his multidisciplinary methodologies. His passionate pursuit of understanding and meaning is the foundation also of his experience of the Sacred from within his relationship with the text.

Abraham Joshua Heschel describes the "holy activity" of Scriptural interpretation which forever transformed Jewish life:

> Jewry found itself in a time of cultural change. The Temple, the state, the aristocracy, the parties had been destroyed. The cultic and political powers, the religious, mystical, poetic, and scholarly energies dissolved almost entirely into the generating of a new fruit: the Talmud. Engagement with the Talmud became the living manifestation of the people, traditional scholarship became a holy activity, education the highest value.[10]

Heschel and Holtz among others describe Rabbi Akiva as the essential source of Rabbinic authority, a unique representation of the Sacred established through Rabbinic interpretation. Akiva takes up the tasks of Moses explaining the text in Deuteronomy 1:5 and Ezra translating the text in Neh. 8:8. Scripture was only accessible when humans read, explained, and translated it, only then could the community engage its Sacred character. Let us use these two stories, as narratives to open a time lost to us, during which the Sacred, as interpreted from Scripture, sustains the community beyond its revelatory origins.

The Sages taught: Four entered the orchard [*Pardes*], i.e., dealt with the loftiest secrets of Torah, and they are as follows: Ben Azzai; and Ben Zoma; *Aḥer*, the other, a name for Elisha ben Avuya; and Rabbi Akiva. Rabbi Akiva, the senior among them, said to them: When, upon your arrival in the upper worlds, you reach pure marble stones, do not say: Water, water, although they appear to be water, because it is stated: "He who speaks falsehood shall not be established before My eyes" (Psalms 101:7). The Gemara proceeds to relate what happened to each of them: Ben Azzai glimpsed at the Divine Presence and died. And with regard to him the verse states: "Precious in the eyes of the Lord is the death of His pious ones" (Psalms 116:15). Ben Zoma glimpsed at the Divine Presence and was harmed, i.e., he lost his mind. And with regard to him the verse states: "Have you found honey? Eat as much as is sufficient for you, lest you become full from it and vomit it" (Proverbs 25:16). *Aḥer* chopped down the shoots of saplings. In other words, he became a heretic. Rabbi Akiva came out safely.[11]

This legend conveys the religious chaos of the early Rabbinic generations, during which the pursuit of the Sacred still entailed life or death risks. The paradigm shift from biblical Israelite culture is illustrated with only Akiva leaving the experience "safely," which of course affirms that his hermeneutic insights are safe and valid for the community. In other words, this story conveys upon Akiva the authority of his system of hermeneutics by which the text will be opened for all generations, but in offering him this position, it also confirms the risks to anyone who does not stay within these communal boundaries. Ricoeur understood these risks:

Only a trial can decide between Yahweh and the "idols of nothing." The works and signs that the revealer "gives" are so many bits of evidence and means of proof in the grand trial of the absolute. Hermeneutics arises there a second time: no manifestation of the absolute without the crisis of false testimony, without the decision which distinguishes sign and idol.[12]

The inexplicable nature of the *Pardes* will become a later reference point as medieval Rabbinic scholars use the word as an acronym: PaRDeS. This represents the four ways to interpret the biblical text: *P'shat*-literal; *Remez*-hint; *Drash*-exegesis; *Sod*-hidden secret. Curiously, Ricoeur seems to understand the challenge that Akiva faced:

In this regard the idea of something secret is the limit-idea of revelation. The idea of revelation is a twofold idea. "The God who reveals himself is a hidden God and hidden things belong to him." . . .The revelation takes place between the secret and the revealed.[13]

The fall of the Temple, end of the priestly cult, and presence of prophets required that God's revealed presence be codified in/through the text which was interpreted by humans with a projected authority of the Divine. The interpretation of Scripture permits the community to experience the authority of Moses' commandments, as now revealed through the rules of interpretation taught by Rabbi Akiva. The Rabbis who authored these narrative texts imagined Akiva using his unique role as the paradigmatic reader, translator, and interpreter of the Scriptural text as a revered model of Rabbinic behavior. The revealed text is the source of the Sacred, now is lived by the community led by its teachers and the interpreters of their texts.

Another significant passage from the Babylonian Talmud, *Menachot 59b*, offers us the religious philosophy foundational to the power, risk, and necessity of interpreting Scripture.

> Rav Yehuda says that Rav says: When Moses ascended on High, he found the Holy One, Blessed be He, sitting and tying crowns on the letters of the Torah. Moses said before God: Master of the Universe, who is preventing You from giving the Torah without these additions? God said to him: There is a man who is destined to be born after several generations, and Akiva ben Yosef is his name; he is destined to derive from each and every thorn of these crowns mounds upon mounds of *halakhot*. It is for his sake that the crowns must be added to the letters of the Torah.
>
> Moses said before God: Master of the Universe, show him to me. God said to him: Return behind you. Moses went and sat at the end of the eighth row in Rabbi Akiva's study hall and did not understand what they were saying. Moses' strength waned, as he thought his Torah knowledge was deficient. When Rabbi Akiva arrived at the discussion of one matter, his students said to him: My teacher, from where do you derive this? Rabbi Akiva said to them: It is a *halakha* transmitted to Moses from Sinai. When Moses heard this, his mind was put at ease, as this too was part of the Torah that he was to receive.
>
> Moses returned and came before the Holy One, Blessed be He, and said before Him: Master of the Universe, You have a man as great as this and yet You still choose to give the Torah through me. Why? God said to him: Be silent; this intention arose before Me. Moses said before God: Master of the Universe, You have shown me Rabbi Akiva's Torah, now show me his reward. God said to him: Return to where you were. Moses went back and saw that they were weighing Rabbi Akiva's flesh in a butcher shop [*bemakkulin*], as Rabbi Akiva was tortured to death by the Romans. Moses said before Him: Master of the Universe, this is Torah, and this is its reward? God said to him: Be silent; this intention arose before Me.[14]

The Rabbinic authors of this legend/fable understand that the community to and for whom the Torah was revealed fully depends upon the new class of sage/Torah interpreter. They created a narrative about themselves in which authority for their product—a post-biblical religion that requires entirely new rituals, new observances, religious ethics, and all done in the Diaspora in which the community is vulnerable to the power of the majority. The power of interpretation is much more than textual explanation, now the process of interpretive engagement imitates the Divine presence.

The Rabbi Akiba, which Heschel presents from within the emerging trauma of Nazi Germany, using the trauma of Jerusalem post 70 CE, is an apt point of reflection. Survival of the Jewish community has always required the leaders to return to the traditional texts from within the world of their work to find the source of adaptation regardless of the threats. Heschel fled his native Poland, and then Berlin, and finally London to find refuge in America. He had to seek new methodologies to sustain the continuity with the European Judaism soon to be destroyed and the assimilated American Jewish community after Auschwitz. Akiva's model emerges in each generation in the search for the Sacred by opening the text to translation, explanation, and interpretation.

The world of the work influences how minds like Ricoeur, Akiva, and Heschel responded to the challenges of trauma to find hope. It is more than merely curious that Ricoeur would find meaning in translating Husserl in order to teach as a German prisoner of war in 1940. His act of intense engagement of learning, thinking, translating, and then teaching was a pattern he would use his entire career.

The European social, economic, and political environments within which Ricoeur's ideas were forged is described in Colin Davis' *Traces of War: Interpreting Ethics and Trauma in Twentieth-Century French Writing*. Paul Ricoeur is included in the section "Prisoners of War Give Philosophy Classes." Using Ricoeur's "Intellectual Autobiography," Davis argues:

> The context suggests that perhaps also the tragedy of the First World War is reawakened by the events of the Second. Moreover, war becomes the intellectual grid through which Ricoeur understands his own development in his early years as a student of philosophy, dealing with the competing demands of rational enquiry and Christian belief: Ricoeur's identity becomes the site of an unfinished, unresolved war.[15]

Davis concludes with a perspective of Ricoeur's legacy with themes that are emphasized by others:

> The great themes of Ricoeur's thought all have direct relevance to the questions raised by his account of the war years, even if they do not broach them directly: history, time, truth, narrative, the configuration of the self, amnesty and forgiveness falsification of the hermeneutic tradition. Conflict, or the undecidability of competing interpretations, is at the heart of hermeneutics, and particularly of Ricoeur's version of it. War, I want to suggest, has permeated the very fabric of his thought. It is what Ricoeur experiences, as a Christian, socialist, pacifist subject who spent five years as a prisoner of war; and it is also what defines,

at the most fundamental level, what it means to be a post-war philosopher, and specifically a philosopher of hermeneutics. . . .This attempt to bring together conflicting positions is absolutely fundamental to Ricoeur's manner of thought and writing . . . . It is as if he wanted to omit no one and nothing, to bring everything together not so much in a grand synthesis as in a peaceful dialogue. Just in terms of its breadth of reference, it is impressive. Among others, Ricoeur refers to great European thinkers (Kant, Hegel), representatives of the German hermeneutic tradition (Schleiermacher, Dilthey), Anglo-American speech act theorists (Austin, Searle), specialists in linguistics (Saussure Helmsley, Benveniste, Chomsky) and structuralists (Lévi-Strauss). At no point does he give a sense that there might be irreconcilable differences between these thinkers and positions. Everyone can be brought together in a generous, all-encompassing discourse.[16]

Ricoeur leaves us with more than his ideas about the transcendence that is possible when fully engaged in the text, his philosophy was lived as his methodology. "What Ricoeur has described as the 'desire to translate,' even the 'pulsion,' the drive to translate is invoked as the unceasing effort to create the conditions for dialogue."[17] Kathleen Blamey was his student and became one of his longtime translators, one who understood the task of illuminating his texts for other readers:

The difficulties and obstacles to translation have to be confronted and addressed within the real world, in the context of natural languages characterized by the condition of dispersion and dislocation. Multiplicity, diversity is not viewed by Ricoeur as an imperfection to be overcome, but as the defining characteristic of the human condition, the fact of human plurality. For this reason, the desire to translate, to connect, to engage with others is always already underway. To express this conviction, in "The Paradigm of Translation," Ricoeur proposes his own interpretation—citing the contemporary French translation by Chouraqui— of the myth of Babel, a recounting casting neither condemnation nor accusation. The narrative of dispersion described here is a given, a state of affairs, and responding to this situation, translation is called for, in Hannah Arendt's words, as "the thing to be done so that human action can simply continue."[18]

THE DIVINITY SCHOOL LEGACY

Paul Ricoeur was not limited by language or circumstances; he intentionally took risks to encounter thinkers and their ideas beyond France and Europe. He accepted the so-called Tillich Chair at the Divinity School of the University of Chicago, where he spent decades thinking, engaging in new dialogues often as he taught, writing, and always modeling his relationship with the text. It was there that he shared his profound hermeneutic insights with, among others, David Tracy, the noted Catholic theologian. Together they engaged in their shared commitment to the responsibility of a thinker's public communal religious thought.

David Tracy's reflections on his colleague's legacy offer a significant affirmation of the themes of Ricœur's unique role in contemporary religious philosophical thinking:

- "For Ricoeur, the radical Freudian hermeneutics of suspicion should also be taken as a serious challenge by any philosophical religious anthropology . . . . For Ricoeur, therefore, hermeneutics will mediate its positive meaning only in a dialectic with Freud, as well as, for Ricoeur, with the other two 'masters of suspicion' Nietzsche and Marx."[19]
- "Ricoeur will attempt to mediate between Gadamerian hermeneutics of basic trust and Habermasian critical theory by establishing a dialectic between those two major forms of contemporary philosophical hermeneutics."[20]
- "Ricoeur's next step in developing his ever more complex hermeneutical philosophy can be understood only by returning to his agreement with and difference from Heidegger and Gadamer."[21]
- "Furthermore, Ricoeur later joined Hannah Arendt and Emmanuel Levinas to criticize Heidegger's refusal to allow for any ethical reading of his ontological analytic of *Dasein* in *Sein* and *Zeit* . . . . Ricoeur himself argued with both Levinas and Arendt over their own too-short routes."[22]
- "Above all, Ricoeur regularly turned to his two favorite classics: the texts of Aristotle and Kant."[23]
- "Dialectic in Ricoeur's most basic use (he occasionally changes) possesses the following elements. In general terms, dialectic for Ricoeur means an interpretation of opposites leading to the conclusion that the original conflicting opposites need not be read simply as conflictual opposites but can be interpreted as diametrically interrelated opposites and sometimes as complementary polarities. At the end of his dialectical analyses, Ricoeur argues that each opposite posits itself by implying its other."[24]
- "Ricoeur's hermeneutical drive to establish a dialectic between initially conflicting opposites is actually one of his most characteristic and frequent philosophical gestures."[25]
- "In this final move, Ricoeur also argues that some original opposites (understanding or explanation; hermeneutics or critical theory; archaeology or teleology—and, in religion, manifestation [Eliade] or proclamation [Barth]) can be philosophically, that is, hermeneutically, interpreted into dialectical but mutually contradictory, opposites by showing how much each opposite is positing itself also implies its other."[26]

Tracy concludes his critical review of Ricoeur's thought and legacy of ideas, "Paul Ricoeur articulated a powerful and subtle, strictly philosophical attention to religion, both as a cultural phenomenon and as a personal conviction. . . . He was a hermeneutical philosopher of religion both rigorous in his analyses and arguments and open to any methods that can clarify the issues under discussion. . . . May his work, in all its complexity, continue to be studied."[27]

The breadth and depth of Ricoeur's conversations is acknowledged as a defining characteristic, and as Tracy concludes, "a hermeneutical philosopher of religion" Ricoeur requires his students and colleagues to be open to the tension between thinkers. The Sacred is not limited by the experience of faith, but rather the willingness to understand differently through the critical encounter with the text. Andre LaCocque, Ricoeur's dialogue and writing partner of a *Thinking Biblically: Exegetical and Hermeneutical Studies*, writes:

> It is in interpreting the Scriptures in question that the community in question interprets itself. A kind of mutual election takes place here between those texts taken as foundational and the community we have deliberately called a community of reading and interpretation. If this circle is not vicious to the eyes of the faithful belonging to such communities, it is because the founding role attached to the sacred texts and the founded condition of the historical community do not designate interchangeable places. . . . Even when this relation surpasses that between authority and obedience to become one of love, the difference in altitude between the word that teaches with authority and the one that responds with acknowledgement cannot be abolished.[28]

Ricoeur believes that the Sacred is not limited by a communal claim of one text over another. His commitment to read and interpret in order to understand all texts is emphasized in his conclusion to "Interpretation Theory." "I say that interpretation is the process by which disclosure of new modes of being—or if you prefer Wittgenstein to Heidegger, of new forms of life—gives to the subject a new capacity for knowing himself."[29] We encounter the Sacred in our willingness to risk the transformative power of each text, which always provides the possibility of "knowing" yourself differently.

Ricoeur is the ultimate expression of multi-disciplinarity, always opening one text in order to engage in a new conversation, new interpretation, another explanation of a previous reading. We learned from our teacher, engage the text, "All you have is the text!" Hence, we must finally, return to Ricoeur himself, the final text he left us, "The Course of Recognition." Here are the three lectures which Ricoeur gave at the *Institut fur de Wissenchaften vom Menschen*, and then developed at the Husserl Archives, Freiburg; we literally conclude our review where and with whom Ricoeur began his own intellectual journey.

In his final "Conclusion," just twenty-four pages, he engages language/ definition, the Greeks, Kant, Hegel, Hannah Arendt, Descartes, Karl Jaspers Merlu-Ponty, Husserl, Derrida, Husserl-Levinas, Simone Weil, and Montaigne. Serious Ricoeur students understand that he is once again and always in conversation with these thinkers, their ideas, and their texts. These conversations had literally filled his entire lifetime and he was not finished but merely pausing for the next generation to continue where he just happened to stop.

> It is in the "between" of the expression "between the protagonists of the exchange" that is concentrated the dialectic of the dissymmetry between me and others and the mutuality of our relations.[30]

How profound a final thought by Ricouer, the "between" and the dialectic between himself and others, "*and the mutuality of our relations.*" (emphasis mine). Ricoeur's instruction to the end, is about the "between" the relational necessity of his thought; and now his legacy, engagement begins with the text, for the ultimate purpose of understanding which would lead to "the mutuality of relations." His final lectures draw from his foundational experiences in translation, explanation, and interpretation of the German thinkers of his youth but build upon his lifetime of interpretation for the purpose of finding transformative meaning in the texts and ideas that continue to challenge him. His goal throughout his life was creating the conversations that might be cornerstones to "the mutuality of our relations," and nothing is more Sacred that such an aspirational vision.

PAUL RICOEUR AND THE "SACRED"

This final image of Ricoeur's thinking that brought together voices from his lifetime of reflection is not offered as a conclusion as if he were bringing all of his thought to an end point but rather emerges as an invitation to his table. He gathers these voices in order to start a conversation and not to end it. He writes with the belief that there is so much more to be said, to discover, to understand. Our book is patterned after that hope with various voices now reflecting on Ricoeur's thought first presented in the collection of *Figuring the Sacred*. We also believe that a focus on the Sacred brings us to one of the core conversations that Paul Ricoeur engages with these many voices even from the earliest texts to the very last.

Paul Ricoeur says in *The Symbolism of Evil* that myth possesses the "power of discovering and revealing the bond between man and what he considers sacred."[31] This comment in an early work by Ricoeur already shows two things about Ricoeur's thought and what we hope is revealed in this book. First, Ricoeur assumes that it is through the text (in this case, the myths) that we connect with the sacred. Second, this bond is a conversation in which an interaction occurs between the human and the sacred. In this early text, Ricoeur also accepts a view of the sacred taken from the history of religions that the sacred is culturally shaped. There is no sense that the sacred transcends the specific mythic or cultural representation.

Of course, Ricoeur develops this understanding more fully in the chapter "Manifestation and Proclamation," which appears in the collection *Figuring the Sacred*.[32] The full scope of the work in that chapter will be one of the several reflections that will be explored in this current book as part of our *Refiguring the Sacred*. In that work Ricoeur builds on the work of Rudolf Otto and identifies the sacred as the "numinous." Thus, though still using the history of religions and especially Mircea Eliade, Ricoeur now defines the sacred as transcendent to the human world. So. if the myth is the connection between the human and what is sacred, this connection represents a sort of translation between what is ineffable and what is part of the profane.

The reflection presented here, then, explores these themes as a prologue to the further analyses found in the chapters in this book. In addition, this portion of our introduction aims to situate the work on the Sacred found in Ricoeur's writing in Ricoeur's overall work as well as in his style of philosophical thought. In order to do the latter, the reflection here will also draw in personal experiences taken from the writer's time spent in the classroom observing Ricoeur as teacher and thinker (in fact, both happening at the same time). This set of observations shows the process of his developing thinking that cannot be fully seen in his writing alone. In incorporating the personal observations, this introduction can also reinforce our belief that Ricoeur set every point of personal contemplation as a conversation, a dialogue between his thinking at the point he found himself in relation to the range of other voices he was engaging at any one time. All of this, of course, was set into the engagement of the reader drawn into a conversation (also, the observing student in the classroom). From this conversation emerges meaning as an ever-developing process.

CONVERSATION

We start with an idea that every conversation is a translation. This would be a logical implication of Ricoeur's claim that meaning lies between the reader and the text. This connection can be offered as a thought exercise exploring the implications of key themes in Ricoeur's thought. This exercise considers "translation" with a broader meaning so that the interaction between partners in dialogue requires a form of translation, converting the spoken word into a meaning that is understood by the listener. Of course, if engaged in a common language, this conversion is an effort to understand, that is, an interpretation. The meaning lies between the two speakers and because interactive with both parties engaged in this process of translation/interpretation. The meaning can be shared to a point but functions rather as two different meanings as constructed by each conversant.

The spoken word becomes a text for the listener to reconstruct in that person's own view of that reality. Though each person is present, the text is actually all that remains as the conversation proceeds. The meaning is in the developing text. If the parties speak in different languages clearly the meaning and the translation must be mediated, perhaps by an interpreter. The translation is then an interpretation that is filtered through the process of constructing meaning. This form of meaning construction is clearly what is often meant as translation. However, the difference in language now creates a problematic that emerges as two languages may not have direct correspondence in words and meanings. Such then becomes the problem in understanding as the translation is an interpretation suggesting a correspondence that may not be exact. The result may produce what Ricoeur has called a "conflict of interpretations."[33] Nevertheless, what remains again is the text now spoken. The text in the end is all we have.

We can make this even more practical and obvious by recalling the process that unfolded for many of us as we sat in the lecture room listening to Ricoeur present in a way that was typical for him and familiar for us. In the lecture the student listens and attempts to follow the logic of Ricoeur's comments. In doing so, the student is reconstructing what Ricoeur is saying and in this sense translating the text to produce a meaning. It would be fair to say that the end result was likely a multitude of constructions as each student would listen and hear differently. Again, Ricoeur's idea that meaning lies between the text and the reader plays out since the listening process results in a merging of horizons. The product is itself a text, perhaps even existing in student notes.[34]

However, the process described above is only part of the dynamic as Ricoeur taught almost always by meticulously reading and interpreting a text. The texts chosen would be texts in a non-English language which would be read by Ricoeur in the original rather than in translation. As students we quickly learned that we should bring the original text to class as a referent such as in our reading of Heidegger's *Sein Un Zeit* since Ricoeur would make reference to the German in this case and sometimes reflect on this in French as well as in English. The assumption is that Ricoeur saw this close reading of a text as his means for teaching thus was fully aware that he was reading the text to invoke an interaction with the students even though it was not always clear that Ricoeur needed this in order for the reading to be productive (he was sometimes captured in his own process of reflection as he was reading with purpose always and each reading was a new engagement and not just a replay or producing what he had already thought in the past or said before to a former class. That is, he was engaged in a conversation with the text and with that the presumed author of the text).

A clear example of this would be Ricoeur's lectures on Aristotle's *Nichomachean Ethics* in which Ricoeur was clearly trying to explore how that text offered insight into the link between action and narrative. But as this is noted, the complexity of the process is revealed as well since the lecture was both an interrelation and a translation engaged in a conversation with the text and the students. Ricoeur was the translator mediating that meaning and producing his text that the students would then take and reconstruct for themselves. We can use the word conversation because the process was an open engagement and not merely intended as a monologue. Meaning emerges then and is not merely assumed or resting on what was before. Ricoeur expected that each class would produce something new both for him and the students. When that did not happen for him, he was disappointed as when he remarked to the class while reading Heidegger that he did not find what he was looking for. The students found plenty as they were listening to Ricoeur on Heidegger and not merely reflecting on Heidegger.

The experience of sitting in the classroom as Ricoeur would read and produce new text (many times taking that and putting it to print) is informative about Ricoeur's writing as a whole in that his writing was a conversational process that was open-ended, expecting that this would produce new insight. Thus, the many texts that were ultimately produced remain these disparate conversations without a clear systematic organization of the results. Clearly, his thought does develop and build toward new thought based on what was done in the past, often actually changing his mind about key things along the way. His treatment of Biblical texts shows this shift in a range of ways. Even so, Ricoeur must be read as he preferred to work as if we are invited into a conversation that is developing along the way not to form a system but rather to address particular concerns, problems, and issues. Thus, we think of this gathering of essays in this current book as a re-figuring not only as a play upon the title of the text published before but rather as a commitment to this process of interpretation/translation as an ongoing open-ended reflection and not as something finished as if a conversation could ever come to a conclusion.

A BRIDGE TOWARD DIALOGUE

This draws us back to the opening comment and to Ricoeur and the Sacred. Ricoeur uses both Otto and Eliade in the analysis in "Manifestation and Proclamation."[35] With Eliade, we have the symbolism that pervades the religions such as the "holy mountain.": With Otto we have the notion of absolute transcendence. Thus, the sacred is presented (made manifest) through the sacred place (the mountain, the tablets of the commands) but is not identical to the symbol (thus, the command not to make graven images). The end result is the encounter with the holy that at once includes the absolute difference and separation of the sacred yet also involves an immanence, a connection.

This sense is present in the figure of Moses as we find in Deuteronomy 1:5 who is not the Sacred but is a mediator. In most cases, Moses passes on as instruction what the Lord commands. In some cases, the people are said to do what Moses says for them to do. The people do not have a direct connection to the Sacred but require this mediator. The notion of mediation is also present in Nehemiah 8—"They read from the scroll of the Teaching of God, translating it and giving the sense; so they understood the reading." The text is interesting in that both translation and interpretation are included in what was needed by the people returning from exile. They no longer were able to understand either the language of the traditions or the sense (the meaning) of what was said. Translation is interpretation and the presentation of the texts (the proclamation) would lead to a manifestation (a giving of the sense of the texts).[36]

This latter point represents what happens within the tradition when the mediator no longer is present, and we cannot get behind the text as Ricoeur argues to reproduce the author. We have the text and those who would read and interpret the text. "The text is all we have." This point seems to be the implication of the reference to Akiba in that Akiba is not really Moses but claims to present what Moses intended. We note that doing this, actually presenting the sense of the Sacred is risky, dangerous. This point, that we have now the task to translate and give the sense, that is we have texts and offer interpretation.

Naturally, this point brings us back again to the Ricoeurian analysis of the process that implies that interpretation is a process, a conversation with the text. Each encounter brings a new sense, a new merging of horizons. We must always ask; how now do we understand since each approach to the text (the text is all we have) begins anew. We have the traditions of interpretation of those who are also brought to the table for discussion, but this reading is now new, made new by the world, our world now brought to the reading of the text. We ask what that is. We read Ricoeur again also in this vein. What does it mean to re-figure the sacred given this new approach, our different world?

RE-THINKING TWENTY-FIVE YEARS LATER

The first part of this book is a first contribution to this re-thinking with five scholars, all with personal and/or professional experience thinking with and about Paul Ricoeur's writing on the Sacred. Each author has written a reflection both on the writings that first appeared in each part of *Figuring the Sacred* and also writing to project what those themes mean for our world today, a new interpretative horizon. Thus, this becomes a refiguring.

The finished texts take on themes from Ricoeur's writing but now set them in new configurations, such as with the chapter by Steven Kepnes thinking his way to Ricoeur and Jewish philosophical and religious thinkers. This refiguring of the conversation is what Ricoeur intended from the outset, not seeing his texts as the endpoint with simple commentaries on his thoughts but rather as a starting point for ever new conversations. Thus, we see with George Taylor a chapter on the imagination now taking the ideas further, exploring new dimensions (even indicating that the work will be continued in a much more detailed work). Timo Helenius takes on Ricoeur's reflections on the Bible by focusing on the theme of self-identification. Dan Stiver reflects on the practical element of religious reflection by considering the poetic as a form of praxis. Stephanie Arel adds a dimension of feminist thought to the way scholars read Ricoeur's work for theological themes focusing on the theme of hope and connecting this to counseling women who have experienced trauma. There is clearly an important statement in this way Stephanie has developed the connection in reminding us that Ricoeur was committed to practical application.

Evidently, the final package does not presume to consider all the rich dimensions of Ricoeur's reflections as were produced in the chapters in *Figuring the Sacred*. Thus, the aim is that these chapters form a beginning to new conversations not just about Ricoeur's thought but from his thought toward ever new developing conversations, a point the authors assume is consummately Ricoeurian. The hope is that the chapters will spur new reflections and additional texts that take up these themes as well as others that follow from the rich thought of Paul Ricoeur on the Sacred.

NOTES

1. Edelheit, Joseph A. and James F Moore, "Introduction," in *Reading Scripture with Paul Ricoeur*, Lantham: Lexington Books, 2021, p. 8.

2. "Deuteronomy 1.5," Sefaria a living library of Jewish texts online https://www.sefaria.org/Deuteronomy.1.5?lang=bi&aliyot=0

3. "Nehemiah 8.8," Sefaria a living library of Jewish texts online https://www.sefaria.org/Nehemiah.8.8?lang=bi

4. Ricoeur, Paul, "Toward a Hermeneutic of the Idea of Revelation," in *Essays on Biblical Interpretation*, Lewis Mudge, ed., Phil., Fortress Press, 1980, p. 85.

5. Holz, Barry, Rabbi Akiva: *Sage of the Talmud*, New Haven, CT: Yale, p. 185.

6. Op.cit, p. 188.

7. Heschel, Abraham Joshua, "Rabbi Akiba" *in In this Hour: Heshel's Writings in Nazi Germany and London Exile*, Phil, The Jewish Publication Society, 2019, p. 57.

8. Ricoeur, "Toward a Hermeneutic of the Idea of Revelation," in *Essays on Biblical Interpretation*, p. 97.

9. Op. cit., p. 100.

10. Heschel, op. cit. p. 57.

11. "Chagigah." Sefaria a living library of Jewish texts online, https://www.sefaria .org/Chagigah.14b?lang=en.

12. Ricoeur, Paul, "The Hermeneutics of Testimony," in *Essays on Biblical Interpretation*, Lewis Mudge ed., Phil, Fortress Press, p. 146.

13. Ricoeur, "Toward a Hermeneutic of the Idea of Revelation," *Essays of Biblical Interp.* p. 93–94.

14. "Menachot 29b," Sefaria a living library of Jewish texts online, https://www .sefaria.org/Menachot.29b?lang=en.

15. Davis, Colin, "Prisoners of War Give Philosophy Classes," in *Traces of War: Interpreting Ethics and Trauma in Twentieth Century French Writing*, Liverpool: Liverpool University Press, 2018, p. 123.

16. Op. cit. p. 129.

17. Blaney, Kathleen, "Resistance and Recognition: Paul Ricoeur on Translation," in *Reading Scripture with Paul Ricoeur*, Edelheit/Moore: Lexington Books, 2021, 40.

18. Op. cit. p. 33.

19. Tracy, David, "Paul Ricoeur: Hermeneutics and the Dialectic of Religious Forms", in *Fragments: The Existential Situations of Our Time*, Chicago, The University of Chicago Press, 2020, p. 214.

20. Op. cit. p. 215

21. Ibid.

22. Op cit. p. 216.

23. Op. cit. p. 218.

24. Op. cit. p. 220.

25. Op. cit. p. 221.

26. Op. cit. p. 229.

27. Op. cit. p. 235.

28. LaCocque, Andre and Paul Ricoeur, *Thinking Biblically: Exegetical and Hermeneutical Studies*, Chicago: The University of Chicago, 1998, p. xvii.

29. Ricoeur, Paul, *Interpretation Theory: Discourse and the Surplus of Meaning*, Fort Worth: Texas Christian University Press, 1976, p. 94.

30. Ricoeur, Paul, *The Course of Recognition*, Cambridge: Harvard University Press, 2005, p. 263.

31. Paul Ricoeur. *The Symbolism of Evil*, New York: Harper and Row, 1969, p. 5.

32. Paul Ricoeur, "Manifestation and Proclamation," in *Figuring the Sacred*, Mark Wallace, ed. Minneapolis, MN: Fortress Press, 1995, pp. 48–67.

33. See, Paul Ricoeur's *The Conflict of Interpretations: Essays in Hermeneutics*, Evanston, IL: Northwestern University Press, 2007.

34. See, Hegel, Georg Wilhelm Friedrich, *Lectures on the Philosophy of Religion*: One-Volume Edition, Berkley, CA: University of California Press; Reprint edition, 1988.

35. Op cit. pp., 49–51.

36. All biblical references in this part are taken from, *The New Revised Standard Version*, New York: Harper Collins, 1993.

BIBLIOGRAPHY

Blaney, Kathleen, "Resistance and Recognition: Paul Ricoeur on Translation," in *Reading Scripture with Paul Ricoeur*, Edelheit/Moore, Lexington Books, 2021, 40.

Davis, Colin, "Prisoners of War Give Philosophy Classes," in *Traces of War: Interpreting Ethics and Trauma in Twentieth Century French Writing*, Liverpool: Liverpool University Press, 2018.

Edelheit, Joseph and James F. Moore, eds. *Reading Scripture with Paul Ricoeur*, Lantham: Lexington Books, 2021.

Hegel, Georg Wilhelm Friedrich, *Lectures on the Philosophy of Religion*: One-Volume Edition, Berkley, CA: University of California Press; Reprint edition, 1988.

Heschel, Abraham Joshua, "Rabbi Akiba" in *In this Hour: Heshel's Writings in Nazi Germany and London Exile,* Phil, The Jewish Publication Society, 2019.

Holz, Barry, Rabbi Akiva: *Sage of the Talmud*, New Haven, CT: Yale.

LaCocque, Andre and Paul Ricoeur, *Thinking Biblically: Exegetical and Hermeneutical Studies*, Chicago: The University of Chicago, 1998.

Ricoeur, Paul. *The Conflict of Interpretations: Essays in Hermeneutics,* Evanston, IL: Northwestern University Press, 2007.

Ricoeur, Paul, *Interpretation Theory: Discourse and the Surplus of Meaning*, Fort Worth: Texas Christian University Press, 1976.

Ricoeur, Paul, "Manifestation and Proclamation" in Figuring the Sacred, Mark Wallace, ed. Minneapolis: Fortress Press, 1995.

Ricoeur, Paul, *The Course of Recognition*, Cambridge: Harvard University Press, 2005.

Ricoeur, Paul. *The Symbolism of Evil*, New York: Harper and Row, 1969.

Ricoeur, Paul, "Toward a Hermeneutic of the Idea of Revelation," in *Essays on Biblical Interpretation,* Lewis Mudge, ed., Phil., Fortress Press, 1980.

Chapter 1

Paul Ricoeur's Biblical Theology and Jewish Theology

Steven Kepnes

Paul Ricoeur's main identity is as a French philosopher in the tradition of phenomenology, post-structuralism, and hermeneutics. However, he had a classical Western philosophical education which included knowledge of the great theological tradition from Augustine to the French Neo-Thomists, Étienne Gilson, and Jacques Maritain. He experienced the European disasters of the Second World War and the Holocaust and was briefly interned in prison. This gave him a sensitivity to the fragility of democracy and the perils of fascism and the need for philosophy to address the ethical issues of the day. Ricoeur was not schooled in Rabbinic Judaism but he did read the great Jewish thinkers of modernity from Buber, to Rosenzweig, to Levinas. As a French philosopher growing up in the heyday of French atheistic existentialism and socialism his interests both in the broad sweep of Western philosophy and particularly in theology made him less than popular in France. And he found a warm welcome at the Divinity School of the University of Chicago at the time when it was still in its theological glory days with figures like Langden Gilkey, Shubert Ogden and Nathan Scott, Mircea Eliade, Martin Marty, and David Tracy.

Ricoeur was definitely a Christian but his work in texts and specifically in biblical texts and their interpretation brought him closer to Judaism than most of his colleagues in the Divinity School. Unlike many of his colleagues who were ministers and priests as well as professors, Ricoeur was a philosopher without a Church portfolio. He therefore was free of the responsibility to speak for a Christian denomination and could move between Catholicism, Protestantism, and through his interest in the work of Eliade, to diverse manifestations of religion in the sweep of world religions. Ricoeur also felt free to speak in a critical almost "prophetic" voice against what he saw as certain problems in Christianity. This is most clearly seen in his insistence that the primary language of Christianity is found in scripture, in the Bible, and not philosophical theology even as we have said, he did respect the theological tradition. However, even as he asserted the primacy of the Bible his position was not the *sola scriptura* of Protestantism, but rather a return to text mediated by literary theory and the hermeneutics of Wilhlem Dilthey and Martin Heidegger and then Hans-Georg Gadamer. This hermeneutics of the text not only brought with it a deep appreciation for the literary structures and rhetorical devices of the Bible but also the insistence that interpreting the Bible required a multiple, ever-changing exegesis that was dependent on the needs of the community of interpreters who read the Bible. Here, Ricoeur's biblical hermeneutics is miles away from Protestant literalism and also, I might say, a far distance from the historical critical approach that was popular in Catholic circles of his day.

Finally, and this is my point, in his respect for the text and its rhetoric and literary devices along with his appreciation of multiple and changing interpretations, Ricoeur's biblical hermeneutics comes close to Jewish hermeneutics. And since his investigations into the biblical text and its interpretations culminate in some rather surprising and perceptive theological insights, which are not necessarily dependent on the New Testament and Christianity, I believe he has much to teach those of us who are interested in Jewish theology and specifically in a biblical Jewish theology. Finally, while being a pathbreaking thinker in hermeneutics with its penchant for multiple and changing interpretations, Ricoeur never totally abandoned the traditional role of philosopher as adjudicator of truth. Thus, he warned that a multiple hermeneutic must still have its limits and even as truth is to be found in the twists and turns of language and literature, the interpreter must be vigilant still to detect the white light of reason and the clarity it brings as it emerges in the encounter with the sacred text.

Most of my review of Ricoeur's biblical hermeneutics, in accordance with the theme of this book, will be taken from the now classic collection of his religious writings *Figuring the Sacred: Religion, Narrative, and Imagination* (1995). I will assume my earlier essay, "Ricoeur's Biblical Hermeneutics: From Poesis to Theology" in which I focused on his book *Essays in Biblical Interpretation* edited by Lewis Mudge (1980) and where I trace a movement from the Bible as a species of "poesis" to the Bible as a form of theology. This present paper will begin from where I left off in my last chapter on Ricoeur and move forward from his interpretation of scripture as poesis to explicate his important theological moves and then turn to its relevance for Jewish theology. I will begin with a presentation of Ricoeur's biblical theology in summary fashion, then return to take each point up at length. In this more in-depth series of discussions, I will try to show the implications of Ricoeur's biblical theology for Jewish theology.

Paul Ricoeur's work reflects a creative synthesis of classical Western philosophy, modern phenomenology, linguistics, literary theory, and hermeneutics. His work attempts to address a series of problems from the nature of human subjectivity and the subject/object split in modern philosophy and science, to the ways in which human experience is imbedded in time, to the failure of theology to get beyond abstract formulations and doctrines. The antidote to this host of problems Ricoeur finds in the phenomenology of lived life, in poetic language, and in texts and their interpretation. All of these are eventually found or refound in a return to the Bible as a multifaceted text of human experience in relation to God.

SIX SUMMARY POINTS

1. I have already said that for Ricoeur the primary language of theology must be biblical and not philosophical. This is the case for Ricoeur because the Bible is both the primary testimony to the God of Judaism and Christianity and because of his starting points in phenomenology and literary theory. Thus Ricoeur has a biblical theology that integrates the insights of the phenomenology of Heidegger as well as the literary theory of post-structuralism.

2. For Ricoeur, the biblical text is unique in that it is a religious and sacred text. This means that it gives access to truth, not in the philosophical sense of verification or adequation or correspondence, but in the religious sense of what he calls "manifestation" of the sacred and "proclamation" of the word of God. The notions of manifestation and proclamation augment his earlier work on poesis in which he articulates the truth of texts in terms of the Aristotelian notion of mimesis and Ricoeur's own work on metaphor as a vehicle to propose new "descriptions of reality."

3. Even as the biblical text is sacred text or scripture, it is still a text and as such, it goes through a process or "work" which subjects it to styles, forms, and genres as well as a process of "distanciation" from its author(s). This distance from its authors—be they divine or human—means that, like all texts, what we have to interpret is not the "mind of the author(s)" but the canonical text as we have it before us. And in addition, we have the history of the text's interpretation in tradition.

4. For Ricoeur, the Bible is a theocentric text. God is found in the rhetorics and "genres" of scripture. But these are multiple, for example, narratives, prophecies, legislation, proverbs, and hymns. Therefore, the Bible gives us not one but multiple theologies in accordance with which of the multiple texts, we focus on.

Ricoeur also insists, however, that even with this multiplicity, God also functions as "coordinator of these varied discourses."[1] This means that despite the multiple discourses and the different theologies that emerge from biblical genres, there is a parallel effort in the Bible to declare and show that God is "One."

5. Even as God is found in the details of the biblical text he is not, finally, limited only to the biblical text, as some "intertextual theologies"[2] might have it. Thus, part of the genius of the biblical text for Ricoeur is to "open up a horizon [for God] that escapes from the closure of discourse."[3] This means that even as biblical literature gives expression to God. God also escapes or transcends the biblical literature and cannot be contained by it.

6. Ricoeur is enough of an ethicist to declare that the multiple theologies and interpretations of God that hermeneutics disclose have its limits. As Ricoeur says, we cannot rest with a model of interpretation of "discourse about discourse" but must insist that there is a final stage of interpretation that requires action in the world. So the word of God in the Bible demands justice. In Jewish terms, interpretation leads to performance of mitsvot as the bridge to justice and holiness.

Given this brief presentation of six basic points, we will now take each point in turn.

THE BIBLE AS THE PRIMARY LANGUAGE OF WESTERN RELIGIONS

Ricoeur's serious move to biblical language and discourse begins with a frustration with purely metaphysical or, as Kant and Heidegger call it, "onto-theology." Onto-theology is the discourse of medieval scholasticism in which the concepts of Being and Essence, Aristotle's First Cause and his categories of knowledge are applied to God. Since God is by definition not an object or finite being in the world, the application of medieval epistemological categories necessarily is not an easy fit, and this leads to a significant tradition of negative or apophatic theologies in which little can be said about God. For some, God becomes reduced to the needs of philosophy for metaphysical principles and warrants in the search for objective truths. For Heidegger, onto-theology contributes to a whole relationship to the world in which subject is distanced from objects, natural and animal life is reduced to things, and the human being is alienated from both her own being and from Being as such. Thus we have the Heideggerian search to find again an originary stance, attitude, and form of participation in the world before the search for objective knowledge of the world. For the later Heidegger, the route to this renewed relationship with Being is found in art and poetic language.

Ricoeur accepts much of the Heideggerian critique but what Heidegger finds in art and poetry Ricoeur comes to find in the Bible. Therefore, Ricoeur sees in the Bible a language to relate to what Husserl calls the *lebenswelt*, the "life world," in which humans live, work, love, and die. In Heidegger's terms, this is the world of "Being-with"—the complex web of relations to things, persons, and society that humans find themselves in before they think or "know" anything in a conscious manner. Heidegger calls this being already in the world before knowing it "fallenness" or "wordliness." This form of being-in-the-world exists before the subject/object distinction and it constitutes the givenness of the particular life world in which we exist as the starting point for all philosophy and theology. So Ricoeur sees the biblical text as presenting a pre-philosophical, pre-modern, and unself-conscious record of the lifeworld of ancient Israel.

Ricoeur thus points us to what he calls the "Heideggerian path" through the "existentials" provided by the analysis of "being-in-the-world, fallenness, care, being-toward-death."[4] Therefore, with Ricoeur, we are to return to the Bible neither for its historical information about life in the ancient Near East nor for knowledge of late Iron Age agriculture and pottery, nor conflicts between social classes in biblical Israel. This information is not totally unhelpful since it does provide some important historical context, but we don't read the Bible for this. Rather, we read the Bible to learn what it was like to live in the ancient biblical world and how people coped with issues of life, death, scarcity and plenty, joy, and suffering in this world. Moreover, we read the Bible to discover how these humans lived in and with and for a deep and lasting relationship with God. And this issue, the theological one, is really the crucial one. For the Bible is not only a poetic text it is a religious text in which God is present at every moment, in every event and in the minds of persons as an everyday participant in the lifeworld. This, I would suggest, adds another dimension to the lifeworld not mentioned or explored by Husserl and Heidegger, which we could call "being-with-God."

The being-with-God disclosed in the Bible is a being-with that is evident in personal, social, economic, agricultural, and natural life. It is this being-with-God, I would suggest, that makes the Bible unrivaled as a religious text in the West and also what makes it, as Ricoeur says, the primary discourse of the religions of Judaism and Christianity in the West. This being-with-God is an unstated presupposition, a background context, a memory, presence, and hope of the lifeworld of ancient Israel that makes the Hebrew Bible the foundational discourse of Judaism.

Now, the connections to Jewish theology here are obvious. The Bible is Torah or Tanak to Jews. And given that metaphysics and onto-theology have never had the prominence in Judaism that it has in Christianity, it is quite natural and uncontroversial to say that Torah is the primal language of Judaism and Jewish theology. Given the primacy of Torah to Judaism, all forms of Judaism are mere interpretations of Torah and one could also say, to take a term from Ricoeur, all forms of Judaism are hermeneutical. In Rabbinic terms, the hermeneutics of Torah is lionized and sacralized as *"Talmud Torah,"* the study of Torah. Talmud Torah is perhaps the central ritual or mitzvah of Rabbinic Judaism. As it is said, the mitzvah of the study of Torah exceeds all other mitzvot (*k'neged kulum*).[5]

Study of Torah in Rabbinic Judaism, however, falls into two classifications, *Aggadah*, narrative, and *Halakhah*, law, and taken together these constitute what is known as "Oral Torah." Each is derived from the Hebrew Bible often referred to by the Rabbis as "Written Torah." A large part of sacred Jewish literature that focuses on interpreting the Written Torah from the first ten centuries of the Common Era is called "Midrash" and this is expanded and further developed in medieval Rabbinic exegesis of the Bible or *parashanut*. With Midrash, we have perhaps, the most creative area of literary and theological discourse in Judaism. We can say, I think, that one of the objectives of this literature is to expand, develop, critique, and praise, in short, interpret, the characters and plot of biblical narrative. In this function, Midrash looks at biblical characters as living human beings caught up in the trials, tribulations, joys, and triumphs of living and being-with-God in their given "life-world." A central feature of Midrash is that it does not view the characters in the Torah as stock figures or mere representations of ideas, virtues, or vices but as real living persons. For Midrash, the figures in the Bible are people, like us, who are complex subjectivities with desires, hopes, foibles, and challenges. Thus, interpreting the lives of these people is often a dual exercise of analysis of another and analysis of self as Ricoeur would say, "as seen through the other." But only when we realize that the figures in the Bible represent real people, living in a "life-world" like us, will we understand the purpose of Midrash as an attempt to explore new possibilities of being in the world with God. Buber called this form of interpretation "existential exegesis" and he also referred to it as "true existence as the nearness to God."[6]

But there is one more feature of Midrash that makes it work as existential exegesis for Jews and that is that the characters of the Bible are not just people from the ancient Near East, these characters are ancestors—Abraham, Isaac, and Jacob, Sarah, Rebecca, Rachel, and Leah. They are "our" fathers and mothers and their geography is the Land of Israel, "our" homeland. As such , every detail is interesting to the Jews as information about "our" past and future and about ourselves. As ancestors and homeland in the stories of the Bible, the characters, times, and places of the land of Israel take on an importance that lends reality to these figures and presents them as part and parcel of the formative lifeworld the "meta-narrative" of Judaism. This life world inhabited by the characters, Abraham, Moses, David, Sarah, Miriam, Deborah et.al. are then of a different quality that figures we might meet in poetry and fiction, history and non-fiction. These are "our people" and our leaders and our guides after whom we name our children and who we regularly meet and meet again as the Torah is read and studied and chanted in shabbat and festivals in synagogue liturgy.

MANIFESTATION AND PROCLAMATION IN THE BIBLE

Like many philosophers of religion in the modern period, Paul Ricoeur was convinced by Immanuel Kant that when we speak of religion and theology we should speak in a different discourse than we use to address the "phenomena" of the natural world. The religious or "noumenal" world is of a different quality than the world of objects. Of course, Kant did not believe that one could gain "knowledge" of the noumena since its expressions did not appear to our intuitions of space and time and the categories of knowledge. However, others used Kant's distinction to suggest that knowledge of the noumenal was possible, albeit through the use of different tools and sensibilities than phenomenal knowledge. Here, often we see thinkers look to feelings (Friedrich Schleiermacher) experience (William James) the I-Thou relation (Martin Buber) wonder (A.J. Heschel) and a *sensis divinitas* (Alvin Plantinga), among others.

When Ricoeur speaks of the unique form of knowledge and truth in religion and theology of the Bible, he likes to utilize the categories "manifestation" and "proclamation." These terms then augment, as I have suggested, his notions of knowledge and truth as "mimesis" and the metaphoric "redescription of reality" he describes in his great book, *The Rule of Metaphor*.[7] Manifestation is a term he takes from historian and phenomenologist of religion Mircea Eliade and proclamation is a term he takes from prophecy. Manifestation is a non-theological term meant to refer to a basic form of religious expression throughout the world religions from animism and indigenous religions to the highly developed religions of the East and West. Manifestation refers to the appearance of the sacred, spirit, or soul, in natural phenomena and events as prosaic as sunrise and sunset, the phases of the moon, and the flight of birds, to special events like an eclipse, an earthquake, or a flood. Manifestation also refers to special places where significant religious events of origin and creation of the world, a temple, a society, and redemption or salvation of a person, people, nation, occur. Manifestation often occurs in moments of transition marked by gates, pathways, bridges, and ladders. It refers to things that are "saturated with efficacy" and power.[8] A manifestation of the sacred also offers humans an orienting point, a center, a deep foundation rooted in the earth and reaching to the heavens. A manifestation of the sacred is often perceived as threatening and fearful since overwhelming power is revealed. But it can also be perceived as extraordinarily wonderful and joyful as well.

Certainly there is no lack of examples of what Ricoeur calls manifestation in the Bible from the creation of the world, to the flood, to the burning bush, the Exodus, and Jerusalem and the Temple as the "navel of the universe." Rudolph Otto refers to manifestation in the Bible as the "Holy" rather than the sacred and we have his wonderful phenomenology of the Holy, as the *mysterium tremendum*, that is at once feared, revered, and loved.[9]

Whereas manifestation is characterized in terms of feelings of fear, awe, joy, and exhilaration, Ricoeur's other category of religious or noumenal knowledge is "proclamation." Proclamation is characterized in terms of language, word, command, law, justice, and images of hope and a new future. In the Bible, it is clear that proclamation, even in the voice of the prophet, comes from God. Most scholars, especially Christian ones, believe that the Bible favors manifestations of the sacred or holy in proclamation more than manifestation. Ricoeur states what has become the classic view that in "Hebraic faith the word outweighs the numinous."[10] Thus, more than the manifestation of the sacred, Judaism is a religion of the word of Torah, ethics, and law. The Israelite prophets are the great mediators of God's multiple moral proclamations which condemn the powerful for foregoing the needs of the poor and demand social justice. For the classical Israelite prophets, even the concern with sabbaths and festivals and the multiple sacrifices is distasteful to God who would rather see justice for the widow, the orphan, the stranger, and the poor.

Certainly, Jewish philosophy and theology, especially in the modern period, have stressed the import of the prophetic word with its penetrating critique of social inequities and righteous demands for justice. This prophetic word remains, unfortunately, only more relevant in our contemporary world. However, it is easy to overlook how manifestation of the sacred and proclamation of the word combine in Israelite religion and Rabbinic Judaism to produce the unique requirements of the system of mitsvot for a holy life. Here, we can follow Ricoeur's own sense that what the Torah is about a way of being in the world.

However, I think that instead of using the terms manifestation of the sacred and proclamation of the word we are better served by the term that Otto introduced, that is, holiness. However, Otto's mysterium trememdum does not adequately convey the Hebrew meaning of Judaism's *kedushah*, as "to be set apart." The notion of *kedushah* suggests that God is the Being that is ultimately set apart from the world even as God is in relation to the world. Furthermore, when the holy is manifested, it should not be taken as an appearance or manifestation of some generic world-soul, or spirit, but indeed, as something that is directly connected to God. Thus, something gains its character of *kedushah* when it manifests a combination of the presence and word of God.

Any discussion of *kedushah* in the Bible must refer to the famous command in Exodus. You shall be a *mamlekhet kohanim, a* kingdom of priests and a *goy kadosh*, a holy nation. This displays the full extent of the command in national as well as religious life. Then we have the central text in the Pentateuch, the Holiness Code of Leviticus 19. "You Shall be Holy for I the Lord your God am holy." Here, we see how holiness is to permeate through all aspects of the lifeworld of Israel. The Holiness Code also suggests that as God is set apart as holy, the people of Israel must be set apart. Furthermore, Leviticus 19 suggests that one could add to the notion of "being with God" the idea of "being holy like God." Being holy is then described in the full text of Leviticus 19 as a matter of acting correctly in ritual, family, agriculture, business transactions, social relations with kin and strangers, with the deaf and blind, and with friends. All of this summed up with the final words of Leviticus 19 *v'ahavtah re'akha kamokhah*, "To love your neighbor as yourself."

Therefore, as I have argued in my book *The Future of Jewish Theology*, holiness as we have it in the Holiness Code of Leviticus, is a combination of ritual and ethics, a kind of holiness as ethos. Here, we have Judaism's recipe for the fulfillment of life's purpose as living or being-in-the-world-as-holy. And here we have a presentation of the purpose of Jewish mitsvot and the whole system of halakhah as directives and guidance for the holy life. This is clearly stated in the basic formula of all Jewish blessings. "Blessed are you Lord our God, Sovereign of the universe who makes us holy (asher kidishanu) with His commandments." So Jews are literally "made holy," become like God, and live the ethos of the holy life with God through the performance of mitsvot. Here we have the Jewish attempt to transform living in the world thoroughly into being with God through the mediation of God's commands.

THE BIBLICAL TEXT AS A "WORK"

If Ricoeur helps Jewish theology make the argument that the Bible or Torah is the primary language of Judaism, he does so not only by pointing to the ways in which it instantiates a form of being in the world as holy but also how it does so. Here, he utilizes literary theories to show us how to look at the Bible as a product or work. Here, we step back from the issues of the uniqueness of biblical literature as religious text to see it as a textual product like other texts. This means that the authors of the Bible needed to employ the techniques, rhetorics, philology, semantics, genres and tropes of textual production of their time to produce the biblical text. As the rabbis say, "the Bible speaks in human language."[11] So the Bible employs the human textual "arts and sciences" of its time. And, for Ricoeur, understanding the Bible requires not only some understanding of ancient textual arts but also knowledge of the contemporary textual sciences of structuralism, narratology, metaphor, and parable. And here, Ricoeur, unlike Heidegger and some his followers, who viewed the methods of the technical sciences as somehow antithetical to the appreciation of art and poetry, embraced these technical methods. This brings us to the role of the sciences, what Wilhelm Dilthey called the *Naturwissenschaften* and the humanities, the *Geisteswissenschaften*.

Ricoeur refers to the *Naturwissenschaften* as methods of "explanation" and the *Geisteswissenschaften* as methods of "understanding." And he suggests that they both contribute to the overall interpretive process and should be used in tandem. As Ricoeur puts it "understanding precedes, accompanies, closes, and thus envelops explanation. In return, explanation develops understanding."[12] Ricoeur discusses just how a comprehensive hermeneutical method can be developed by employing these two different interpretive approaches in a three stage process that includes (1) "naïve understanding," (2) "explanation," and (3) "understanding proper."[13] In naive understanding we attempt to read a text openly and naively to get an intuitive sense of its meaning. In explanation, we employ historical criticism, knowledge of textual composition, rhetorics, and philology, to unpack context and literary structures. And in understanding proper we return to reread the text for a grasp of the "life-world" that is opened up by the text.

Ricoeur's comprehensive hermeneutical method is relevant to Judaism where the *Wissenschaft des Judentums*, the Science of Judaism, is often opposed to more humanistic and philosophical and theological approaches to the study of Jewish texts. Ricoeur's argument would be that scientific and philosophical-theological approaches need not be opposed. And this means that the whole field of biblical criticism can be seen as an aid to and not a hindrance to the understanding of the Bible. I have reviewed some of the ways in which Ricoeur uses literary theory and biblical criticism in my previous essay "Ricoeur's Biblical Hermeneutics" and need not repeat again what I said there.[14] However, there are a number of additional issues relevant to Jewish theology that I will now discuss.

One of the most important things that we learn from the application of literary theory to the Bible is that, like all texts, the biblical text goes through a process of production. After this process the text is separate from its author. The text goes through a process of what Ricoeur calls "distanciation" from its author.[15] One of the special things, then, about all written texts is that the process of distanciation separates the text from not only its author but the original audience as well. And this makes the text available for others in different times and places to read and interpret it. However, what those people have to read and interpret is not the "mind of the author" who produced the text but the text itself, and this is particularly the case with ancient texts when the authors of the text are no longer living. And precisely because of this distance of the text from its author and original audience, and also because of the use of ways of writing and linguistic codes and techniques of the time of production, the interpreter needs to use explanatory historical and literary analyses as keys to the codes. Ricoeur says this in a more technical fashion as follows. "The exteriorization into material marks and the inscription in the codes of discourse makes not only possible but necessary the mediation of understanding by explanation."[16] So here, Ricoeur presents a compelling argument, I think, for why methods of explanation, why biblical criticism, is relevant to the theological understanding of the Bible.

However, as we showed above, the stage of explanation is only one step in the hermeneutical process and to end with this step as some biblical criticism does, is to miss what is unique about the biblical text as scripture, as sacred text. Thus, we use explanation to set context "behind the text" but we do not end there. We do not end there because what we want to get to is the "life world" in front of the text that the text opens to us. Here, as I said above, Heidegger is helpful in describing some of the aspects of the human lifeworld as being with things, people, self, and God. And I suggested, as well, that traditional Jewish Midrash and exegesis can also help here. But even this step is not enough since Ricoeur insists that true understanding of a text requires a deep interaction of reader and text in what Buber has called an "existential exegesis" and what Hans-Georg Gadamer calls a "fusion of horizons" of the lifeworld and the text and the life world of the reader. This involves what Gadamer and Ricoeur call "application" of the meaning of the text to one's life. Thus, Ricoeur stresses that genuine interpretation, especially of religious texts like the Bible, requires a change in both one's worldview and behavior.

But another point to make here is that because interpretation is dependent upon what Robert Jauss calls the "reader's response"[17] to a text or what C. S. Peirce calls the "interpretant,"[18] of the text, the meaning of a text will necessarily change with every "community of interpreters" or even every single interpreter. In this view of textual meaning, a text is like a transmitter of a series of signals or signs that need to be read and interpreted by a receiver, a person or community of persons. Interpretation of a text then is never fixed but dependent upon the receptors of the text as a system of signs. As Gadamer then says, "one will understand in different way if one understands at all."[19] This suggests that understanding is different not only from the original audience but from each successive audience. The model of transmitter and receiver makes this point well but when we add to it Gadamer's sense that understanding involves a "fusion of horizons" of the life world of the text and the life world of the reader or interpreter, we see that understanding will necessarily take on a new and different character with every interpreter since the life-world of the interpreter continually changes with the times.

THE BIBLE AND DIVINE AUTHORSHIP

But now there is one further issue that Ricoeur's hermeneutic theory raises for our understanding of the nature of biblical texts and their interpretation. This is made obvious in the parallel he draws between the Bible and other non-biblical texts in their production. Here, he suggests that like all literature, once the text is produced, it exists independently or "at a distance" from its authors. But tradition has it that the author of the Bible is not human but divine. Certainly, in some of his essays on biblical interpretation when he speaks of the Bible as a form of poesis like other poetry and literature, the Bible appears more like literature than sacred scripture. But Ricoeur also seems to suggest something like divine authorship with his notion of proclamation. The Bible proclaims the word of God. Buber puts it this way. The prophet says, "The word of God came to me, Go and Proclaim in the hearing of Jerusalem."[20] Also, Ricoeur sometime speaks of the word as divine "revelation" and he refers especially of the New Testament as "kerygma." So there does seem to be some ambiguity in Ricoeur's position on the divine authorship of the Bible and perhaps he wants to leave it that way.

Certainly, for the Jewish tradition and for Jewish theology, the Torah has to be understood as in some way revealed by God. Without this, mitsvah and halakhah are just ancient Jewish cultural practice or traditional practices of the ancestors that have little relevance today. And without some notion of divine authorship of the Torah, the motivation for the study of Torah as a religious activity and Midrash as a search for God in the text of the Torah makes little sense.

Maimonides has it that the doctrine of Torah from God or "Torah from Heaven" given through Moses, is a Jewish article of faith. Maimonides does not extensively argue or logically demonstrate this position. "We do not know exactly how it reached us, but only that it came to us through Moses."[21] I have suggested that this means that the divine nature of Torah is a given axiom of Judaism that must be accepted in order for the whole system of law and belief to operate. Like the axioms of geometry and natural science, the academic disciplines, and the "self-evident" principles of democracy, "Torah from Heaven," is a given principle, a presupposition that we give our assent to without extensive logical demonstration.[22]

Obviously, there are a large variety of Jewish views on revelation that range from that of Maimonides to modern existential views like those of Martin Buber and others. These existential views of revelation suggest that the Torah issued from a wordless encounter of God with Moses. And that Moses then transformed this encounter into speech. Then, of course, we have a variety of views of Torah as constructed by four documents from four human schools, that are woven together by some unknown human redactor.[23]

Whatever of these views of revelation we take, we might consider what divine authorship means for a hermeneutical approach to the Bible. First, as I have suggested already, hermeneutical approaches in general want to preserve a space to view the Bible as sacred, as scripture. One well-known way to state this is with Rudolph Bultmann's "hermeneutical circle"—we believe in order to understand, and understand in order to believe. This suggests that the Bible cannot yield its religious meaning fully if the reader does not come to the text with an assumption of belief. Without this assumption, the Bible appears as an old text from an ancient culture with little relevance for us today. As I have suggested, when we see the Bible as sacred, as revealed by God, every chapter, verse, and word, has potential spiritual meaning. And this serves to motivate Torah study as a religious activity.

But if the Bible is Torah, revealed by God, then additional implications can be stated. As living and steadfast, God not only revealed the Torah but God remains accessible through Torah as God's living word, His *mayim haim*. Thus, there is a difference between the human author of a work of literature and the divine author of Torah. We cannot really commune with a dead author of literature but, we can commune with the living God of scripture through interpreting His word and behaving in accordance with His mitsvot. Also by accepting this view of the Bible as revealed I see no reason why we could not still say that God uses the techniques and genres of literature just as God uses Moses as an instrument of His revelation.

THE GOD-REFERENCE OF SCRIPTURE

Although Ricoeur does not, as far as I know, directly endorse a straightforward notion of divine revelation of the Bible, he does say a number of things that point in that direction. As I have said, his notion of "proclamation" suggests that the words of the prophets are divine words uttered in the mouths of the prophets. One could say, I think, that for Ricoeur, whether or not God "revealed" the entire Bible is hard to say with certainty, but that the Bible gives expression to the human search, need, experience, and reception of the word of God is much easier to assert. So even if the divine authorship of the Bible is uncertain, in Ricoeur's more technical terms, the Bible definitely has a "God-referent." And this God-referent already makes the text of the Bible unique among world literature. As Ricoeur puts this: "One of the traits that makes for the specificity of the biblical discourse, we all know, Is the central place of God-reference in it."[24] The significance of this remark cannot be overstated, first because the world of post-structuralism within which Ricoeur works has largely abandoned all notion of reference in any text. That is, the rule of post-structural theory is that texts do not "refer" to anything in the world outside them but only to other texts.[25]

Furthermore, as Ricoeur continues to explicate his view of the God-reference in the Bible, he asserts that not just the Torah or Pentateuch gives expression to God, but, indeed, the entire Hebrew Bible, what Jews call the Tanak, gives expression to God. "The signification of this [God] reference of biblical discourse is implicated . . . in the multiple unified significations of the literary forms of narration, prophecy, hymn, wisdom, and so forth"[26]

So here, Ricoeur makes the interesting claim that biblical theology is expressed in multiple different ways, according to which literary genre and rhetorical strategies are employed. Thus, we find different theologies in narration than we do in prophecy, the writings, psalms, wisdom, and hymnic literature. Ricoeur remarks that where the book of Exodus focuses on covenant and the particular historical issues of salvation from slavery and revelation at Sinai, the wisdom literature of Proverbs and Ecclesiastes points to timeless issues "which overflow the framework of the covenant . . . and bears on the human condition in general."[27] And where Deuteronomy presents a just correlation between reward and punishment for obedience and disobedience to God's commandments, the book of Job addresses the issue of evil and "unjust suffering"[28] that remains a challenge to the doctrine of reward and punishment and explores the eternal problem of theodicy.

Given the variety of books in the Bible that derive from different times and places, it is not surprising that the Bible would give expression to a variety of theologies. But beyond the historical and geographical issues of difference, Ricoeur points us to the difference in literary genres and styles as keys to a biblical theological pluralism. With this Ricoeur opens a host of new possibilities for theological investigation that is dependent upon careful study of biblical literary techniques. Much of this work has been started in the literary approach to study of the Bible in both Jewish and "Old Testament" studies. Indeed, this is one of the more creative areas of contemporary biblical studies. However, most of this work stops short of theological exploration and remains in the sphere of "Bible as Literature" which refuses to seriously engage in the theological issues that the Bible is concerned with.[29] Here, the Bible becomes an example of ancient Near Eastern literature to be compared to other world literatures without reference to the significant theological ideas it gives expression to. What is unique about Ricoeur's suggestion is that literary study of the Bible provides a key specifically to theological reflection. And in paying attention to the variety in biblical literary expression, we see that "the originary expression of faith" which the Bible gives expression to "is not simple but multiple. It is not a simple tone but polyphonic"[30]

UNITY AND TRANSCENDENCE

While endorsing theological pluralism in the Bible, Ricoeur still sees a concerted effort to sketch a theological unity that "proceeds from the concurrence and convergence" of what he calls each of the "partial discourses"[31] of scripture. This, I take it, is Ricoeur's nod to the issue of biblical monotheism. So even as he sees multiple theologies in scripture, and even as he has to acknowledge elements of biblical theology that portray God in multiple roles, for instance as warrior, legislator, redeemer, savior, lover, and healer, all these are roles that issue from the same one God.[32]

In the end, I think we can say that Ricoeur's theology remains close to the Jewish assertion of Deuteronomy 6:4 and the Shema prayer of Judaism. "Hear O Israel the LORD our God the LORD is One." Ricoeur also spends significant time on the Name of God given to Moses in Exodus 3:14 as a unifying concept of biblical theology.[33] In making this assertion about the ultimate unity of God, however, especially after arguing for the theological pluralism in the Bible, Ricoeur once more sets forth a program for a future biblical theology that would be charged with highlighting the "concurrence and convergence" among the different theologies and integrating them into some kind of dynamic whole. Ricoeur himself does not do this, but his work suggests it as a future program.

Ricoeur labors to show us just how biblical literature, through its use of multiple genres, gives expression to God. Here, he endorses the use of literary theory to display the various techniques of the Bible as literature. However, when viewing the Bible as an expression of God, Ricoeur sees how the semantics and syntax of biblical literature is, at times marshalled against itself to declare that God, finally, transcends literature. Ricoeur therefore, speaks of the "double power" of Biblical language. This is the power to point to God with language and, at the same time, to assert that God exists outside of and beyond language. Thus Ricoeur says.

> To understand the word "God" is to follow the direction of the meaning of the word.
>
> By direction of the meaning I mean its double power to gather all the significations that issue from the partial discourses and to open up a horizon that escapes from the closure of discourse.[34]

Here, I think Ricoeur is looking at the plurality of biblical theological discourses that the Bible at times tries to place into a unified monotheism, as a sign that God cannot be, finally, bottled up and contained by discourse. The very multiplicity of theologies in the Bible then is theologically productive not, as some have suggested, because it points to a biblical polytheism, but because it points to a God that transcends all easy attempts to contain God in discourse.

As well as pointing to the different genres of biblical literature that resist easy systematization Ricoeur refers us to individual chapters, phrases, metaphors and images for God in which we see God emerging from odd uses of language. Here, one could say that out of the prosaic and ordinary lifeworld of Israel's attempt to "Be-with" God, there emerges a 'theology of interruption,' a theology of the extra-ordinary, which is revealed through what Ricoeur calls "ruptures in ordinary speech."[35] Here, in strange images, semantic and syntactic oddities and narrative gaps, a space is opened for the transcendent God to appear. Here, we may think of the burning bush, the seeing of thunder and hearing of lightning at Sinai, Jacob's pillow made of rock and the ladder with angels ascending and descending (they should be descending and ascending) and Elijah's "still small sound" (I Kings 19:12).

In some ways each of these participates in what Ricoeur calls the "metaphoric function" of scripture whereby two incongruent meanings are placed in juxtaposition to reveal a new third meaning different from one's ordinary association with either juxtaposed element. Thus, the bush aflame that is yet not consumed juxtaposes the flammable branches with the fire that would normally burn it up to yield a sense of an eternal flame as a metaphor for God. And God as a still small sound juxtaposes the normal meaning of a sound as hearable with the sound of silence to express the extraordinary nature of the voice of God. As Ricoeur describes the power of metaphor, it is the power of language to disclose a new possibility in reality that we would normally not perceive or think of. Biblical literature is filled with metaphoric expression so it can "tell us something new about reality."[36] The metaphoric function of the Bible is then to expand the possibilities in our world with new visions, new sights, sounds, ideas, and hopes that only God can make possible.

Although Ricoeur does not use the famous name of God as an example of this, it seems to me that there is no better example. Thus, when Moses is given God's name in Exodus. 3:14 as *Ehyeh Asher Ehyeh* we have a phrase that both makes some sense and defies sense. The expression *Ehyeh Asher Ehyeh* could suggest that God is the philosopher's Absolute Being, "I am that I am, "as the King James translation has it. However, grammatically we really have a verbal form "Ehyeh" that is better translated as "I will be." So then the meaning is something like "I will Be as/or what I will Be." This then carries the sense of a God who becomes as opposed to a God who is a static unchanging Being—a becoming God in process as opposed to an eternal unchanging God. But there is also the possibility that *Ehyeh Asher Ehyeh* refers to the human perception of God that changes with God's presence at different times. Thus, Martin Buber suggests the translation, "I will be present as I will be present." And we also have the Midrash that suggests that the Name refers to God as existing in all tenses of time—past, present, future—at once (Midrash Exodus Rabbah on Exod. 3:14).

"I will be present as I will be present" is a rather long and strange "Name" for anything including for God. But it is also a brilliant name for God for it at once points to God and frustrates the desire for a name that might really give us a sense of who God actually is. Especially in the context of the Bible where names often are used to signify an essential aspect or character trait of a figure (e.g., Abraham is father of many, Isaac, he will laugh, Sarah, princess) the Bible is careful not to give us God's nature in God's name. When the long name of God is then given in a short form of YHWH, we are left with an index that points to God without really giving us any real content or nature of God. Therefore, the name of God does exactly what Ricoeur suggests. It gives us a word-phrase that at once points to God and suggests that we cannot contain God in words, that is, *YHVH*, short for *Ehyeh Asher Ehyeh*, in Ricoeur's terms: "opens up a horizon that escapes from the closure of discourse."[37]

THE SCOPE AND LIMITS OF HERMENEUTICS

What Ricoeur takes away from the Bible in attending to the specifics and particularities of biblical literature is a rich interchange between the biblical text, the moral person and God. The Bible presents us with a triangular relationship which Franz Rosenzweig describe as God, World, Person. The Bible tells the stories of people who exist in rich relationship to others, to society, and to God. The prophets function like social philosophers constantly reminding the people of their moral obligations to each other and to society and the presence of God in their everyday and historical experience. Nature, agriculture, animals, and plants are living beings that can manifest the Holy God at any moment. And family is as fundamental a unit of religious life as Temple, nation, and economy. This picture of the biblical world is not merely a picture of an ancient civilization, it is, for Ricoeur relevant still to us today. Thus, everyday life today and the social and political world today require the person of faith to act. We read the Bible not for fun but to hear again the word of God commanding us to intervene in the world. But like biblical persons we also get tired, worn-down, disillusioned, and fearful for the future and so we also read the Bible for a sense of perspective on our world, which however depressing is really nothing like the fragile, unpredictable, imperiled world of ancient Israel. And most importantly, we read the Bible for its divine word of hope, "unconditional trust," and what Ricoeur calls, "the utmost possibilities of my own freedom."[38]

In this last issue, the issue of my freedom as a person, Ricoeur perhaps gives us his own very modern interpretation of the biblical world, which probably did not include the kind of possibility of individual freedom, separate from family, world, and society, that we as moderns have today. But, again, it is a tribute to both the flexibility of the biblical text and the power of theological interpretation that as Ricoeur says, the person of faith "accepts being interpreted as he or she interprets the world of the [biblical] text."[39] Here, again, a line has been crossed from language to the person so that interpretation is not just a play with textual meaning but an enterprise in which the self remakes itself in accordance with the word he or she is interpreting.

Ricoeur's hermeneutical theology then includes a dynamic relationship between language and being, word and action, holy and profane, person and society. Certainly, the very meaning and purpose of the hermeneutical approach to theology means that language and text take on a primary mediating role in the religious life of the relationship to God and the world. As Ricoeur says, for hermeneutical philosophy, religion "never appears as an immediate experience but always as mediated by a certain language that articulates it."[40] In Jewish terms, this can be simply put this way. Torah mediates God and world. However, it is also true in Ricoeur's terms and my view of Jewish theology that language or Torah does not take God and the world thoroughly in. There is no final unity, no grand summing up. As Rosenzweig suggests, God, World, Human, and Torah are realities that stand in relation to one another in the rich web of Jewish religious life.

That language (or Torah) does not absorb the world and God means that hermeneutics has its limits. Ricoeur points to what he calls a "danger" in hermeneutics and that is that everything becomes "discourse about discourse."[41] Here, I think that Ricoeur, as philosopher is clearing a space for deliberation on which interpretation is best and also which interpretation is true. Here, philosophy as reasoning argument emerges to help establish ration criteria that can adjudicate among different interpretations.

Ricoeur also makes the point another way by referring to the hermeneutical philosopher Hans-Georg Gadamer who has said that "understanding and explication without application is not interpretation."[42] What this means is that hermeneutical understanding, if it is to be genuine, must include a final stage in which the interpreter *applies* the meaning of her interpretation to life. So that interpretation ends in action, not in the play of thought and text alone.

Finally, Ricoeur gives one more fruitful ways of understanding the limits of hermeneutics with his notion of religious faith. "Faith is the limit of all hermeneutics and the nonhermeneutical origin of all interpretation. The ceaseless movement of interpretation begins and ends in the risk of a response that is neither engendered nor exhausted by commentary."[43] Here, I believe that Ricoeur is saying that the ultimate origin of religious faith is neither language nor interpretation but God. So for the person of faith who desires to "be-with-God," it is God who is the "necessary and unique thing from whose basis I orient myself in all that I do."[44]

NOTES

1. Ricoeur, "Philosophy and Religious Language," *Figuring the Sacred*, Mark Wallace, ed. (Minneapolis: Fortress Press, 1995), p. 45.

2. George Lindbeck, *The Nature of Doctrine* (Philadelphia: Westminster, 1984), p. 114.

3. Ricoeur, *Figuring*, p. 46.

4. Ricoeur, *Essays on Biblical Interpretation*, p. 71.

5. *Babylonian Talmud, Peah 8a*.

6. Martin Buber, *Good and Evil* (Saddle River, NJ: Prentice-Hall, 1952), p. 6.

7. Paul Ricoeur, *The Rule of Metaphor* (Toronto: University of Toronto Press, 1977).

8. Ricoeur, *Figuring*, p. 50.

9. Rudolph Otto, *The Idea of the Holy* (Oxford: Oxford University Press, 1958).

10. Ricoeur, "Manifestation and Proclamation," *Figuring*, p. 56.

11. Babylonian Talmud, *Berakhot* 31b.

12. Paul Ricoeur, "Explanation and Understanding," in The Philosophy of Paul Ricoeur C. Reagan and D. Stewart eds. (Boston: Beacon Press, 1978), p. 158.

13. Ibid., p. 154.

14. My most thought-provoking discussion of the relation of explanation and understanding in hermeneutics is found in my *The Text as Thou: Martin Buber's Dialogical Hermeneutics and Narrative Theology* (Bloomington: Indiana University Press, 1992), chs. 2–4.

15. Paul Ricoeur, "The Hermeneutical Function of Distanciation," *Philosophy Today* 17:2/9 (Summer, 1973), pp. 129–42.

16. Ibid., p. 153.

17. Robert Jauss, *Toward an Aesthetic of Reception* (Minneapolis, University of Minneapolis Press, 1982).

18. Charles Sanders Peirce, *Collected Papers* C. Hartshorne and P. Weiss eds. (Cambridge: Harvard University Press, 1931), p. 228.

19. Hans Georg Gadamer, *Truth and Method* (New York: Crossroad, 1982), p. 264.

20. Ricoeur, "Naming God," *Figuring*, p. 225.

21. Maimonides *Commentary on the Mishna*, Helek, Sanhedrin, Ch. 10.

22. Steven Kepnes, "Reviving Jewish Theology: From A Soft Maimonidean to a Practical Biblical Metaphysics," *Modern Theology* (August, 2022).

23. For a wonderful summary of modern Jewish views of revelation from Orthodox to Liberal, see Alan Brill, "Jewish Models of Revelation," in S. Kepnes, ed. *Cambridge Companion to Jewish Theology* (Cambridge: Cambridge University Press, 2020).

24. Ricoeur, "Naming God," *Figuring*, p. 44.

25. In the world of theology, George Lindbeck has used the term intertextuality to argue that if we want to know about the nature of God in Christianity or Judaism, we need to focus solely on the series of intertextual references that are used to speak of God in the sacred texts of the tradition. "The proper way to understand the way the word God signifies, for example, is by understanding how the word operates within a religion." (*Nature of Doctrince*, 114) This view has some affinities with Ricoeur's view about the primacy of language in giving expression to what we mean by God. But it also has been used to suggest that God is limited to His intertextual references and cannot be said to "exist" outside language. Linbeck says that intertextuality means that "scripture . . . absorbs the universe" (*Nature of Doctrine,* 117) And his notion of intertextual theology suggests that scripture absorbs God as well.

26. Ricoeur, "Philosophy and Religious Language," *Figuring*, p. 45.

27. Ricoeur, "Naming God," *Figuring*, p. 227.

28. Ibid.

29. A good example of a highly insightful literary analysis of the Bible that does not engage theological issues in any real depth is the work of Robert Alter. In his *Art of Biblical Narrative* (New York: Basic Books, 2011), and *Art of Biblical Poetry* (New York: Basic Books, 1987) we see important advances in the application of literary tropes, type-scenes, figures of speech, etc. to the Bible as literature. However, when issues of meaning are addressed Alter is much more likely to turn to historical criticism than theology to bring clarity to a difficult text.

30. Ricoeur, "Naming God," *Figuring*, p. 224.

31. Ricoeur, "Philosophy and Religious Language," *Figuring*, p. 45.

32. We could also articulate this more philosophically to say that even as God appears to have a body, voice, moods of anger and compassion, He is finally, incorporeal, and his bodily manifestations are only appearances used by the incorporeal God to gain the attention of humans for specific purposes. This of course is a complex issue especially for the Jewish philosophers who want to deny any bodily manifestation to God what so ever. But the rabbis are less worried about this issue and we see that God in the Talmud often is imagined as father, rabbi, teacher, judge, and so on. The theologian Alan Brill has summarized the Rabbinic position well by showing how God's different roles and guises are different "modalities" of appearance. Alan Brill, Modern Theology.

33. Ricoeur, "Naming God," *Figuring,* p. 217ff.

34. Ricoeur, "Philosophy and Religious Language," *Figuring*, p. 45.

35. Ricoeur, "Manifestation and Proclamation," *Figuring*, p. 60.

36. Ricoeur, *Interpretation Theory* (Forth Worth: TCU Press, 1976), p. 53.

37. Ricoeur, "Naming God," *Figuring*, p. 46.

38. Ibid, p. 47.

39. Ibid, p. 46.

40. Ibid.
41. Ricoeur, "Patoral Praxeology, Hermeneutics, and Identity," *Figuring*, p. 304.
42. Ibid.
43. Ricoeur, "Naming God," *Figuring*, p. 46
44. Ibid., p. 47.

BIBLIOGRAPHY

Martin Buber, *Good and Evil*. Saddle River, NJ: Prentice-Hall, 1952.

Hans Georg Gadamer, *Truth and Method*. New York: Crossroad, 1982.

Robert Jauss, *Toward an Aesthetic of Reception*. Minneapolis: University of Minneapolis Press, 1982.

Steven Kepnes, *The Text as Thou: Martin Buber's Dialogical Hermeneutics and Narrative Theology*. Bloomington: Indiana University Press, 1992.

———, *The Future of Jewish Theology*. London: Wiley Blackwell, 2013.

———, "Ricoeur's Biblical Hermeneutics: From Poesis to Theology," *Reading Scripture with Paul Ricoeur*. Edited by Joseph Edelheit and James Moore. Lanham, MD: Lexington Books, 2021.

Steven Kepnes, "Reviving Jewish Theology: From A Soft Maimonidean to a Practical Biblical Metaphysics," *Modern Theology* (August, 2022).

George Lindbeck, *The Nature of Doctrine*. Philadelphia: Westminster Press, 1984.

Rudolph Otto, *The Idea of the Holy*. Oxford: Oxford University Press, 1958.

Paul Ricoeur, "The Hermeneutical Function of Distanciation," *Philosophy Today* 17:2/9 (Summer, 1973), pp. 129–42.

———. *Interpretation Theory*. Forth Worth: Texas Christian University Press, 1976.

———, *The Rule of Metaphor*. Toronto: University of Toronto Press, 1977.

———, "Explanation and Understanding," in *The Philosophy of Paul Ricoeur*. Edited by C. Reagan and D. Stewart. Boston: Beacon Press, 1978.

———, *Essays in Biblical Interpretation*. Edited by Lewis Mudge. Philadelphia: Fortress. 1980.

———, *Figuring the Sacred: Religion, Narrative, and Imagination*. Minneapolis: Augsburg Press, 1995.

BIBLIOGRAPHY

Chapter 2

Ricoeur and the Religious Imagination

George H. Taylor

Paul Ricoeur claims that there are four types of productive imagination: the poetic, the epistemological, the social and cultural, and the religious.[1] In this chapter, I want to take on the task of investigating what Ricoeur means by the religious imagination.[2] The framework for my argument is provided by Ricoeur's essay on "Philosophy and Religious Language" in *Figuring the Sacred*. In that essay Ricoeur claims that in part the religious imagination is a regional hermeneutic internal to a more general poetic imagination, and yet he also claims that the religious imagination serves to ground the poetic imagination. For purposes of space, I cannot address the latter claim here. Instead, I restrict myself to the wager that despite criticisms in the secondary literature that Ricoeur makes the religious imagination too much subordinate to the poetic imagination, in fact understanding the religious imagination in relation to the poetic imagination deepens rather than reduces the meaning of the religious imagination.

In the *Lectures on Imagination*, Ricoeur claims that the imagination can be described across two axes, a horizontal axis attentive to the object side (the noematic) that runs from reproductive to productive imagination and a vertical axis attentive to the subjective side (the noetic) that proceeds from belief at the bottom to critical distance at the top.[3] As we shall see, the vertical axis also addresses imagination as a power, ranging from a capability, a power to, to a distorted form of belief, a power over. In other work, I have argued that internal to Ricoeur's interpretation of the productive imagination, he allows for two different types. The first is *seeing as*, where a transposition has occurred, and a new sense of reality arises. The second is the *as if*, a realm of new possibilities, imaginative variations, where alternatives to present reality are offered but the alternatives' reality is not yet determined.[4] Ricoeur's central notion of "manifestation," a fundamental element of the poetic, covers both. For his development of *seeing as*, Ricoeur explicitly draws on Kant's notion of the schematism to show how the imagination conjoins the conceptual and the experiential, extending the latter side beyond the empirical to the pre-objective.[5] Ricoeur in fact argues that the relation between the conceptual and the experience is not simply schematized but also *depicted*.[6] The verbal and conceptual are linked to the sensible as not only intuitive but visual. The nature of the productive imagination as depiction will relate to his subsequent attention to figuration. I will draw on these characterizations of imagination to apply to the religious imagination.

The chapter proceeds in three parts. Part one uses "Philosophy and Religious Language" to establish Ricoeur's general argument about the characterization of religious imagination as a regional hermeneutic internal to the poetic imagination. Part two examines the role of the religious imagination from within the context of religious belief and focuses particularly on the example of religious—and prototypically Christian—hope. The claim here is that internal to faith, the religious imagination combines both *seeing as* and the *as if*. Part three turns to question the role of religious imagination for those outside a faith community and asks whether and how Ricoeur's focus on a religious hermeneutics as the proposal of a world allows for religious inspiration or conversion.

THE RELIGIOUS IMAGINATION AS A FORM OF POETIC IMAGINATION

In part one, we develop Ricoeur's basic argument on the religious imagination as a subcategory of the poetic imagination. Our primary text for development of this interrelation is Ricoeur's article on "Philosophy and Religious Language." The article was first published in 1974. It should be noted that although Ricoeur explicitly references the imagination, as we shall see, only once in the article, the attention to the poetic implicates the role of the imagination throughout, both regarding the poetic text and that text's interpretation.

For the bulk of the article, Ricoeur considers ways in which poetic hermeneutics offers a general hermeneutics into which religious hermeneutics can be located as a "regional" hermeneutic, a subcategory variant.[7] We should concentrate first, then, on the nature of the poetic. The poetic "comes to" language; it begins elsewhere, in a gift.[8] In another text, drawing upon Martin Heidegger, Ricoeur characterizes language as a mediation and so not a point of departure; it occurs in a process that precedes and envelops it.[9] In poetic language we find manifestation, the incursion of rupture and opening, the appearance of something new, another reality.[10] The hermeneutic, interpretive aspect is central: something comes to language that we seek—with halting, limited capacity—to capture within language. We do not begin with the literal but in hermeneutic interpretation. In Ricoeur's famous line: "Between absolute knowledge and hermeneutics, it is necessary to choose."[11] The implications are fundamental for religious understanding. If in Kantian language the productive imagination "gives us more to think about," the same is true for the sacred in relation to its manifestations.[12] Here too we always begin in interpretation, including the interpretation of biblical testimony, points receiving later attention. Daniel Frey recognizes, even as he challenges, that for Ricoeur the pure Christ event is never discoverable, because always encompassed within a hermeneutic logic.[13] From a different perspective, Dan Stiver has emphasized that the credibility of theological stances is enhanced if envisaged as participating in a similar dynamic as more general poetic claims of manifestation, of "coming to" language.[14]

If for us a first point of "Philosophy and Religious Language" is that the poetic "comes to" language, the second point is that it comes to *language*. Notable here is the juxtaposition to Ricoeur's prior focus on the religious symbol in *The Symbolism of Evil*. As well known, in the conclusion of that text Ricoeur argues that "[t]he symbol gives rise to thought."[15] Ricoeur's newer, broader attention to language seems to emphasize the more prominent role of the poetic, with the religious again a regional hermeneutic of this larger force. We also need to consider what for Ricoeur the poetic coming to language entails. As part of its semantic autonomy, a text's meaning is separable from whatever might have been the psychology of the author that inspired the text.[16] Instead, a text unfolds a "proposed world," what Ricoeur calls "the world of the text."[17] The poetic as a form of manifestation offers "a dimension of revelation in a nonreligious, nontheistic, nonbiblical sense of the word."[18] The text opens "new possibilities of being-in-the-world" and these possibilities are offered "not through the modality of givenness, but rather through the modality of possibility." These possibilities are "imaginative variations"—the only explicit reference to imagination in this text—worked upon the real.[19] Elsewhere Ricoeur asserts that "the new being announced by biblical texts can be interpreted as fundamentally imaginary." Before these texts appeal to the will, they "appeal to an imagination which they open to new and radical possibilities."[20] Ricoeur's advocacy of "the world of the text" is of course another famous aspect of his hermeneutics, but once more the implications require some subtle analysis. Later we shall examine more closely the import of the world of the religious text as offered in the modality of possibility and imaginative variation. In these pages of "Philosophy and Religious Language," Ricoeur also adverts to the way *fiction* offers the "privileged path" to the poetic redescription of reality in the world of the text, but he does not address here the implications for religious understanding, something we will pick up in part two.[21] Ricoeur suggests too that poetic manifestation requires a new definition of truth but does not pursue that here, and this is a topic we shall postpone until later also.[22]

Particularly in the last several pages of the article, Ricoeur turns to the application to biblical texts of this hermeneutics of poetic texts. The world of the religious text is emphasized, and the question of the inspiration of the writings is set aside. Whatever religious experience may mean, it is articulated in language and most adequately interpreted in terms of its linguistic expression.[23] Similarly, on the side of the reader or listener, attention also remains on the world of the text and not on reader decision in front of the text: "above and beyond emotions, disposition, belief, or nonbelief, is the proposition of a world that in the biblical language is called a new world, a new covenant, the kingdom of God, a new birth."[24] Revelation in the biblical context, "if the expression is meaningful," means revelation of a biblical world, not a psychological reduction.[25] "For a hermeneutical philosophy, faith never appears as an immediate experience but always as mediated by a certain language that articulates it."[26] Although Ricoeur refers to the force of the religious text's world as one "of rupture and opening," the rupture remains at the level of possibility, of a "projected world," "the reality of the possible."[27] This vocabulary seems quite different from Ricoeur's language from "Listening to the Parables of Jesus," also first published in 1974, where he pursues how the meaning of a parable "invades us, overwhelms us, beyond our control and our grasp . . . as a gift."[28] As we proceed, my claim is that the vocabulary of "Philosophy and Religious Language" on the modality of possibility instead better represents—rightly or wrongly—Ricoeur's mature thought on the religious imagination from a perspective outside belief, something we will examine in greater depth in part three.[29]

THE RELIGIOUS IMAGINATION FROM THE PERSPECTIVE OF A BELIEVER

Part two offers comparisons and contrasts to Ricoeur's analysis in "Philosophy and Religious Language." It proceeds from a perspective internal to belief rather than in consideration of a perspective that is external. We shall return to the external perspective in part three.

The Interrelation of Reproductive and Productive Religious Imagination

The religious imagination provides a distinctive form of interrelation between reproductive and productive aspects. While in poetic manifestation we typically look to the appearance of the new and so productive in that sense, religious imagination involves a greater integration of reproductive fidelity to the past, an originative religious event, context, or meaning. To my knowledge, Ricoeur does not directly address the responsiveness of the productive religious imagination to the reproductive imagination except to the extent it revisits his broader thematic, now in the religious context, of the way the imagination moves from form to form. In his article on biblical imagination, Ricoeur returns to a Kantian inspired notion of the imagination as "a rule-governed form of invention," with the interplay of rule and free play offering a power of redescription.[30] In other writings in the religious arena, Ricoeur emphasizes how imagination functions as both structuring and destructuring, destructuring of prior forms to reopen them.[31] In both of these contexts, Ricoeur refers to the functions of redescription and destructuring as a power of fiction, a topic to which we return in the final section of this part. I also think of Ricoeur's frequent personal observation that his own faith stance is "chance transformed into destiny by a continuous choice."[32] Movement forward—a productive imagination—is framed in relation to the chance faith circumstances of his birth—a reproductive imagination. For us, the larger point is the grounding of religious faith in reproductive imagination, even as it permits productive imagination, as we shall investigate.

Hope

Within Ricoeur's philosophy, several commentators argue that the notion of hope, a "passion for the possible," is the key to his corpus.[33] Brian Treanor and Henry Venema have indeed entitled a book collection on Ricoeur with the name *A Passion for the Possible*. I do not weigh in on the absolute primacy of hope as a Ricoeur motif but rather use Ricoeur's discussion of hope as a valuable vehicle for examination of the religious imagination within the context of belief.[34] I engage first in an elaboration of Ricoeur's approach to hope and then evaluate how this approach illumines the meanings of the horizontal and vertical axes of the religious imagination. My primary thesis here is that the nature of hope demonstrates how the productive religious imagination offers a distinctive *combination* of *seeing as* and the *as if*.

Viewed initially apart from Ricoeur and within a more general hermeneutic of the imagination, hope seems a matter of the *as if*. It suggests the availability of not being bound by current structures, including current political and social structures, something that is part of the contribution of manifestation as the possible. Yet hope as an appeal to the possible can also come across as vague and platitudinous, merely an assertion: well, *x* or *y* is "possible": "the future is here," "the revolution is on our doorstep," "history is on our side," and so on. Ricoeur has criticized utopias, for example, to the extent that they offer escapism—merely the possible—and no efforts to legitimate their possibility by showing how they might move us from where we are to where we could or should be.[35]

Something different occurs with hope in the context of religious belief. Ricoeur, in fact, defines religion by the question of what may we hope for.[36] In defining hope as the "passion for the possible," a phrase that he draws from Kierkegaard, Ricoeur argues that the formulation retains "the mark of the future which the promise puts on freedom."[37] (We shall return later to the "passion for the possible" as a passion.) He repeats in several works the emphasis on hope as a promise and in so doing amplifies the nature of what a promise means.[38] The promise entails that fulfillment has the nature of a given.[39] Ricoeur quotes *Ephesians* on the "covenants of promise"—an oath, a pact, something binding—and *Romans* on the divine grace that through Jesus Christ came as a "free gift."[40] Ricoeur cites Jürgen Moltmann on the Resurrection as a Promise for all.[41] While the orientation of a promise is futural, something has been given now, already.[42] Hope in the context of religious belief is not simply an aspiration for a future hypothetical, an abstract possibility, something *as if*, because the hope has received assurance. A transposition has occurred; a new reality has been disclosed, even if its contours remain for future clarification. The religious believer *sees as*. Ricoeur expands upon the nature of the religious promise in other vocabulary that is well known and underscores that something has been given, that life has been transformed. The God of hope offers the "economy of the gift."[43] This economy of the gift is one of surplus; the logic of hope is that of superabundance, an economy of superabundance.[44] Grace superabounds.[45]

The secondary literature on Ricoeur reinforces that religious hope offers confirmed possibility. Hope offers "redeemed possibility," "accomplishment," "promise of fulfillment," "true description," "sure promises of God for the future," "promise of a future."[46] Jürgen Moltmann, who is an important source for Ricoeur, himself references Kierkegaard's phrase and asserts that "hope becomes a 'passion for the possible' . . ., because it can be a passion for what has been made possible."[47] In the Christian promise "the hidden future already announces itself and exerts its influence on the present through the hope it awakens."[48] A promise has been given.[49] "Hope's assurance springs from the credibility and faithfulness of the God of promise."[50] In his larger discussion of Ricoeur, Kevin Vanhoozer looks to Moltmann to render more precise that the resurrection is "God's 'deed' of promise," with the deed being "an actual event that is also the promise of a possible future."[51]

In his discussion of hope as the passion for the possible, Ricoeur is explicit that this hope encompasses a "creative imagination of the possible."[52] That the religious imagination is "creative" is noteworthy and will receive later attention. That hope involves imagination returns us to a theme touched upon previously and now deserving special weight: the claim that the role of imagination pertains to a *grace* of imagination, one that is the *grace* of possibility.[53] The grace of imagination brings about an "upsurge" of the possible.[54] In an article on "The Language of Faith," Ricoeur returns to the vocabulary of the grace of imagination and of the surging up of the possible and asserts that "the fundamental theme of Revelation is this awakening and this call, into the heart of existence, of the imagination of the possible."[55] The religious imagination partakes of a gift of the divine.

Theologically, we may say that religious hope—where the new reality appears, the transposition occurs—is not simply a function of hope but of hope grounded in faith. Religious hope is not simply *as if*—mere possibility—because of the transposition, a *seeing as*, a faith that reality is now different. We find some support for this interrelation of faith and hope in Ricoeur's writings. He discusses the "faith" that humanity is founded by a creative word, "The Good News" as the establishment of human possibility by a creative word.[56] He distinguishes between religious and poetic imagination in that for the latter there is no commitment, simply an open imagination, while in the former there is an element of both promise and commitment.[57] More overt attention to the relation between faith and hope appears in secondary commentary. Quite astutely, Don Ihde contends that faith "remains hidden within hope," for hope is oriented not to any historical possibility but rather to "certain possibilities, those which respond to and fulfill hope."[58] More broadly, Moltmann maintains that while faith binds humans to Christ, hope opens faith to the comprehensive divine future. Moltmann quotes Calvin: "Hope is nothing else than the expectation of those things which faith has believed to have been truly promised by God. . . . [F]aith is the foundation upon which hope rests, hope nourishes and sustains faith."[59] Ricoeur may claim that "religion is constituted less by faith than by hope," because faith falls short and hope participates in superabundance, but that does not challenge the nature of their interrelation.[60] Faith offers the basis for the transposition, the *seeing as*, that makes hope not simply possibility, the *as if*, but something given, a gift.

At first glance, then, the nature of hope is quite different from the perspective toward religious imagination offered by Ricoeur in "Philosophy and Religious Language." Within the sphere of hope, the believer does not regard the world of the religious text simply as a "proposed" world, where new possibilities of being are solely imaginative variations, hypothetical, possible but uncertain, just the *as if*. As we have emphasized, the context of hope is one where transposition has occurred, *seeing as*. And yet within hope a considerable dimension of the *as if* remains, a distinctive form that builds upon and grows out of the *seeing as* that has occurred, one that reaffirms the interrelation between faith and hope. Religious imagination is not just the grace of the imagination; it is as well the *creative* imagination of the possible.[61] Moltmann writes analogously of "creative hope."[62] The Resurrection is not an event that closes but one that opens.[63] Hope opens what existing systems would like to close or keep closed.[64] With the notions of the divine economy of the gift and superabundance, God is the source of unknown possibilities, an excess of meaning, meaning that Christians will never finish working through.[65] The imagination offers us "the power to open us to new possibilities."[66] The religious imagination distinctively *combines seeing as* and the *as if*. The "passion for the possible" within the context of the religious imagination reforms what the possible means. A truth has been given on which the possible rests.

The religious imagination retains a component of *as if*, because it is uncertain how the divine promise on which hope relies will unfold over time. It is unknown how the eschatological promise will manifest.[67] In the next section we shall consider the implications for the religious imagination of this continuing function of the *as if*, in the nature of productive religious imagination as incorporative of fiction and figuration. Before doing so, one final area in our consideration of hope remains. Generally speaking, our discussion thus far has been oriented to the horizontal axis of the religious imagination, trying to assess the interrelation between the reproductive and productive religious imagination and in particular what the productive religious imagination means. We now redirect our attention to the implications of the vertical axis of the religious imagination. We start here by returning to Ricoeur's emphasis on hope as a "passion for the possible" and address the nature of hope as a passion. Ricoeur clarifies that the orientation here is psychological, so speaking to the subject side of imagination and its implications for consciousness.[68] Hope as the "*creative* imagination of the possible"(italics in original) is linked to imagination as the "*power* of the imagination."[69] We return to the conception of imagination as a power. In some of his more religiously oriented texts on the grace of imagination, Ricoeur revisits more general vocabulary of the imagination's "mytho-poetic core," but there are nevertheless religious valences, as he writes of humans as created and recreated by a word that engenders this core.[70] The notion of engendering is paramount, a theme that Ricoeur elsewhere ratifies in terms such as regeneration, primordial power, and historical impulse.[71] The core of hope has a kerygmatic center.[72] The power engendering the religious imagination offers a positive characterization of imagination as *power of*. As a function of *power of*, we have not only a responsibility to act—a matter of the horizontal axis—but a power to act, a power of what Richard Kearney calls human "can-be."[73] Internal to the vertical axis, the nature of religious imagination as a function of faith and commitment challenges whether at the height of this axis it can absent itself from belief.

This last matter points to a final set of topics concerning the vertical axis of the religious imagination that concludes this section on hope. These issues involve the range in the degrees of commitment of belief that arise across this axis. The query is no longer oriented to the ways in which religious commitment leads, say, to social and ethical stances, an issue for the productive imagination on the horizontal axis, but to the degrees of commitment of belief on its own.[74] Religious imagination too must be fearful of capture by deception, of capture by belief, of belief in false gods, as the bottom of the vertical axis warns. Ricoeur writes, "The field of hope has exactly the same extension as that of transcendental illusion. I hope at the very place where I am deceived by the so-called absolute objects: I as a substance, freedom as an object in the world, 'God' as a supreme being, as the cause of all causes, as the whole of all partial reality."[75] Believers must watch against idolatry and leave God simply as a name, not an image.[76] Any assumption of accord between history and divine promise falls prey to a guilty natural theology.[77] Mysticism and religious fanaticism mislead in their totalization.[78] In our entry into the hermeneutic circle between belief and understanding, we must always probe whether the circle is vicious or healthy.[79] Hope must always retain some sense of the beyond and not yet, so that it avoids becoming a fetish.[80] Even if the top of the vertical axis of the religious imagination is not one of unbelief (as Ricoeur claims), the prospects of critical distance, of checks on belief, must be retained.

Fiction and Figuration in the Religious Imagination

Ricoeur challenges the presupposition that the Bible is a fixed, closed book, one hostile to a "radically original creation of meaning" and imaginative openness.[81] Instead, we return to the world of the text—now religious text—where hermeneutics is required to explicate that which relates us indirectly to reality and where a productive imagination is at work in the text.[82] The new being that biblical texts announce should be interpreted as "fundamentally imaginary," and these texts in turn appeal to reader's or interpreter's imagination "which they open to new and radical possibilities."[83] In this concluding section of this part, we assess the implications of the religious imagination—in text and in interpretation—as fictions and figurations. How are they not simply false?

For Ricoeur, the interconnection between the imagination in biblical resources and the imagination of interpretation begins in the biblical text itself. Biblical meaning is inseparable from the forms in which it appears.[84] Ricoeur has been particularly acute in this assessment. We must comprehend that biblical language is composed of "speech acts"—"invocation, worship, lamentation, disputation"; rhetorical tropes—"metaphor, metonymy, synecdoche, irony"; and literary genres—"narrative, law, prophecy, hymn, wisdom sayings."[85] Attention to these forms returns us, at a deepened level, to the nature of the biblical text as poetic, with a productive imaginative capacity, a capacity that in turn calls for interpretation.[86]

Ricoeur emphatically and repeatedly characterizes this productive bibli-cal capacity as a form of *redescription*, a breaking with existing reality that brings forward a new dimension of reality. This redescription is a form of *fiction*, a fiction not as that which deviates from reality and so is false but as that which productively opens up new reality.[87] For Ricoeur the productive imagination as fiction is connected to ontology; here the extension is to reli-gion and theology.[88] In the religious imagination, the fictional as redescription functions in two ways. First, as in the parable, the example is itself fictional—a fictional story—that operates metaphorically to transpose reality—a form of *seeing as*—to indicate what the kingdom of God is like.[89] Ricoeur speaks of religious language as involving the "intensification" of the metaphorical func-tion and the "limit-metaphor."[90] Second, the religious imagination may also combine *seeing as* and the *as if*, where the *as if* is the fictional, building upon a claimed truth, the *seeing as*, and seeking to tease out and work through the implications and extensions of the claimed truth. More broadly, as we have discussed, the nature of religious imagination as hope is similar: it is faith in a truth whose parameters remain to unfold. The theological imagination acts to extend existing religious truths to consider future possibles. Human practice can seek to make some of these future possibles real. Mark Wallace suggests that biblical faith offers "true fictions."[91]

We can better comprehend the availability of the fictional in religious language when we perceive that in turn it rests on the availability of the *figurative* in religious texts. To some extent the figurative here is a matter of religious language as figurative. For example, in our previous reference to Ricoeur's analysis of biblical language as speech acts, rhetorical tropes, and literary genres, he sums these attributes as figurative.[92] More broadly, the claim is that *religious thought* is itself figurative. It engages in "figura-tive thinking" (a translation of *Vorstellung*).[93] Figurative religious thought includes not only narrative and symbol but conceptions such as "Trinity, Creation, Fall, Incarnation, and Salvation," all of which remain pictorial and so figurative.[94] Most significantly for Ricoeur, the notion of the figurative as picturing returns us to the heart of the productive imagination, where innova-tion is not simply schematized but pictured.[95] No longer is picturing a matter of reproductive imagination of an existing image; instead, as Ricoeur argues in "Biblical Hermeneutics," the "figure" offers a mode of being that can be *displayed*, an expression of something new, a productive imagination.[96] In his larger consideration of the interrelation between figurative and concep-tual thought, Ricoeur questions whether the human mind can ever be simply conceptual or instead whether the conceptual continues to need the support of the figurative and thinking in pictures.[97] In this view, again, the religious and theological are not isolable or outmoded modes of thinking but partake of approaches common across thought.

In the secondary commentary on Ricoeur, Dan Stiver and Mark Wallace are especially astute in their appreciation of the figurative in Ricoeur's thinking on religion. In *Ricoeur and Theology*, Stiver has a chapter on "Figuration and Theology" in which he argues for Ricoeur's "figurative turn."[98] Wallace is prescient in entitling his collection of Ricoeur articles on religion precisely *Figuring the Sacred*. His introduction to that volume amplifies the rationale for that title. On the one hand, he urges more broadly, "The role of figurative texts in the formation of human subjectivity is the unifying theme that underlies Ricoeur's writing." More specifically, he continues, religion speaks to the "imaginative potential of myth, symbol, and story."[99] Religious faith lives out "the figures of hope unleashed by the imagination."[100] Ricoeur, Wallace says, maintains "the integrity of figurative modes of religious discourse."[101] Similarly motifs appear in other of Wallace's writings. He praises the way that Ricoeur's "figural ontology" provides a basis, as we have discussed, for the productive, imaginative capacity of figuration in the biblical context.[102] He recognizes the "scriptural figuration of the divine life" and the way that through the Bible's "figurative variations on reality, the imagination is appealed to so that we might see the world as the text depicts it."[103] For Ricoeur, the religious promise is never unadorned truth but always figured. It is offered in the form of fiction, a matter of productive imagination. Figuration runs all the way down.

A final few points remain as we conclude this section on fiction and figuration in the religious imagination. To this stage, we have emphasized the role of productive imagination within the religious text. Yet this form of productive imagination must be complemented by productive imagination in the reader or interpreter. In part, this ability is a capacity to receive; it is also a capacity of the interpreter's productive imagination itself. This is perhaps most easily discerned in the imaginative capacity of biblical authors, who are themselves interpreters. It is also available in all believing interpreters. The act of reading a biblical text, Ricoeur says, is "guided by a productive imagination at work in the text" but is also itself a "creative operation" applying and extending biblical meaning. The act of reading "realizes the union of fiction and redescription that characterizes the imagination."[104] The interpretive role is not simply one of reading but also of practice, seeking imaginatively to implement the divine insight in personal, social, and ecclesial ways.[105] This act of reading and interpretation will become more problematical when in the next part we move out of the context of religious belief, the frame of this part.

We also need to be alert to adverse consequences of the fictional and figurative on the vertical axis of the religious imagination: the dangers of being captured by various figurations. We elaborated similar concerns in the arena of hope. In commenting on the revelation in Exodus of the name of God as "I am that I am," Ricoeur argues that it is "the dissolution of all anthropomorphisms, of all figures and figurations, including that of the father. The name against the idol. All nonmetaphoric sonship, all literal descent, is thus reduced. . . . [I]t is the name without image and without idol."[106] Elsewhere Ricoeur writes similarly that the name of God in the Old Testament "excludes the figure"; it is the "demythologization of the figure of the idol."[107]

I conclude this part by referencing how Ricoeur encapsulates the interrelation between what I am calling the *as if* and the *seeing as* within the religious imagination. In a little discussed text comparing and contrasting faith with ideology and utopia, Ricoeur argues ultimately that faith is rooted more deeply than the oscillation or conflict between ideology and utopia, because it shares both. "The root of faith," he says, "is somewhere near that point where Expectation"—hope, the utopian, the future *as if*—"springs forth out of Memory," memory in the granting of the promise, the ideological as constitutive, as *seeing as*.[108] We find in the religious imagination the intertwining between reproductive and productive imagination and an intertwining between *seeing as* and the *as if*. "[T]he God of hope and the God of creation are one and the same God at both extremes of the economy of the gift."[109]

THE RELIGIOUS IMAGINATION FROM A PERSPECTIVE OUTSIDE BELIEF

In part three, we turn to the religious imagination from a perspective outside belief. We return more directly to Ricoeur's vocabulary in "Philosophy and Religious Language," where religious belief was not presumed, and that article's claim that interpretation of a religious text delineates the "world of the text" as a "proposed world." We evaluate whether the model advanced in this article reflects Ricoeur's approach across his writings on religious interpretation (again, outside a faith perspective) and conclude that it does. Our orientation in this initial section is simply descriptive, an attempt to capture Ricoeur's model. Our thesis is that this orientation marks the imagination in the religious text as one solely of *as if*, with transposition to a new truth, *seeing as*, dependent upon the role of refiguration of the text undertaken by the reader or interpreter. In the final section of this part, we consider how other parts of Ricoeur's corpus on the poetic imagination might offer an alternative orientation that reincorporates *seeing as*, transposition, as more a work coming out of the text. In this part, consistent with Ricoeur's stance, the religious imagination and the religious hermeneutic are again treated as regional variants of the poetic imagination and a general hermeneutic.

The Projected World of the Religious Text

Our initial point in this part reiterates Ricoeur's broad emphasis that a biblical hermeneutic is a regional hermeneutic of a general hermeneutic category.[110]

Religious texts are forms of poetic texts.[111] Ricoeur reaffirms these assertions from "Philosophy and Religious Language" in similar language elsewhere. In "Naming God" and "Toward a Hermeneutic of the Idea of Revelation," for instance, Ricoeur discusses a provisional "assimilation of biblical texts to poetic texts," biblical hermeneutics again as regional hermeneutic, and the poetic as a form of revelation in a nonreligious sense.[112]

A second point, also recalled from "Philosophy and Religious Language" but needing greater elaboration, is that "faith never appears as an immediate experience but always as mediated by a certain language that articulates it."[113] Religious experience "comes to language" and should be interpreted on the basis of its linguistic character.[114] A decisive move here is a distinction between the author and the text created by the author. On the one hand, Ricoeur rejects the reduction of the biblical message to any form of the author's psychological inspiration, the insufflation of meaning. Ricoeur frequently reiterates this emphasis.[115] The author's meaning is not reducible to psychological inspiration, and the author's inspiration is not available to us. There is no unmediated psychological communion between the biblical author and reader. Meaning must be located in the text. As a text, the Gospel creates a distance from any event that it proclaims: "distance is given at the beginning."[116] There is no transparency between the event and the reader or between the author and the reader. The text mediates between both. Any aspiration toward "literal meaning" must locate that meaning in the text.[117] On the reader's side, exegesis is not turned at the outset toward existential appropriation but toward a more objective elaboration of meaning.[118] Revelation is a matter of the issue of the text, an issue of the biblical word.[119] While in this context, Ricoeur reasserts that we must choose between hermeneutics—here a hermeneutics of biblical testimony—and absolute knowledge, it appears to be more emphatically the case that for Ricoeur no choice is available because of the lack of immediacy to originary religious events.[120]

As in "Philosophy and Religious Language," Ricoeur often adverts to manifestation as "revelatory," a force of "rupture" or "breaking through" and "opening." [121] Manifestation "shatters our ordinary beliefs about the 'real' world."[122] From this vocabulary, we might presume that manifestation in the religious context necessarily involves a form of transposition, a way of *seeing as*, the disclosure of a new reality. Yet it is critical to appreciate that for Ricoeur the "reality" newly manifested in the religious text is instead a "reality of the possible."[123] The manifestation offers the "proposing" of a world, a "projected" world, one that the reader might inhabit.[124] As we shall shortly discuss, manifestation's proposing of a world, this reality of the possible, has quite different valences than in the context of existing religious belief.

Before taking that step, we need to reclaim that what the religious text proposes is a *world*. This world is an implication of the religious text as language. This world separates from the presumed author and from the beliefs or non-beliefs of the reader and instead requires interpretation of the issue of the text, the world it unfolds.[125] As we have cited before from "Philosophy and Religious Language" and as Ricoeur reasserts elsewhere, "above and beyond emotions, disposition, belief, or nonbelief, is the proposition of a world that in the biblical language is called a new world, a new covenant, the kingdom of God, a new birth."[126] Ricoeur's reference to the *world* of the biblical text is frequent.[127] Certainly for Ricoeur, as we have seen, the naming of God by religious language renders that language distinctive and intensified, not simply a regional hermeneutic or poetics but unique.[128] Yet this naming of God does not appear to disrupt Ricoeur's hermeneutic concentration on interpretation of the world of the religious text.[129]

The poetic nature of religious language for Ricoeur seems accepted in secondary commentary, even if in expression of disagreement.[130] Ricoeur's emphasis on biblical interpretation as oriented to the *world* of the religious text also seems a common understanding in the secondary literature.[131] These points of agreement in the understanding of Ricoeur's mature orientation are significant for my argument in this part, because I want that argument to rest on a considered view of Ricoeur's approach rather than something idiosyncratic. What seems less a common understanding are the implications of Ricoeur's approach for the religious imagination. We need to address Ricoeur's more specific vocabulary in characterizing the world of the religious text. In the language of "Philosophy and Religious Language," the religious text offers "a *proposed* world, a world that I *might* inhabit and wherein I might *project* my ownmost *possibilities*."[132] It is the "*proposition* of a world."[133] New "*possibilities* of being-in-the-world are opened up."[134] This is the vocabulary not of *seeing as*, where a transposition has occurred and we see reality in a new way, but that of *as if,* the *possible* world, a *possible* new reality. Recall with new emphasis that in "Philosophy and Religious Language," Ricoeur speaks of the poetic as offered in the "modality of *possibility*," a manifestation by means of *imaginative variation*.[135] Attention in the secondary literature to Ricoeur's vocabulary of the *possibility* and *projection* of a world is sparser.[136]

The consequences of Ricoeur's perspective for the religious imagination are significant. It remains the case that the productive imagination functions in the religious text; the text is the vehicle of manifestation. But it is through the *interpreter*'s imagination in the act of reading that is realized "the union of fiction and redescription that characterizes the imagination in the most pregnant sense of this term."[137] The "poem of the Exodus and the poem of the resurrection" are addressed to our imagination.[138] Biblical "metaphorization" "exercises the reader's productive imagination."[139] To listen to the parables is to "let one's imagination be opened to the new possibilities" they disclose.[140] Our imagination is "the power to open us to new possibilities."[141] In his essay on revelation, Ricoeur contends that it is our imagination that responds to the text as a poem and that "alone can encounter revelation no longer as an unacceptable pretension, but a nonviolent appeal."[142] Ricoeur's reference to revelation as a nonviolent appeal appears also at several other junctures in this essay.[143]

The language of revelation as a nonviolent appeal and that of the reader's imagination as opening to new possibilities is the language of imagination as *as if*, of possibilities being proposed rather than of *seeing* reality *as*, in a new, transposed way. For the nonbeliever approaching the religious text, the context is quite different than the religious believer perceiving the possible, the *as if*, as an outgrowth of an existing truth, a prior *seeing as*. In the situation of the nonbeliever, it is dependent upon the reader to actualize—or not—the text's meaning. Any *event* of meaning is a product of the reading.[144] The reader's imagination is invited to continue the biblical itineraries of meaning.[145] We move from the operation of imagination in the biblical text to the reader's "work of imagination *about* the text."[146] Ricoeur's mature methodological stance in analyzing religious texts seems parallel to his approach in *Time and Narrative*. The text proposes a world—*configures* a world—and the reader interprets it—*refigures* it. It is left to the reader's judgment—a voluntary act—whether and how to appropriate the message of the religious text.

Criticism of Ricoeur from a Christian perspective by those otherwise sympathetic to him has been forceful here. Daniel Frey objects that Ricoeur's laicization of religious language incorporates it into a philosophy of imagination where language speaks imaginatively instead of revealing a new truth by means of divine action, a revelation otherwise unknown to us.[147] For Brian Gregor, it is not simply that the biblical text names God but that God names in and through the text. The regenerating power of the Bible is different from other poetic texts.[148] Underscoring the consequences of the religious text as manifestation of the *possible*, Kevin Vanhoozer asks why one should hearken to the biblical message rather than any other poetic text.[149] Might not other poetic texts similarly solicit the imagination's interest?[150] "To suggest that the work of the Holy Spirit has its approximation in the phenomenon of imaginative appropriation is, in my opinion, to miss the whole point of the Gospels, namely, that it is only thanks to a divine initiative of deed and word that the possibility of resurrection freedom becomes ours."[151] For Christianity, Vanhoozer argues, it is the Spirit and "not the imagination" that is "the power that appropriates the kerygma."[152]

I would like to determine whether Ricoeur's approach can be more responsive to these concerns. My own methodological stance does not proceed from a religious vantage point. I do not assume a perspective of faith but rather proceed from an independent methodological place. I hope to show that this independence has some benefits, as it may assist the credibility that my argument is not simply faith-based. I will proceed on the basis of the following

evaluation. It seems ironic that while, as we have shown, in Ricoeur's philosophical poetics of the mid-1970s, he does not hesitate to describe how a text
manifests a new world and how the reader is transfigured by it—the reader
sees as—he does not want to employ this same vocabulary and orientation in
discussing the imaginative interpretation by a nonbeliever of a religious text.
For Ricoeur, the reader of the religious text is not transfigured by it, does
not undergo an experience of conversion. Just as I criticize Ricoeur's larger
theory of productive imagination for moving, in *Time and Narrative*, to
grant too great a weight in interpretation to the role and control of the reader,
similarly within the reading of a religious text, it seems limited as a matter of
description to characterize the reader simply as refiguring the proposed text
rather than ever being transposed and transfigured by and through it. In very
interesting ways, at least in parts of his work, Ricoeur seems more open to the
imagination of general poetic revelation than to present religious revelation.

In the section that follows in this part, I want to argue that resources for a
contrary position advancing *seeing as* in the reading of the religious text may
lie within Ricoeur. But to conclude the present section and set the stage for
the section to come, one last step remains. It may be objected that my presentation of Ricoeur's stance is one-sided. What about, for instance, the language
of Ricoeur's article, "Listening to the Parables of Jesus," and its depiction of
how the meaning of a parable "invades us, overwhelms us, beyond our control
and our grasp . . . as a gift."[153] I hope it is apparent that this form of presentation does not reflect Ricoeur's mature view as I have tried to describe it and as
the secondary sources generally endorse. The quotation is quite different than
an evaluation of the world of the text and revelation as a "nonviolent appeal."
Even by the end of this essay, Ricoeur's argument is similar to his mature
analysis. In the essay, he describes the parable's poetic power as a power of
an event, but it is an event where one "*let[s]* one's imagination to be opened
to the new *possibilities* disclosed."[154] Similarly, while some of Ricoeur's
earlier vocabulary on "limit-expressions" and "limit-experiences" in religion
encompass not just the possible, the *as if*, but *seeing as*, yet in his mature
work, the description of limit-experiences is quite different, ascribing them
as "possible world[s]" or as "imaginative variations."[155] For my purposes,
we must elaborate Ricoeur's mature views on the religious imagination and
determine whether, from a perspective outside faith, there are resources in
Ricoeur more responsive to the religious imagination as *seeing as* rather than
just *as if* that can encompass rather than reject these mature views.

Seeing as a Work of the Text

Throughout this chapter, we have accepted Ricoeur's argument that no unmediated access to an author—whether an author earthly or divinely inspired—is

available due to the text acting as a form of inextricable mediation. We have no direct access to whatever may be the source of the author's gift, whether divine or secular inspiration, individual psychology, or subjectivity. In the development of his theory, Ricoeur also appears to suspend the role of the subjective, intuitive, or psychological on the side of the reader, as themselves attempts to seek immediacy and therefore misconstruals of what is available in interpretation, which is instead the working through the mediation of the world of the text. Due to the nature of textual mediation, in Ricoeur's view, the world of the text, including the religious text, is the proposal of a world, a proposal that is *as if*. The text configures a meaning, and a reader or interpreter refigures it.

If we accept that we have no direct access to an author, the question for the present section is whether we can find resources in Ricoeur outside of his reflections on the world of the text that can demonstrate how a transposition, a transfiguration of belief, can both occur in the reader or interpreter and occur in a way consistent with notions of religious imagination as divine action. We now attempt, then, to respond to objections in the secondary literature that Ricoeur's poetics of the imagination superimposes itself on what should be a distinctive, religious imagination.[156] We make the attempt, though, by returning to the ways that the workings of the poetic imagination may in fact illuminate the workings of the religious imagination.

In "Listening to the Parables of Jesus," Ricoeur writes of the religious experience that "happens to us, . . . beyond our control and our grasp, beyond our willing and our planning, . . . the Event . . . as a gift."[157] Ricoeur also speaks early of the religious imaginative moment as going further than the abstract and cerebral and encompassing the heart, "in short . . . the whole human being."[158] This aspect of the imagination needs particular development. In another early essay, on "The Metaphorical Process," Ricoeur especially elaborates, as he does not elsewhere, the role of feeling. Feelings are not merely emotive—something simply subjective—but have a cognitive dimension. They help complete imagination because they make thought *ours*; there is "felt participation."[159] We are "included in the process as knowing subjects."[160] Feeling speaks to the subject side of imagination. Ricoeur writes elsewhere of the *force* of imagination, its power, which feeling also encompasses and adds to the subject axis contributions of imagination.[161] The notion of feeling as thought made ours, of felt participation, indicates that our perspective has changed. There is *apperception*, the "sudden insight," an "instantaneous grasping," a transposition, an event.[162] We *see as* rather than *as if*.

Yet can the references to feeling, force, and apperception, which all come from the early Ricoeur, be retained in light of the mature theory of the religious imagination that Ricoeur advances? My claim here, pivotal to my thesis, is that if we expand on Ricoeur's discussion of what is called the *psycholinguistic*, in both a technical and more extensive understanding of the term, we can recover the ways that an interpreter is transposed by the gift to the imagination, ways that Ricoeur's mature thought does not address and is not responsive to. I attempt to use Ricoeur, then, against himself. Let me set the stage for this discussion by indicating that the psycholinguistic wants to contest that imaginative transposition is simply a language event. Transposition is not a function of the operation of language itself in the act of reading. One might respond by suggesting that this observation in fact supports Ricoeur's later insistence on the role of reader refiguration. Yet Ricoeur's examination of the psycholinguistic offers a recoverable perspective internal to his earlier work on metaphor and imagination.

Ricoeur's principal discussion of the psycholinguistic and its extensions comes in but two places, in his article on "The Metaphorical Process" and in some pages in *The Rule of Metaphor*.[163] As he observes, the problem is an outgrowth of Kant's reflections on the schematism as the conjunction between the logical—the conceptual—and the sensible—the senses.[164] The logical side is semantic, the actions of language, but the sensible side is psychological, involving feeling.[165] The poetic offers an intersection between meaning and the senses.[166] The act of transposition in metaphor involves then a mixed approach of language and psychology, something psycholinguistic.[167] There is an incursion of the psychological into the semantic. Metaphor and imagination are not simply semantic, not simply actions of language. Significantly, Ricoeur characterizes psycholinguistics not as prior to language but as embodied in language and therefore "postlinguistic." Psycholinguistics then satisfies Ricoeur's concern to avoid the merely subjective, merely impressionistic, merely intuitive, merely im-mediate.[168] The psycholinguistic is mediated; it occurs through the medium of language although is not simply a product of language. Extensions of Ricoeur's argument on the psycholinguistic lead to his conception of *seeing as*. *Seeing as* is itself "half thought and half experience;" it combines the sensible and the conceptual or linguistic.[169] In anticipation of Ricoeur's later vocabulary, we should note that for Ricoeur "*to figure* is always *to see as*."[170] Figuration too includes both a conceptual side and a sensible side.[171] The psychological, sensible, feeling side of psycholinguistics, *seeing as*, and figuration offer the subject side of imagination, the vertical axis.

Ricoeur's exploration and extension of the psycholinguistic help refine what "comes to" language. For Ricoeur, a succeeding step is the recognition that what comes to language on the "sensible" side is not just the product of the physical senses but also something potentially quite more profound. A "more deeply rooted operation of feeling" acts to "insert us within the world in a nonobjectifying manner."[172] The poetic imagination schematizes the pre-objective.[173] Revealed through the pre-objective are "deep structures of reality."[174] Revealed are deep feelings that go beyond emotion or passion, a coming to language of experiences that are not completely of language even if articulated through language.[175]

We know that in some early formulations in the 1970s, Ricoeur seems to allow that what may come to language in religious terms is divine manifestation. We have referenced his 1974 essay, "Listening to the Parables of Jesus," on "the Event . . . as a gift."[176] In "Biblical Hermeneutics," Ricoeur claims "that the *eruption of the unheard in* our discourse and *in* our experience constitutes precisely one dimension *of* our discourse and *of* our experience."[177] (It is true even here that the eruption as divine action is less than evident.) Then there is the 1993 essay, "L'enchevêtrement de la voix et de l'écrit dans le discours biblique," and the claim that faith consists in the belief that the interior witness to the Holy Spirit and the inspiration attributed to Scriptures owe to the work of the same Spirit. Ricoeur's posture here too is unclear, as he notes that the belief may be recognized not only by the faithful but also by those acting in "imagination and sympathy in the suspense of belief."[178] In any event, as we have previously delineated, these passages do not comport with Ricoeur's mature reflections on the religious imagination.

By contrast, my claim is that Ricoeur's analysis of the psycholinguistic and its extensions, though a product of his earlier work, does remain relevant to the evaluation of his mature work, as it applies both to the poetic imagination and the religious imagination. The psycholinguistic thread requires expansion beyond the object side of imagination to its subject side, to feeling, experience, consciousness, and the power that comes to bear in those experiences. The poetic imagination is a gift that comes from elsewhere; the religious imagination may too. The subject side of the imagination may allow for divine action in that "kernel of opacity" that is the transposition to a new reality.[179] Something beyond language comes to language. There may indeed be a "grace of imagination," a conversion of the religious imagination.[180]

As I have stated, my own wager has been that detailed analytic examination of the operation of the poetic imagination in Ricoeur allows for greater, more delineated insight into the operation of the religious imagination also, in ways that are sympathetic to the secondary accounts but seek to respond to them on the basis of greater precision.[181] Admittedly, the conclusion pointing to the possibility of divine action does not extend to the *reality* of divine action but offers only its *possibility*.[182] Yet, this conclusion will hopefully be of interest to religious believers who, as we have seen, otherwise may find Ricoeur's accounts searching in their probity but unsatisfying, even as they find a conclusion resting on possibility ultimately unsatisfying as well. The chapter further does not address the question, critical for Christian believers, whether Jesus's crucifixion and resurrection were real historical events that decisively changed human prospects.[183] This conclusion will be unsatisfying for believers also. Hopefully, the chapter will remain of value for arguments about the nature of the religious imagination that offer more of a bridge to religious belief.

Gives Rise to Thought

In this final, brief section of part three, we return to give emphasis to a side of Ricoeur's approach to the religious imagination that we have witnessed throughout. In the language of *The Symbolism of Evil*, the religious imagination "gives rise to thought."[184] Throughout our accounts of both the poetic and religious imagination, we have seen how for Ricoeur the imagination is not simply a mystical event but is describable in considerable detail, up to the moment of opacity in the transposition. At this juncture, we may say that Ricoeur offers two great contributions to elaboration of the poetic and religious poetic: on the one hand, an unfolding of the availability of manifestation itself, and on the other an extensive analysis of the role of thought in its elaboration, including his own thought in making this assessment. At a historical time when many religious believers seem to feel obligated to decide between faith or critical distance, Ricoeur offers a valuable alternative path that argues for their interrelation.

That the religious imagination gives rise to thought is not an optional mode, a process of thinking that we can choose or decline to undertake. Throughout his corpus on religious interpretation, Ricoeur's vocabulary is replete with notions that the figurative "requires" movement to the conceptual, that this movement is not "superimposed from outside" but motivated by the nature of the figurative itself.[185] The speculative is "not extrinsic" to the figurative but generated as a manner of an "inner dialectic," an "inner dynamism" that directs the figurative toward the speculative.[186] There is no religious event that does not also have "meaning."[187] Speculative thought is involved even in the naming of God.[188] As we have discussed, on the side of thought the religious imagination seeks to think through the implications of religious events and moments of inspiration, seeks to work out doctrinal and theological significance. Religious interpretation "promotes the meaning, forms the meaning," teases out the projects for existence.[189] Religious interpretation also considers ethical implications. As Ricoeur writes in "Biblical Hermeneutics": "It is the task of ethics to articulate its coherent discourse by listening to what the poets say."[190] At the same time, the side of thought remains cautioned by the religious imagination not to be caught by theological idolatry; thought must retain affiliation with its imaginative beginnings.[191] Finally, as we saw in part two on productive imagination as fiction and figuration, one of the signal attributes of Ricoeur's contribution is not only an overcoming of a divide between the religious imagination and thought but an articulation of this relationship through a distinct formulation of thought, "another reason."[192] "[I]f we give to poetic language the function of redescription through fictions, then we can say that the logical space opened by Kant between *Denken* and *Erkennen*, between 'Thought' and 'Knowledge,' is the place of indirect discourse, of symbols, parables, and myths, as the indirect presentation of the Unconditioned."[193] On the vertical axis of the religious imagination, faith need not be insular and captured but remains integrally open to thought and critical reflection.

NOTES

1. Paul Ricoeur, *Lectures on Imagination*, ed. George H. Taylor, Robert D. Sweeney, Jean-Luc Amalric, and Patrick F. Crosby (Chicago: University of Chicago Press, 2024), 243.

2. Reference to the "religious imagination" is shorthand for what Ricoeur typically refers to as the religious imagination from a Christian perspective.

3. Ricoeur, *Lectures on Imagination*, 7–10.

4. See, for example, George H. Taylor, "Editor's Introduction," in *Lectures on Imagination*, xxxiv, xxxvii–iii.

5. Ricoeur, *Lectures on Imagination*, 71–74; Paul Ricoeur, *The Rule of Metaphor: Multi-Disciplinary Studies of the Creation of Meaning in Language*, trans. Robert Czerny with Kathleen McLaughlin and John Costello, S. J. (Toronto: University of Toronto Press, 1977; London: Routledge, 2003 [different pagination]), 213/253; Paul Ricoeur, "The Metaphorical Process as Cognition, Imagination, and Feeling," *Critical Inquiry* 5 (Autumn 1978): 149, republished in *On Metaphor*, ed. Sheldon Sacks (Chicago: University of Chicago Press, 1979), 147 [hereafter identified by pagination in both publications]; Paul Ricoeur, "The Function of Fiction in Shaping Reality," in *A Ricoeur Reader: Reflection and Imagination*, ed. Mario J. Valdès (Toronto: University of Toronto Press, 1991), 126; Paul Ricoeur, "Imagination in Discourse and in Action," in *From Text to Action: Essays in Hermeneutics, II*, trans. Kathleen Blamey and John B. Thompson (Evanston, IL: Northwestern University Press, 1991), 173.

6. Ricoeur, *Lectures on Imagination*, 240.

7. Paul Ricoeur, "Philosophy and Religious Language," in *Figuring the Sacred: Religion, Narrative, and Imagination*, ed. Mark I. Wallace, trans. David Pellauer (Minneapolis: Fortress Press, 1995), 45. Ricoeur's location of religious language within poetic language, at least in an initial sense, is a frequent theme. See Paul Ricoeur, "Poétique et symbolique," in *Initiation à la pratique de la théologie*, volume 1, ed. Bernard Lauret and François Refoulé (Paris: Cerf, 1982), 39; Paul Ricoeur, "Poetry and Possibility," in *A Ricoeur Reader: Reflection and Imagination*, ed. Mario J. Valdès (Toronto: University of Toronto Press, 1991), 454.

8. Ricoeur, "Philosophy and Religious Language," 35.

9. Paul Ricoeur, "Contribution d'une réflexion sur le langage à une théologie de la parole," *Revue de théologie et de philosophie*, 18 (1968): 345.

10. Ricoeur, "Philosophy and Religious Language," 45.

11. Paul Ricoeur, "Appropriation," in *Hermeneutics and the Human Sciences: Essays on Language, Action and Interpretation*, ed. John B. Thompson (Cambridge, UK: Cambridge University Press, 1981), 193.

12. Paul Ricoeur, "Manifestation and Proclamation," in *Figuring the Sacred*, 50.

13. Daniel Frey, *La religion dans la philosophie de Paul Ricoeur* (Paris: Hermann, 2021), 303. Using the vocabulary of metaphor, Frey argues himself that "truth can be as metaphoric as one wants, but there is no metaphor unless all is not metaphor and therefore no metaphoric truth unless there are cores reputed true in themselves." Daniel Frey, "La religion dans l'oeuvre de Ricoeur," *Études Ricoeuriennes/Ricoeur Studies* 13, no. 2 (2022): 20 (my translation).

14. Dan R. Stiver, *Theology After Ricoeur: New Directions in Hermeneutical Theology* (Louisville, KY: Westminster John Knox Press, 2001), 232: "The promising import of hermeneutical philosophy is precisely that it is a general epistemology that arises virtually from within the faith context." Stiver extends the argument more broadly to the greater proximity between faith and reason, an important consideration that I do not pursue here. Stiver, 14. For Gilbert Vincent too, Ricoeur acts as an arbiter between reason and belief, attempting to find in their different traditions dialogical resources that enlarge the cultural horizon of each. He suggests that Ricoeur is engaged in advocacy of a generous conception of laicity, an approach that, as I have mentioned, Daniel Frey later rejects. Gilbert Vincent, *La religion de Ricoeur* (Paris: Les Éditions de l'Atelier, 2008), 147; Frey, *La religion dans la philosophie de Paul Ricoeur*, 211.

15. Paul Ricoeur, *The Symbolism of Evil*, trans. Emerson Buchanan (Boston: Beacon Press, 1967), 348.

16. For explicit reference to semantic autonomy in the context of biblical interpretation, see Paul Ricoeur, "Philosophical Hermeneutics and Theological Hermeneutics," *Sciences Religieuses/Studies in Religion* 5, no. 1 (Summer 1975): 18.

17. Ricoeur, "Philosophy and Religious Language," 43–44.

18. Paul Ricoeur, "Naming God," in *Figuring the Sacred*, 222. Ricoeur argues that poetic and religious language proceed equally as manifestation and revelation of a world. Paul Ricoeur, "Foi et philosophie aujourd'hui," *Foi-Éducation* 42, no. 100 (1972): 7.

19. Ricoeur, "Philosophy and Religious Language," 43. For quite similar language, see Ricoeur, "Philosophical Hermeneutics and Theological Hermeneutics," 26.

20. Paul Ricoeur, "Preface," in *Studies in the Philosophy of Paul Ricoeur*, ed. Charles E. Reagan (Athens, OH: Ohio University Press, 1979), xviii.

21. Ricoeur, "Philosophy and Religious Language," 43.

22. Ricoeur, "Philosophy and Religious Language," 35–36.

23. Ricoeur, "Philosophy and Religious Language," 35.

24. Ricoeur, "Philosophy and Religious Language," 44. While during this time period Ricoeur did consider reader appropriation of the text, only later did he develop the theme of reader "refiguration" of a text. Ricoeur, "Appropriation"; Paul Ricoeur, *Time and Narrative*, volume 1, trans. Kathleen McLaughlin and David Pellauer (Chicago: University of Chicago Press, 1984), 70–87.

25. Ricoeur, "Philosophy and Religious Language," 44, 46.

26. Ricoeur, "Philosophy and Religious Language," 46. Ricoeur acknowledges that his approach to religious language participates in a larger theological trend giving priority to "linguisticality" and subordination of existential interpretation, a reaction to Bultmann's remaining caught in subjectivist, romanticist hermeneutics. Paul Ricoeur, "From Existentialism to the Philosophy of Language," in *The Rule of Metaphor*, 320/378.

27. Ricoeur, "Philosophy and Religious Language," 45. For similar language, see Ricoeur, "Philosophical Hermeneutics and Theological Hermeneutics," 27.

28. Paul Ricoeur, "Listening to the Parables of Jesus," in *The Philosophy of Paul Ricoeur: An Anthology of His Work*, ed. Charles E. Reagan and David Stewart (Boston: Beacon Press, 1978), 241. Originally published in *Criterion* 13, no. 3 (1974): 18–22.

29. I am aware that the contrasts I am alleging between these two essays raise the challenge that I in fact misunderstand Ricoeur's contentions and that these two essays can be reconciled. At least implicitly, the remainder of my argument, particularly in part three, will seek to refute this possible challenge.

30. Paul Ricoeur, "The Bible and the Imagination," in *Figuring the Sacred*, 144.

31. Paul Ricoeur, "Pastoral Praxeology, Hermeneutics, and Identity," in *Figuring the Sacred*, 311.

32. Paul Ricoeur, "Biblical Readings and Meditations," in *Critique and Conviction: Conversations with François Azouvi and Marc de Launay*, trans. Kathleen Blamey (New York: Columbia University Press, 1998), 145; Paul Ricoeur, *Oneself as Another*, trans. Kathleen Blamey (Chicago: University of Chicago Press, 1992), 25.

33. See, for example, Barnabas Aspray, *Ricoeur at the Limits of Philosophy: God, Creation, and Evil* (Cambridge, UK: Cambridge University Press, 2022), 43; Brian Treanor and Henry Isaac Venema, "Introduction: How Much More Than the Possible?," in *A Passion for the Possible: Thinking with Paul Ricoeur*, ed. Brian Treanor and Henry Isaac Venema (New York: Fordham University Press, 2010), 2; Kevin J. Vanhoozer, *Biblical Narrative in the Philosophy of Paul Ricoeur: A Study in Hermeneutics and Theology* (Cambridge: Cambridge University Press, 1990), 6. As we shall discuss, for Ricoeur's reference to the "passion for the possible," see Paul Ricoeur, "Freedom in the Light of Hope," in *The Conflict of Interpretations*, ed. Don Ihde (Evanston, IL: Northwestern University Press, 1974), 407.

34. For an example of an alternative to the primacy of hope, see Paul Ricoeur, "Paul the Apostle: Proclamation and Argumentation," trans. David Pellauer, in *Paul and the Philosophers*, ed. Ward Blanton and Hent De Vries (New York: Fordham University Press, 2013), 276: "Is love not . . . placed even higher than the law and hope?" I do not dispute that Ricoeur's inquiry of hope is philosophical, but as we shall develop, it has theological bases. I agree, then, with Daniel Frey that for Ricoeur the imagination of the possible is inseparable from a theological hope. Frey, *La religion dans la philosophie de Paul Ricoeur*, 112.

35. Paul Ricoeur, *Lectures on Ideology and Utopia*, ed. George H. Taylor (New York: Columbia University Press, 1986), 310.

36. Paul Ricoeur, "Fatherhood: From Phantasm to Symbol," trans. Robert Sweeney, in *The Conflict of Interpretations*, 481.

37. Ricoeur, "Freedom in the Light of Hope," 407. Ricoeur returns similarly to the language of the "passion for the possible" elsewhere. Paul Ricoeur, "Guilt, Ethics, and Religion," in *The Conflict of Interpretations*, 437.

38. Ricoeur includes the importance of promise not only in Christian but in Jewish sources (Ricoeur, "Foi et philosophie aujourd'hui," 8).

39. Paul Ricoeur, "The Demythization of Accusation," trans. Peter McCormick, in *The Conflict of Interpretations*, 345.

40. Ricoeur, "Paul the Apostle," 265 (citing *Ephesians* 2:12); Ricoeur, "Freedom in the Light of Hope," 410 (quoting *Romans* 5:12–20).

41. Ricoeur, "Foi et philosophie aujourd'hui," 9.

42. We might reference Ricoeur's discussion of promise in *Oneself as Another*. The making of a promise is itself a pledge, an illocutionary act, a doing in the saying. Ricoeur, *Oneself as Another*, 42–43.

43. Paul Ricoeur, "Love and Justice," in *Figuring the Sacred*, 325; Paul Ricoeur, "Ethical and Theological Considerations on the Golden Rule," in *Figuring the Sacred*, 299. Ricoeur contends that the concept of a gift has no place in Kant, since it is a "category of the Sacred." Ricoeur, "Freedom in the Light of Hope," 421.

44. Paul Ricoeur, *Plaidoyer pour l'utopie ecclésiale*, ed. Olivier Abel and Alberto Romele (Genève: Labor et Fides, 2016), 16; Ricoeur, "Foi et philosophie aujourd'hui," 9; Ricoeur, "Freedom in the Light of Hope," 410. See also Ricoeur, "Guilt, Ethics, and Religion," 437; Paul Ricoeur, "Hope and the Structure of Philosophical Systems," in *Figuring the Sacred*, 216.

45. Ricoeur, *Plaidoyer pour l'utopie ecclésiale*, 17, 58–59.

46. James Fodor, *Christian Hermeneutics: Paul Ricoeur and the Refiguring of Theology* (Oxford: Clarendon Press, 1995), 337; Frey, *La religion dans la philosophie de Paul Ricoeur*, 268; William Schweiker, "Imagination, Violence, and Hope: A Theological Response to Ricoeur's Moral Philosophy," in *Meanings in Texts and Actions: Questioning Paul Ricoeur*, ed. David E. Klemm and William Schweiker (Charlottesville, VA: University Press of Virginia, 1993), 213; Peter de Vries, *Paul Ricoeur's Hermeneutics and the Discourse of Mark 13: Appropriating the Apocalyptic* (Lanham, MD: Lexington Books, 2016), 36; Dan R. Stiver, *Life Together in the Way of Jesus Christ: An Introduction to Christian Theology* (Waco, TX: Baylor University Press, 2009), 431; Vanhoozer, *Biblical Narrative in the Philosophy of Paul Ricoeur*, 245.

47. Jürgen Moltmann, *Theology of Hope: On the Ground and the Implications of a Christian Eschatology,* trans. James W. Leitch (New York: Harper & Row, 1967), 20.

48. Moltmann, *Theology of Hope*, 18.

49. Moltmann, *Theology of Hope*, 88.

50. Moltmann, *Theology of Hope*, 119. Moltmann distinguishes Christian eschatology from the utopian as the latter can be unfulfilled. "Without faith's knowledge of Christ, hope becomes a utopia and remains hanging in the air." Moltmann, *Theology of Hope,* 20. In this view, the utopian remains a mere possibility, not an assured one.

51. Vanhoozer, *Biblical Narrative in the Philosophy of Paul Ricoeur*, 282.

52. Ricoeur, "Freedom in the Light of Hope," 408; Ricoeur, "Guilt, Ethics, and Religion," 437.

53. Paul Ricoeur, "Être protestant aujourd'hui," *Cahiers d'Etudes du Centre Protestant de recherche et de rencontres du Nord* 26 (1968): 11; Ricoeur, *Plaidoyer pour l'utopie ecclésiale*, 26.

54. Paul Ricoeur, *Freud and Philosophy: An Essay on Interpretation*, trans. Denis Savage (New Haven, CT: Yale University Press, 1970), 36. See also *Freud and Philosophy*, 551.

55. Paul Ricoeur, "The Language of Faith," in *The Philosophy of Paul Ricoeur*, 237. See Vanhoozer, *Biblical Narrative in the Philosophy of Paul Ricoeur,* 7: "Possibility is thus intimately connected to the imagination which projects it."

56. Ricoeur, "The Language of Faith," 238.

57. Ricoeur, "Poetry and Possibility," 455–56.

58. Don Ihde, "Editor's Introduction," in Ricoeur, *The Conflict of Interpretations*, xxiv.

59. Moltmann, *Theology of Hope*, 20 (quoting John Calvin, *Institutes of the Christian Religion*, ed. John T. McNeill (Philadelphia: Westminster Press, 1960), 590).

60. Ricoeur, "Fatherhood: From Phantasm to Symbol," 481.

61. Ricoeur, "Freedom in the Light of Hope," 408; Ricoeur, "Guilt, Ethics, and Religion," 437. John Wall emphasizes this aspect of the religious imagination. John Wall, *Moral Creativity: Paul Ricoeur and the Poetics of Possibility* (Oxford: Oxford University Press, 2005), 155.

62. Moltmann, *Theology of Hope*, 338.

63. Ricoeur, "Freedom in the Light of Hope," 406.

64. Ricoeur, "Fatherhood: From Phantasm to Symbol," 497; Ricoeur, "Hope and the Structure of Philosophical Systems," 211.

65. Ricoeur, "Ethical and Theological Considerations on the Golden Rule," 299; Ricoeur, "Freedom in the Light of Hope," 411; Ricoeur, *Plaidoyer pour l'utopie ecclésiale*, 17.

66. Paul Ricoeur, "The Logic of Jesus, the Logic of God," in *Figuring the Sacred*, 281.

67. Ricoeur acknowledges at one point that there may be a divine design but if so, it is an "unassignable" one, "a design which is God's secret." Paul Ricoeur, "Toward a Hermeneutic of the Idea of Revelation," in *Essays on Biblical Interpretation*, ed. Lewis S. Mudge (Philadelphia: Fortress Press, 1980), 87. He does not pursue in this context the implications of the comment on human ethics or on such theological themes as divine omniscience and predestination.

68. Ricoeur, "Freedom in the Light of Hope," 407.

69. Ricoeur, "Freedom in the Light of Hope," 408 (emphases added).

70. Ricoeur, "Être protestant aujourd'hui," 11; Ricoeur, *Plaidoyer pour l'utopie ecclésiale*, 26.

71. Ricoeur, "Ethical and Theological Considerations on the Golden Rule," 297; Ricoeur, "The Demythization of Accusation," 346–47; Ricoeur, "Foi et philosophie aujourd'hui," 9.

72. Ricoeur, "Freedom in the Light of Hope," 409; Alain Thomasset, S.J., "L'imagination dans la pensée de Paul Ricoeur. Fonction poétique du langage et transformation du sujet," *Études théologiques et religieuses* , no. 4 (2005): 528.

73. Paul Ricoeur, "The Addressee of Religion: The Capable Human Being," in *Philosophical Anthropology, Writings and Lectures, Volume 3*, ed. Johann Michel and Jérôme Porée, trans. David Pellauer (Cambridge, UK: Polity, 2016), 289.

74. Ricoeur, "Poetry and Possibility," 455–56.

75. Ricoeur, "Hope and the Structure of Philosophical Systems," 212.

76. Ricoeur, "Foi et philosophie aujourd'hui," 8; Ricoeur, "Hope and the Structure of Philosophical Systems," 204. Elsewhere Ricoeur comments positively on scholarship in the comparative history of religions that focuses on "noniconicity," that is, "devotion to a Name without an image; no figure, statue, material image." Paul Ricoeur, *Living up to Death*, trans. David Pellauer (Chicago: University of Chicago Press, 2009), 80.

77. Paul Ricoeur, "Preface to the First Edition (1955)," in *History and Truth,* trans. Charles A. Kelbley (Evanston, IL: Northwestern University Press, 1965), 6–7.

78. Ricoeur, "The Demythization of Accusation," 345.

79. Paul Ricoeur, "Phénoménologie de la religion (1993)," in *Lectures 3: Aux frontières de la philosophie* (Paris: Seuil, 1994), 268.

80. John Van den Hengel, "Faith and Ideology in the Philosophy of Paul Ricoeur," *Église et Théologie* 14 (1983): 82. Van den Hengel contends that for Ricoeur "objectivations are in a constant process of being overcome by faith itself." Van den Hengel, 89. For Moltmann, hope by its own virtues "alone keeps life – including public, social life – flowing and free." It resists "institutional stabilizing." Moltmann, *Theology of Hope*, 324.

81. Ricoeur, "The Bible and the Imagination," 144.

82. Paul Ricoeur, "Interview, June 19, 1982, Chatenay-Malabry," in Charles E. Reagan, *Paul Ricoeur: His Life and His Work* (Chicago: University of Chicago Press, 1996), 101; Ricoeur, "The Bible and the Imagination," 145.

83. Ricoeur, "Preface," in *Studies in the Philosophy of Paul Ricoeur*, xviii.

84. Paul Ricoeur, "Philosophical Hermeneutics and Biblical Hermeneutics," in *From Text to Action*, 90.

85. Paul Ricoeur, "From One Testament to the Other," trans. Barnabas Aspray, *Modern Theology* 33, no. 2 (April 2017): 240–41. Ricoeur also attends these dimensions of religious discourses in the opening pages of "Philosophy and Religious Language," which we have not previously referenced. Ricoeur, "Philosophy and Religious Language," 35–36.

86. Ricoeur, "Biblical Hermeneutics," *Semeia* 4 (1975): 32.

87. Ricoeur, "Biblical Hermeneutics," 34; Ricoeur, "The Bible and the Imagination," 144; Ricoeur, "Manifestation and Proclamation," 58; Ricoeur, "Toward a Hermeneutic of the Idea of Revelation," 101–102.

88. Ricoeur, *Lectures on Imagination*, 285.

89. Ricoeur, "Biblical Hermeneutics," 32, 89, 103; Ricoeur, "Manifestation and Proclamation," 57–58.

90. Ricoeur, "Biblical Hermeneutics," 108, 122.

91. Mark I. Wallace, "Introduction," in *Figuring the Sacred*, 14.

92. Ricoeur, "From One Testament to the Other," 240–41.

93. Paul Ricoeur, "The Status of *Vorstellung* in Hegel's Philosophy of Religion," in *Meaning, Truth, and God*, ed. Leroy S. Rouner (Notre Dame, IN: University of Notre Dame Press, 1982), 70.

94. Ricoeur, "The Status of *Vorstellung* in Hegel's Philosophy of Religion," 87.

95. Ricoeur, "The Metaphorical Process," 149/147.

96. Ricoeur, "Biblical Hermeneutics," 92.

97. Ricoeur, "The Status of *Vorstellung* in Hegel's Philosophy of Religion," 70–71, 84. See also Ricoeur, "From One Testament to the Other," 240.

98. Dan R. Stiver, *Ricoeur and Theology* (London: T&T Clark, 2012), 61–90 (chapter), 61 ("figurative turn").

99. Wallace, "Introduction," in *Figuring the Sacred*, 14.

100. Wallace, "Introduction," in *Figuring the Sacred*, 8.

101. Wallace, "Introduction," in *Figuring the Sacred*, 19.

102. Mark I. Wallace, "Ricoeur, Rorty, and the Question of Revelation," in *Meanings in Texts and Actions*, 235.

103. Mark I. Wallace, "From Phenomenology to Scripture? Paul Ricoeur's Hermeneutical Philosophy of Religion," *Modern Theology* 16, no. 3 (July 2000): 311; Mark I. Wallace, *The Second Naiveté: Barth, Ricoeur, and the New Yale Theology* (Macon, GA: Mercer University Press, 1990), 124. For additional attention to Ricoeur on figuration, see, for example, Thomasset, "L'imagination dans la pensée de Paul Ricoeur," 528 and Vanhoozer, *Biblical Narrative in the Philosophy of Paul Ricoeur*, 52.

104. Ricoeur, "The Bible and the Imagination," 145.

105. See, for example, Stiver, *Ricoeur and Theology*, 113, 140.

106. Ricoeur, "Fatherhood: From Phantasm to Symbol," 486.

107. Ricoeur, *Plaidoyer pour l'utopie ecclésiale*, 79.

108. Paul Ricoeur, "Ideology, Utopia, Faith," in *Protocol of the Seventeenth Colloquy of the Center for Hermeneutical Studies in Hellenistic and Modern Culture*, ed. W. Wuellner (Berkeley, CA: Center for Hermeneutical Studies in Hellenistic and Modern Culture, 1976), 28. This essay is an abbreviated translation of a 1976 article that has recently become more widely available as published in a Ricoeur collection, where the original of the citation can be located within its full context. Paul Ricoeur, "L'herméneutique de la sécularisation: Foi, Idéologie, Utopie," in *La Religion pour penser: Écrits et conférences 5*, ed. Daniel Frey (Paris: Seuil, 2021), 183. For what is to my knowledge a rare reference to this passage, see Alain Thomasset, S.J., "Biblical Hermeneutics, the Art of Interpretation, and Philosophy of the Self: A Tribute to Paul Ricoeur and Paul Beauchamp," in *Reading Scripture with Paul Ricoeur*, ed. Joseph A. Edelheit and James F. Moore (Lanham, MD: Lexington Books, 2021), 84 note 20.

109. Ricoeur, "Love and Justice," 325. See also Ricoeur, "Ethical and Theological Considerations on the Golden Rule," 299: "The God of beginnings is the God of hope." John Wall elaborates on this passage. Wall, *Moral Creativity*, 155–56.

110. Ricoeur, "Philosophy and Religious Language," 45.

111. Ricoeur, "Philosophy and Religious Language," 43.

112. Ricoeur, "Naming God," 221, 222, 232; Ricoeur, "Toward a Hermeneutic of the Idea of Revelation," 99, 104.

113. Ricoeur, "Philosophy and Religious Language," 46.

114. Ricoeur, "Philosophy and Religious Language," 35.

115. See, for example, Ricoeur, "Philosophical Hermeneutics and Biblical Hermeneutics," 96; Ricoeur, "Philosophical Hermeneutics and Theological Hermeneutics," 27 (same): 31–32; Paul Ricoeur, "Preface to Bultmann," trans. Peter McCormick, in *The Conflict of Interpretation*, 398; Ricoeur, "Toward a Hermeneutic of the Idea of Revelation," 93.

116. Ricoeur, "Preface to Bultmann," 387.

117. Ricoeur, "Preface to Bultmann," 387.

118. Ricoeur, "Preface to Bultmann," 397; Ricoeur, "Toward a Hermeneutic of the Idea of Revelation," 93.

119. Ricoeur, "Naming God," 221.

120. Paul Ricoeur, "The Hermeneutics of Testimony," in *Essays on Biblical Interpretation*, 153.

121. Ricoeur, "Toward a Hermeneutic of the Idea of Revelation," 102, 104; Ricoeur, "Philosophy and Religious Language," 45; Ricoeur, "Philosophical Hermeneutics and Theological Hermeneutics," 27.

122. Ricoeur, "Reply to Lewis S. Mudge," in *Essays on Biblical Interpretation*, 44.

123. Ricoeur, "Philosophy and Religious Language," 45; Ricoeur, "Philosophical Hermeneutics and Theological Hermeneutics," 27.

124. Ricoeur, "Naming God," 223; Ricoeur, "Philosophical Hermeneutics and Theological Hermeneutics," 27; Ricoeur, "Toward a Hermeneutic of the Idea of Revelation," 102.

125. Ricoeur, "Naming God," 220–21.

126. Ricoeur, "Philosophy and Religious Language," 44; Ricoeur, "Philosophical Hermeneutics and Biblical Hermeneutics," 95–96; Ricoeur, "Philosophical Hermeneutics and Theological Hermeneutics," 26–27.

127. Beyond the references already mentioned, see, for example, Ricoeur, "Naming God," 232; Ricoeur, "Philosophical Hermeneutics and Theological Hermeneutics," 28–29; Ricoeur, "Reply to Lewis S. Mudge," 44.

128. Ricoeur, "Naming God," 232–33; Ricoeur, "Foi et philosophie aujourd'hui," 7; Ricoeur, "Philosophy and Religious Language," 45–46; Ricoeur, "Toward a Hermeneutic of the Idea of Revelation," 104.

129. Ricoeur, "Toward a Hermeneutic of the Idea of Revelation," 104.

130. See, for example, Fodor, *Christian Hermeneutics*, 134–35, 258–59; Frey, *La religion dans la philosophie de Paul Ricoeur*, 132, 206, 341; Adam Graves, *The Phenomenology of Revelation in Heidegger, Marion, and Ricoeur* (Lanham, MD: Lexington Books, 2021), 202; Brian Gregor, *Ricoeur's Hermeneutics of Religion: Rebirth of the Capable Self* (Lanham, MD: Lexington Books, 2019), 133, 137; W. David Hall, *Paul Ricoeur and the Poetic Imperative: The Creative Tension Between Love and Justice* (Albany: SUNY Press, 2007), 74–79; David E. Klemm, "Ricoeur, Theology, and the Rhetoric of Overturning," *Literature and Theology* 3, no. 3 (November 1989):

273; David E. Klemm, "Searching for a Heart of Gold: A Ricoeurian Meditation on Moral Striving and the Power of Religious Discourse," in *Paul Ricoeur and Contemporary Moral Thought*, ed. John Wall, William Schweiker, and W. David Hall (New York: Routledge, 2002), 108; Gregory J. Laughery, *Living Hermeneutics in Motion: An Analysis and Evaluation of Paul Ricoeur's Contribution to Biblical Hermeneutics* (Lanham, MD: University Press of America, 2002), 43–49; David Pellauer, "Paul Ricoeur on the Specificity of Religious Language," *Journal of Religion* 61, no. 3 (1981): 275–76, 277, 280; Stiver, *Theology After Ricoeur*, 201; Vanhoozer, *Biblical Narrative in the Philosophy of Paul Ricoeur*, 148–49, 155–56; Wallace, "Ricoeur, Rorty, and the Question of Revelation," 240; Wallace, *The Second Naiveté*, 70. As we have anticipated and shall shortly return to discuss, a major point of disagreement with Ricoeur lies in whether his emphasis on the poetic in religious language properly allows for the role of divine as opposed to poetic activity as the impetus leading to interpreter transformation.

131. See, for example, Frey, *La religion dans la philosophie de Paul Ricoeur*, 318, 340; Gregor, *Ricoeur's Hermeneutics of Religion*, 118, 133; Brian Gregor, "Epistles as Revelation," in *Reading Scripture with Paul Ricoeur*, 212; Gilles Marmasse, "Ricoeur et le concept hégélien de *Vorstellung* religieuse," in *Ricoeur et la pensée allemande: De Kant à Dilthey*, ed. Gilles Marmasse and Roberta Picardi (Paris: CNRS Éditions, 2019), 194–95; Stiver, *Ricoeur and Theology*, 82–83; Thomasset, "L'imagination dans la pensée de Paul Ricoeur," 539–40; Alain Thomasset, S.J., "Toward a Hermeneutic and Narrative Moral Theology: Paul Ricoeur's Contribution to New Approaches in Christian Ethics," in *Between Suspicion and Sympathy: Paul Ricoeur's Unstable Equilibrium*, ed. Andrzej Wierciński (Toronto: The Hermeneutic Press, 2003), 318; Vanhoozer, *Biblical Narrative in the Philosophy of Paul Ricoeur*, 134, 138, 215; Wallace, *The Second Naiveté*, 59–60, 121–22. We return to exceptions later.

132. Ricoeur, "Philosophy and Religious Language," 43 (emphases added); Ricoeur, "Philosophical Hermeneutics and Theological Hermeneutics," 25 (same); Ricoeur, "Toward a Hermeneutic of the Idea of Revelation," 103 ("proposed world").

133. Ricoeur, "Philosophy and Religious Language," 44 (emphasis added).

134. Ricoeur, "Philosophy and Religious Language," 43 (emphasis added). See also Ricoeur, "Appropriation," 192: "the projection of a world, the proposal of a mode of being-in-the-world."

135. Ricoeur, "Philosophy and Religious Language," 43.

136. See, for example, Gregor, *Ricoeur's Hermeneutics of Religion*, 137; Klemm: "Ricoeur, Theology, and the Rhetoric of Overturning," 277–78; David E. Klemm, "The Word as Grace: The Religious Bearing of Paul Ricoeur's Philosophy," *Faith and Philosophy: Journal of the Society of Christian Philosophers* 10, no. 4 (October 1993): 513; Stiver, *Ricoeur and Theology*, 82–83; Richard R. Topping, *Revelation, Scripture and Church: Theological Hermeneutic Thought of James Barr, Paul Ricoeur and Hans Frei* (Aldershot, UK: Ashgate, 2007), 33–34, 47; Vanhoozer, *Biblical Narrative in the Philosophy of Paul Ricoeur*, 141, 155, 234; Wallace, "From Phenomenology to Scripture?," 302; Wallace, "Ricoeur, Rorty, and the Question of Revelation," 239; Wallace, *The Second Naiveté*, 80.

137. Ricoeur, "The Bible and the Imagination," 145.

138. Ricoeur, "Toward a Hermeneutic of the Idea of Revelation," 117; Ricoeur, "The Logic of Jesus, the Logic of God," 281.

139. Ricoeur, "The Bible and the Imagination," 160.

140. Ricoeur, "Listening to the Parables of Jesus," 245.

141. Ricoeur, "The Logic of Jesus, the Logic of God," 281.

142. Ricoeur, "Toward a Hermeneutic of the Idea of Revelation," 117.

143. Ricoeur, "Toward a Hermeneutic of the Idea of Revelation," 95, 97, 99.

144. Ricoeur, "Appropriation," 185.

145. Ricoeur, "The Bible and the Imagination," 149.

146. Ricoeur, "The Bible and the Imagination," 166 (emphasis in original).

147. Frey, *La religion dans la philosophie de Paul Ricoeur*, 67, 68, 189, 211.

148. Gregor, *Ricoeur's Hermeneutics of Religion*, 137. See also Fodor, *Christian Hermeneutics*, 302; Klemm, "Ricoeur, Theology, and the Rhetoric of Overturning," 277–78; Topping, *Revelation, Scripture and Church*, 33, 52, 119.

149. Vanhoozer, *Biblical Narrative in the Philosophy of Paul Ricoeur*, 225.

150. Vanhoozer, *Biblical Narrative in the Philosophy of Paul Ricoeur*, 234.

151. Vanhoozer, *Biblical Narrative in the Philosophy of Paul Ricoeur*, 278. See also 181, 226–27.

152. Vanhoozer, *Biblical Narrative in the Philosophy of Paul Ricoeur*, 265.

153. Ricoeur, "Listening to the Parables of Jesus," 241.

154. Ricoeur, "Listening to the Parables of Jesus," 245 (emphases added).

155. Ricoeur, "Biblical Hermeneutics," 122–28; Paul Ricoeur, *Time and Narrative*, volume 3, trans. Kathleen Blamey and David Pellauer (Chicago: University of Chicago Press, 1988), 271, 130.

156. See, for example, Richard Topping's objection that in Ricoeur: "Too much emphasis falls on meaning as established and won by hard-fought human interpretative effort and too little on meaning as a gift of grace, achieved through the action of God in Jesus Christ – of which the Bible is a fit and perspicuous inscripturation made effective for the Church by the Spirit." Topping, *Revelation, Scripture and Church*, 186.

157. Ricoeur, "Listening to the Parables of Jesus," 241.

158. Ricoeur, "Manifestation and Proclamation," 67.

159. Ricoeur, "The Metaphorical Process as Cognition, Imagination, and Feeling," 156/154.

160. Ricoeur, "The Metaphorical Process as Cognition, Imagination, and Feeling," 156/154. On the same page, Ricoeur maintains that the imagination has an illocutionary – performative – force. David Klemm is especially attentive to the implications for the religious imagination of Ricoeur's comments on feeling in this early article. See Klemm, "Philosophy and Kerygma," 64; Klemm, "Ricoeur, Theology, and the Rhetoric of Overturning," 280; Klemm, "Searching for a Heart of Gold," 108–109; Klemm, "The Word as Grace," 514. See also Michele Kueter Petersen, *A Hermeneutics of Contemplative Silence: Paul Ricoeur, Edith Stein, and the Heart of Meaning* (Lanham, MD: Lexington Books, 2021), 265 (citing Klemm); Stiver, *Theology After Ricoeur*, 203.

161. Ricoeur, "Philosophy and Religious Language," 45; Ricoeur, "Philosophical Hermeneutics and Theological Hermeneutics," 27; Ricoeur, "Toward a Hermeneutic of the Idea of Revelation," 93; Ricoeur, "The Metaphorical Process as Cognition, Imagination, and Feeling," 156/154.

162. Ricoeur, "The Function of Fiction in Shaping Reality," 125; Ricoeur, *Lectures on Imagination*, 238, 271; Ricoeur, "The Metaphorical Process as Cognition, Imagination, and Feeling," 148/146; Ricoeur, "Appropriation," 185. Ricoeur refers to the concept of apperception on numerous occasions. See, for example, Ricoeur, "Imagination in Discourse and in Action," 173; Ricoeur, *The Rule of Metaphor*, 116/135, 195/230–31.

163. See Ricoeur, *The Rule of Metaphor*, 200-15/237–54.

164. Ricoeur, "The Function of Fiction in Shaping Reality," 126; Ricoeur, "The Metaphorical Process as Cognition, Imagination, and Feeling," 147/145; Ricoeur, *The Rule of Metaphor*, 208/246–47.

165. Ricoeur, "The Metaphorical Process as Cognition, Imagination, and Feeling," 143/141.

166. Ricoeur, *The Rule of Metaphor*, 209/247.

167. Ricoeur, *The Rule of Metaphor*, 200/237, 204/241. See also Ricoeur, *Lectures on Imagination*, 234.

168. Ricoeur, *The Rule of Metaphor*, 200/237.

169. Ricoeur, *The Rule of Metaphor*, 212/251. Although not central to our present theme, it is worth noting that not only does metaphor draw from the senses but it itself offers a sensible moment, as it sets something before our eyes. Ricoeur, *The Rule of Metaphor*, 207/245. As we previously noted in Ricoeur, a step beyond schematization is iconic augmentation, a *depiction*, something appears. Ricoeur, "The Metaphorical Process as Cognition, Imagination, and Feeling," 150/148. Here we have an enriched conception of *seeing as*. *Seeing as* as transposition involves both thinking and *seeing* something anew. Ricoeur, "The Metaphorical Process as Cognition, Imagination, and Feeling," 147/145. In the transposition, an intersection exists between saying – in language – and *seeing as*. Ricoeur, *The Rule of Metaphor*, 207/245. As observed in the text, *seeing as* relates to the vocabulary of figuration, as figuration provides figures of.

170. Ricoeur, *The Rule of Metaphor*, 61/70.

171. In "The Metaphorical Process," Ricoeur explicitly relates his conception to *Vorstellung*, which is picture-thinking. Ricoeur, "The Metaphorical Process as Cognition, Imagination, and Feeling," 144/142, 151/149.

172. Ricoeur, "The Metaphorical Process as Cognition, Imagination, and Feeling," 157/155. See Klemm, "Searching for a Heart of Gold," 109; Klemm, "The Word as Grace," 515.

173. Ricoeur, *Lectures on Imagination*, 285.

174. Ricoeur, "The Metaphorical Process as Cognition, Imagination, and Feeling," 153/151.

175. Ricoeur, "Poétique et symbolique," 54.

176. Ricoeur, "Listening to the Parables of Jesus," 241.

177. Ricoeur, "Biblical Hermeneutics," 127. In another essay from 1974, "Manifestation and Proclamation," Ricoeur argues that manifestation and proclamation can

be reconciled, as proclamation includes manifestation as "the power to set forth the new being it proclaims." Ricoeur, "Manifestation and Proclamation," 65. This seems not a matter of divine action.

178. Paul Ricoeur, "L'enchevêtrement de la voix et de l'écrit dans le discours biblique," in *Lectures 3*, 325–26. In his critique of whether Ricoeur allows for divine action through the biblical text, Brian Gregor pays important attention to this passage. On the one hand, the text "opens the possibility that someone can speak to me – and us – in and through the text." On the other it is also a rare passage in Ricoeur and one limited in its own terms: "Beyond these words of acknowledgment, Ricoeur never ventures." Gregor, *Ricoeur's Hermeneutics of Religion*, 145, 216–17.

179. Ricoeur, *Lectures on Imagination*, 273.

180. On the grace of imagination, see Ricoeur, "Être protestant aujourd'hui," 11; Ricoeur, *Freud and Philosophy*, 36, 551; Ricoeur, "Language of Faith," 237. Ricoeur, *Plaidoyer pour l'utopie ecclésiale*, 26. Daniel Frey offers a brief reference to this phrase also. Frey, *La religion dans la philosophie de Paul Ricoeur*, 196. On the conversion of the religious imagination, Ricoeur offers an early statement: ""conversion" . . . implies a shift in the direction of the look, a reversal in the vision, in the imagination, in the heart."" Conversion of the imagination is also cited in the secondary literature. Richard B. Hays, "The Conversion of the Imagination, Scripture and Eschatology in 1 Corinthians," *New Testament Studies* 45, no. 3 (1999): 395; Gregor, *Ricoeur's Hermeneutics of Religion*, 137; Garrett Green, *Imagining God: Theology and the Religious Imagination* (Grand Rapids, MI: Eerdmans, 1998), 38.

181. Green notes that for Barth the whole inquiry into the nature of the religious imagination is misguided. In Barth's perspective, "[w]e do not understand revelation by learning how people are able to receive it but rather by learning that it comes precisely to those who are *un*able to receive it," since revelation is entirely and completely a gift of God. Green, *Imagining God*, 32.

182. See Vanhoozer, *Biblical Narrative in the Philosophy of Paul Ricoeur*, 8 (making this distinction).

183. Ricoeur, "Toward a Hermeneutic of the Idea of Revelation," 80 (observing this point). Daniel Frey specifically argues for the insufficiency of an approach of imagination and sympathy in the face of the claim of a revealed truth. Frey, *La religion dans la philosophie de Paul Ricoeur*, 188–89. Hans Frei argues frontally for the insufficiency of imagination: "the use of imagination in regard to Jesus cannot adequately represent his presence to us as the resurrected Lord." Hans W. Frei, *The Identity of Jesus Christ: The Hermeneutical Bases of Dogmatic Theology* (Eugene, OR: Cascade Books, 2013), 51, 153. Frei also maintains that explaining how a transition from literary description to historical and religious affirmation might be possible let alone actual "is what we claimed from the beginning to be impossible, certainly in the context of our analysis of the unity of Christ's identity and presence, if indeed at all." Frei, *The Identity of Jesus Christ*, 146.

184. Ricoeur, *The Symbolism of Evil*, 348.

185. Ricoeur, "Biblical Hermeneutics," 129; 133; Ricoeur, "From One Testament to the Other," 240.

186. Ricoeur, "The Status of *Vorstellung* in Hegel's Philosophy of Religion," 73, 86. See also, Ricoeur, "From One Testament to the Other," 240: "the speculative and conceptual mode is not imposed from outside on the affirmations that will remain in the figurative mode, but . . . it is already constitutive of what one could call their wisdom dimension."

187. Ricoeur, "Preface to Bultmann," 396.

188. Ricoeur, "From One Testament to the Other," 241.

189. Ricoeur, *The Symbolism of Evil*, 350. See generally, Ricoeur, *Lectures on Imagination*, 238: insight does not exclude thought as, quite the contrary, restructuring semantic fields "demands the greatest thought."

190. Ricoeur, "Biblical Hermeneutics," 144.

191. Paul Ricoeur, "From Interpretation to Translation," in *Thinking Biblically: Exegetical and Hermeneutical Studies* (with André LaCocque), trans. David Pellauer (Chicago: University of Chicago Press, 1998), 358, citing the critique of Jean-Luc Marion.

192. Ricoeur, "From Interpretation to Translation," 359.

193. Ricoeur, "Biblical Hermeneutics," 142–43.

BIBLIOGRAPHY

Aspray, Barnabas. *Ricoeur at the Limits of Philosophy*. Cambridge, UK: Cambridge University Press, 2022.

Calvin, John. *Institutes of the Christian Religion*, edited by John T. McNeill. Philadelphia: Westminster Press, 1960.

de Vries, Peter. *Paul Ricoeur's Hermeneutics and the Discourse of Mark 13*. Lanham, MD: Lexington Books, 2016.

Fodor, James. *Christian Hermeneutics*. Oxford: Clarendon Press, 1995.

Frei, Hans W. *The Identity of Jesus Christ*. Eugene, OR: Cascade Books, 2013.

Frey, Daniel. *La religion dans la philosophie de Paul Ricoeur*. Paris: Hermann, 2021.

Frey, Daniel. "La religion dans l'oeuvre de Ricoeur." *Études Ricoeuriennes/Ricoeur Studies* 13, no. 2 (2022): 8–25.

Graves, Adam. *The Phenomenology of Revelation in Heidegger, Marion, and Ricoeur*. Lanham, MD: Lexington Books, 2021.

Green, Garrett. *Imagining God: Theology and the Religious Imagination*. Grand Rapids, MI: Eerdmans, 1998.

Gregor, Brian. "Epistles as Revelation: Expanding Ricoeur's Account of Biblical Discourse." In *Reading Scripture with Paul Ricoeur*, edited by Joseph A. Edelheit and James F. Moore, 203–24. Lanham, MD: Lexington Books, 2021.

Gregor, Brian. *Ricoeur's Hermeneutics of Religion*. Lanham, MD: Lexington Books, 2019.

Hall, W. David. *Paul Ricoeur and the Poetic Imperative*. Albany: SUNY Press, 2007.

Hays, Richard B. "The Conversion of the Imagination: Scripture and Eschatology in 1 Corinthians." *New Testament Studies* 45, no. 3 (1999): 391–412.

Ihde, Don. "Editor's Introduction," in Paul Ricoeur, *The Conflict of Interpretations*, edited by Don Ihde, ix–xxv. Evanston, IL: Northwestern University Press, 1974.

Klemm, David E. "Ricoeur, Theology, and the Rhetoric of Overturning." *Literature and Theology* 3, no. 3 (November 1989): 267–84.

Klemm, David E. "Searching for a Heart of Gold: A Ricoeurian Meditation on Moral Striving and the Power of Religious Discourse." In *Paul Ricoeur and Contemporary Moral Thought*, edited by John Wall, William Schweiker, and W. David Hall, 97–116. New York: Routledge, 2002.

Klemm, David E. "The Word as Grace: The Religious Bearing of Paul Ricoeur's Philosophy." *Faith and Philosophy: Journal of the Society of Christian Philosophers* 10, no. 4 (October 1993): 503–20.

Laughery, Gregory J. *Living Hermeneutics in Motion: An Analysis and Evaluation of Paul Ricoeur's Contribution to Biblical Hermeneutics.* Lanham, MD: University Press of America, 2002, republished in slightly revised form as *Paul Ricoeur and Living Hermeneutics: Exploring Ricoeur's Contribution to Biblical Interpretation.* Destinée S. A., 2018.

Marmasse, Gilles. "Ricoeur et le concept hégélien de *Vorstellung* religieuse." In *Ricoeur et la pensée allemande*, edited by Gilles Marmasse and Roberta Picardi, 183–201. Paris: CNRS Éditions, 2019.

Moltmann, Jürgen. *Theology of Hope: On the Ground and the Implications of a Christian Eschatology.* Translated by James W. Leitch. New York: Harper & Row, 1967.

Pellauer, David. "Paul Ricoeur on the Specificity of Religious Language." *Journal of Religion* 61, no. 3 (1981): 264–84.

Petersen, Michele Kueter. *A Hermeneutics of Contemplative Silence: Paul Ricoeur, Edith Stein, and the Heart of Meaning.* Lanham, MD: Lexington Books, 2021.

Ricoeur, Paul, "The Addressee of Religion: The Capable Human Being." In *Philosophical Anthropology: Writings and Lectures, Volume 3*, edited by Johann Michel and Jérôme Porée, 269–89. Translated by David Pellauer. Cambridge, UK: Polity, 2016.

Ricoeur, Paul, "Appropriation." In *Hermeneutics and the Human Sciences: Essays on Language, Action and Interpretation*, edited by John B. Thompson, 182–93. Cambridge, UK: Cambridge University Press, 1981.

Ricoeur, Paul, "The Bible and the Imagination." In *Figuring the Sacred: Religion, Narrative, and Imagination*, edited by Mark I. Wallace, 144–66. Translated by David Pellauer. Minneapolis: Fortress Press, 1995.

Ricoeur, Paul, "Biblical Hermeneutics." *Semeia* 4 (1975): 29–148.

Ricoeur, Paul, "Biblical Readings and Meditations." In *Critique and Conviction: Conversations with François Azouvi and Marc de Launay*, 139–70. Translated by Kathleen Blamey. New York: Columbia University Press, 1998.

Ricoeur, Paul, "Contribution d'une réflexion sur le langage à une théologie de la parole." *Revue de théologie et de philosophie*, 18 (1968): 333–48.

Ricoeur, Paul, "The Demythization of Accusation." Translated by Peter McCormick. In *The Conflict of Interpretations*, edited by Don Ihde, 335–53. Evanston, IL: Northwestern University Press, 1974.

Ricoeur, Paul, "Ethical and Theological Considerations on the Golden Rule." In *Figuring the Sacred: Religion, Narrative, and Imagination*, edited by Mark I. Wallace, 293–302. Translated by David Pellauer. Minneapolis: Fortress Press, 1995.

Ricoeur, Paul, "Être protestant aujourd'hui." *Cahiers d'Etudes du Centre Protestant de recherche et de rencontres du Nord* 26 (1968): 1–14.

Ricoeur, Paul, "Fatherhood: From Phantasm to Symbol," translated by Robert Sweeney, in *The Conflict of Interpretations*, edited by Don Ihde, 468–97. Evanston, IL: Northwestern University Press, 1974.

Ricoeur, Paul, "Foi et philosophie aujourd'hui." *Foi-Éducation* 42, no. 100 (1972): 1–12 (discussion 12–13).

Ricoeur, Paul, "Freedom in the Light of Hope," in *The Conflict of Interpretations*, edited by Don Ihde, 402–24. Evanston, IL: Northwestern University Press, 1974.

Ricoeur, Paul, *Freud and Philosophy: An Essay on Interpretation*. Translated by Denis Savage. New Haven, CT: Yale University Press, 1970.

Ricoeur, Paul, "From Existentialism to the Philosophy of Language." Toronto: University of Toronto Press, 1977.

Ricoeur, Paul, "From Interpretation to Translation." In *Thinking Biblically: Exegetical and Hermeneutical Studies* (with André LaCocque), 331–61. Translated by David Pellauer. Chicago: University of Chicago Press, 1998.

Ricoeur, Paul, "From One Testament to the Other." Translated by Barnabas Aspray. *Modern Theology* 33, no. 2 (April 2017): 235–42.

Ricoeur, Paul, "The Function of Fiction in Shaping Reality." In *A Ricoeur Reader: Reflection and Imagination*, edited by Mario J. Valdès, 117–36. Toronto: University of Toronto Press, 1991.

Ricoeur, Paul, "Guilt, Ethics, and Religion." In *The Conflict of Interpretations*, edited by Don Ihde, 425–39. Evanston, IL: Northwestern University Press, 1974.

Ricoeur, Paul, "The Hermeneutics of Testimony." In *Essays on Biblical Interpretation*, edited by Lewis S. Mudge, 119–54. Philadelphia: Fortress Press, 1980.

Ricoeur, Paul, "L'enchevêtrement de la voix et de l'écrit dans le discours biblique (1992)." In *Lectures 3: Aux frontières de la philosophie*, 307–26. Paris: Seuil, 1994.

Ricoeur, Paul, "L'herméneutique de la sécularisation: Foi, Idéologie, Utopie." In *La Religion pour penser: Écrits et conférences 5*, edited by Daniel Frey, 155–87. Paris: Seuil, 2021.

Ricoeur, Paul, "Hope and the Structure of Philosophical Systems." In *Figuring the Sacred: Religion, Narrative, and Imagination*, edited by Mark I. Wallace, 203–16. Translated by David Pellauer. Minneapolis: Fortress Press, 1995.

Ricoeur, Paul, "Ideology, Utopia, Faith." In *Protocol of the Seventeenth Colloquy of the Center for Hermeneutical Studies in Hellenistic and Modern Culture*, edited by W. Wuellner, 21–28. Berkeley, CA: Center for Hermeneutical Studies in Hellenistic and Modern Culture, 1976. [Discussion: 40–56.]

Ricoeur, Paul, "Imagination in Discourse and in Action." In *From Text to Action: Essays in Hermeneutics, II*, 168–87. Translated by Kathleen Blamey and John B. Thompson. Evanston, IL: Northwestern University Press, 1991.

Ricoeur, Paul, "Interview, June 19, 1982, Chatenay-Malabry." In Charles E. Reagan, *Paul Ricoeur: His Life and His Work*, 100–109. Chicago: University of Chicago Press, 1996.

Ricoeur, Paul, "The Language of Faith." In *The Philosophy of Paul Ricoeur: An Anthology of His Work*, edited by Charles E. Reagan and David Stewart. Boston: Beacon Press, 1978, 223–38.

Ricoeur, Paul, *Lectures on Ideology and Utopia*, edited by George H. Taylor. New York: Columbia University Press, 1986.

Ricoeur, Paul, *Lectures on Imagination*, edited by George H. Taylor, Robert D. Sweeney, Jean-Luc Amalric, and Patrick F. Crosby. Chicago: University of Chicago Press, 2024.

Ricoeur, Paul, "Listening to the Parables of Jesus." In *The Philosophy of Paul Ricoeur: An Anthology of His Work*, edited by Charles E. Reagan and David Stewart. Boston: Beacon Press, 1978, 239–45. Originally published in *Criterion* 13, no. 3 (1974): 18–22.

Ricoeur, Paul, *Living Up to Death*. Translated by David Pellauer. Chicago: University of Chicago Press, 2009.

Ricoeur, Paul, "The Logic of Jesus, the Logic of God." In *Figuring the Sacred: Religion, Narrative, and Imagination*, edited by Mark I. Wallace, 279–83. Translated by David Pellauer. Minneapolis: Fortress Press, 1995.

Ricoeur, Paul, "Love and Justice." In *Figuring the Sacred: Religion, Narrative, and Imagination*, edited by Mark I. Wallace, 315–29. Translated by David Pellauer. Minneapolis: Fortress Press, 1995.

Ricoeur, Paul, "Manifestation and Proclamation." In *Figuring the Sacred: Religion, Narrative, and Imagination*, edited by Mark I. Wallace, 48–67. Translated by David Pellauer. Minneapolis: Fortress Press, 1995.

Ricoeur, Paul, "The Metaphorical Process as Cognition, Imagination, and Feeling." *Critical Inquiry* 5 (Autumn 1978): 143–59. Republished in *On Metaphor*, edited by Sheldon Sacks, 141–57. Chicago: University of Chicago Press, 1979.

Ricoeur, Paul, "Naming God." In *Figuring the Sacred: Religion, Narrative, and Imagination*, edited by Mark I. Wallace, 217–35. Translated by David Pellauer. Minneapolis: Fortress Press, 1995.

Ricoeur, Paul, *Oneself as Another*. Translated by Kathleen Blamey. Chicago: University of Chicago Press, 1992.

Ricoeur, Paul, "Pastoral Praxeology, Hermeneutics, and Identity." In *Figuring the Sacred: Religion, Narrative, and Imagination*, edited by Mark I. Wallace, 303–14. Translated by David Pellauer. Minneapolis: Fortress Press, 1995.

Ricoeur, Paul, "Paul the Apostle: Proclamation and Argumentation" [with separate endnotes section, pp. 568–71]. Translated by David Pellauer. In *Paul and the Philosophers*, edited by Ward Blanton and Hent De Vries, 256–78. New York: Fordham University Press, 2013.

Ricoeur, Paul, "Phénoménologie de la religion (1993)." In *Lectures 3: Aux frontières de la philosophie*. Paris : Seuil, 1994, 263–71.

Ricoeur, Paul, "Philosophical Hermeneutics and Biblical Hermeneutics." In *From Text to Action: Essays in Hermeneutics, II*, 89–101. Translated by Kathleen Blamey and John B. Thompson. Evanston, IL: Northwestern University Press, 1991.

Ricoeur, Paul, "Philosophical Hermeneutics and Theological Hermeneutics." *Sciences Religieuses/Studies in Religion* 5, no. 1 (Summer 1975): 14–33.

Ricoeur, Paul, "Philosophy and Religious Language." In *Figuring the Sacred: Religion, Narrative, and Imagination*, edited by Mark I. Wallace, 35–47. Translated by David Pellauer. Minneapolis: Fortress Press, 1995.

Ricoeur, Paul, *Plaidoyer pour l'utopie ecclésiale*, edited by Olivier Abel and Alberto Romele. Genève: Labor et Fides, 2016.

Ricoeur, Paul, "Poétique et symbolique." In *Initiation à la pratique de la théologie*, volume 1, edited by Bernard Lauret and François Refoulé, 37–61. Paris: Cerf, 1982.

Ricoeur, Paul, "Poetry and Possibility." In *A Ricoeur Reader: Reflection and Imagination*, edited by Mario J. Valdès, 448–62. Toronto: University of Toronto Press, 1991.

Ricoeur, Paul, "Preface." In *Studies in the Philosophy of Paul Ricoeur*, edited by Charles E. Reagan, xi-xxi. Athens, OH: Ohio University Press, 1979.

Ricoeur, Paul, "Preface to Bultmann." Translated by Peter McCormick. In *The Conflict of Interpretations*, edited by Don Ihde, 381–401. Evanston, IL: Northwestern University Press, 1974.

Ricoeur, Paul, "Preface to the First Edition (1955)." In *History and Truth*, 3–14. Translated by Charles A. Kelbley. Evanston, IL: Northwestern University Press, 1965.

Ricoeur, Paul, "Reply to Lewis S. Mudge." In *Essays on Biblical Interpretation*, edited by Lewis S. Mudge, 41–45. Philadelphia: Fortress Press, 1980.

Ricoeur, Paul, *The Rule of Metaphor: Multi-Disciplinary Studies of the Creation of Meaning in Language*. Translated by Robert Czerny with Kathleen McLaughlin and John Costello, S. J. Toronto: University of Toronto Press, 1977. Republished with different pagination: London: Routledge, 2003.

Ricoeur, Paul, "The Status of *Vorstellung* in Hegel's Philosophy of Religion." In *Meaning, Truth, and God*, edited by Leroy S. Rouner, 70–88. Notre Dame, IN: University of Notre Dame Press, 1982.

Ricoeur, Paul, *The Symbolism of Evil*. Translated by Emerson Buchanan. Boston: Beacon Press, 1967.

Ricoeur, Paul, *Time and Narrative*, volume 1. Translated by Kathleen McLaughlin and David Pellauer. Chicago: University of Chicago Press, 1984.

Ricoeur, Paul, *Time and Narrative*, volume 3. Translated by Kathleen Blamey and David Pellauer. Chicago: University of Chicago Press, 1988.

Ricoeur, Paul, "Toward a Hermeneutic of the Idea of Revelation." In *Essays on Biblical Interpretation*, edited by Lewis S. Mudge, 73–118. Philadelphia: Fortress Press, 1980.

Schweiker, William. "Imagination, Violence, and Hope: A Theological Response to Ricoeur's Moral Philosophy." In *Meanings in Texts and Actions*, 205–25, edited by David E. Klemm and William Schweiker. Charlottesville, VA: University Press of Virginia, 1993.

Stiver, Dan R. *Life Together in the Way of Jesus Christ*. Waco, TX: Baylor University Press, 2009.

Stiver, Dan R. *Ricoeur and Theology.* London: T&T Clark, 2012.

Stiver, Dan R. *Theology After Ricoeur.* Louisville, KY: Westminster John Knox Press, 2001.

Taylor, George H. "Editor's Introduction." In Paul Ricoeur, *Lectures on Imagination,* edited by George H. Taylor, Robert D. Sweeney, Jean-Luc Amalric, and Patrick F. Crosby, xi–xl. Chicago: University of Chicago Press, 2024.

Thomasset, Alain, S.J. "Biblical Hermeneutics, the Art of Interpretation, and Philosophy of the Self: A Tribute to Paul Ricoeur and Paul Beauchamp." In *Reading Scripture with Paul Ricoeur,* edited by Joseph A. Edelheit and James F. Moore, 75–86. Lanham, MD: Lexington Books, 2021.

Thomasset, Alain, S.J. "L'imagination dans la pensée de Paul Ricoeur. Fonction poétique du langage et transformation du sujet." *Études théologiques et religieuses* 80, no. 4 (2005): 525–41.

Thomasset, Alain, S.J. "Toward a Hermeneutic and Narrative Moral Theology: Paul Ricoeur's Contribution to New Approaches in Christian Ethics." In *Between Suspicion and Sympathy,* edited by Andrzej Wierciński, 315–32. Toronto: The Hermeneutic Press, 2003.

Topping, Richard R. *Revelation, Scripture and Church: Theological Hermeneutic Thought of James Barr, Paul Ricoeur and Hans Frei.* Aldershot, UK: Ashgate, 2007.

Treanor, Brian and Henry Isaac Venema. "Introduction: How Much More Than the Possible?" In *A Passion for the Possible,* edited by Brian Treanor and Henry Isaac Venema, 1–21. New York: Fordham University Press, 2010.

Van den Hengel, John. "Faith and Ideology in the Philosophy of Paul Ricoeur." *Église et Théologie* 14 (1983): 63–89.

Vanhoozer, Kevin J. *Biblical Narrative in the Philosophy of Paul Ricoeur.* Cambridge: Cambridge University Press, 1990.

Vincent, Gilbert. *La religion de Ricoeur.* Paris: Atelier, 2008.

Wall, John. *Moral Creativity.* Oxford: Oxford University Press, 2005.

Wallace, Mark I. "From Phenomenology to Scripture? Paul Ricoeur's Hermeneutical Philosophy of Religion." *Modern Theology* 16, no. 3 (July 2000): 301–13.

Wallace, Mark. "Introduction." In Paul Ricoeur, *Figuring the Sacred.* edited by Mark I. Wallace, 1–32. Translated by David Pellauer. Minneapolis: Fortress Press, 1995.

Wallace, Mark I. "Ricoeur, Rorty, and the Question of Revelation." In *Meanings in Texts and Actions,* edited by David E. Klemm and William Schweiker, 234–54. Charlottesville, VA: University Press of Virginia, 1993.

Wallace, Mark I. *The Second Naiveté.* Macon, GA: Mercer University Press, 1990.

Chapter 3

The Bible

A Polyphonic Medium for Self-Identification

Timo Helenius

The Bible is mythopoetic literature, but it also stands for a peculiar experience that calls for verbalization at both individual and collective levels. It is an artifact of human culture that can be explored merely as such, but it also aims to express a radical experience of encounter that is both historical and, according to the testimonies of those involved, at the same time transcends all temporal categories. It is no wonder that Paul Ricoeur—a philosopher particularly interested in phenomenological and hermeneutical questions—is also interested in asking whether the fact of the Bible is able to shed light on the question of radical human experience and the relating need for interpretation of that experience through the medium of symbolization and narrativization that allows for further interpretative actions to emerge: the Bible is literally revelatory in the world of the reader. Through its myths and symbols, it discloses new avenues of understanding—or narrativizing—one's own existence or the experience of being alive. In other words, the Bible summons for a refiguration of the (collective or individual) self that is enriched by the novel aspects opened up in the applicative reception of the biblical narratives and stories that themselves rely on linguistic means facilitating all necessary cultural subjectivity.

FIGURING THE SACRED

Before taking on the question of Ricoeur's use and reading of the Scriptures, there are some aspects we should be aware of in terms of the anthology that comprises the specific essays we will explore. First, the matter of deciding whether the included essays represent Ricoeur's "religious writings" as Mark Wallace puts it in his introduction or whether the essays are writings about linguistic and textual material that can be called religious.[1] Even though there is a longstanding discussion about Ricoeur's personal openness to the Christian faith tradition, we will respect his explicit reservations against setting aside a professional philosophical approach. Insofar as Ricoeur's essays can be said to be religious, they are so only to the extent of Ricoeur's philosophical insistence of a recurring actualization of an originary orientation for the renewal of grounding—or a holistic—"incarnatory" meaning.[2] Second, the collection of essays included in *Figuring the Sacred* do not therefore deviate and are not isolated from the rest of Ricoeur's work but they rather complement it by putting it in test and, in some cases, by providing substantial and invigorating material for more general philosophical thought (in a similar manner than in *The Symbolism of Evil* that resulted in the hermeneutical wager). Third, this leads us to acknowledge that the question of religious language is resolved in the context of Ricoeur's overall philosophical pursuit. The religious use of language is not dealt with as an isolated or a wholly separate linguistic convention but, in spite of allowing for its distinctness, rather as a regional or a parochial linguistic practice. Religious language, inclusive of the Scriptures, does not in any way constitute a special or an anomalous case in terms of linguistic practices, but it is such a practice among other practices that provides ample material for philosophical analysis because of its internal need for finding suitable expression and narrative framing.[3] Fourth, our focus—that will be placed on Ricoeur's use of scriptural material—is therefore not similar to that of the Yale School narrative theology (Frei, Lindbeck, Hauerwas) as the Bible is not approached as the medium for self-identification but as one of potentially many.[4] When studying biblical narrative Ricoeur is not pursuing narrative theology whereas he philosophically explores the power of linguistic redescription in the Bible that takes use of the narrative structure. In other words, the Bible serves as relevant historical material witnessing and aiding the human quest of coming up or disclosing a suitable narrative framing for the self in both its individual and communal forms.

These acknowledgments are made apparent and justified in *Figuring the Sacred*. The name of the collection of essays already indicates that the emphasis is not in the Sacred, as could be hastily concluded, but in the human imaginative-intellectual activity of figuration. In this sense the task of the work resembles or in some ways comes close to Richard Kearney's *Poétique du possible: Phenomenologie herméneutique de la figuration*—a doctoral thesis in philosophy written in the 1980s under Ricoeur's supervision. Moreover, the selected essays of *Figuring the Sacred* are grouped in such a manner that it makes evident the overall philosophical task in the context of which also religious scriptures are explored. Part one, accordingly, addresses the question of religious language and religious linguistic practices that rely on equivocation as in symbols, but also manifestly on narration as in myths. Ricoeur's key interest is in linguistic expressivity or a discourse that can be called religious; his phenomenologico-hermeneutical thesis is that religious experience is articulated in a language—it "comes to language through specific modes of discourse"[5]—that conveys an ultimately irreducible meaning as well as a claim of truthfulness pertaining to the world of the text (that, in turn, invites a novel structure of being-in-the-world or an existentially revealing redescription of the lifeworld). Due to this particular interest in the revelatory power and potential of language, he is firmly focused on the Abrahamic tradition (Judaism, Christianity, Islam) that has a special emphasis on the divine "word" calling for as much reception as interpretation, especially in textual form. According to Ricoeur, such a linguistically manifesting tradition that ties in the narrative and kerygmatic dimensions clearly warrants an analysis in the field of philosophical hermeneutics.

Part two provides further philosophical context when bringing together Ricoeur's critical engagements in terms of philosophers' thoughts about religion (Kant, Rosenzweig, Heidegger, Nabert, Levinas) and, included in this discussion, Ricoeur's own thoughts about the role and profile of philosophy of religion. Ricoeur's reading of Kant's *Religion within the Limits of Reason Alone* as "a philosophical hermeneutics of religion"[6] arises out of Kant's focus on religion (instead of God), the analysis of servile will (in contrast with Kant's notion of freedom in his critical works), and the problematization of hope and the possibility of regeneration through the examination of radical evil. The essay—which is later in the anthology complemented with an analysis on Hegel, bringing forth Ricoeur's "post- Hegelian Kantianism"[7]—concludes with Ricoeur's brief statement concerning the philosophical need of a hermeneutics of religion as exemplified through his close reading of Kant's text. Ricoeur's essay on Rosenzweig's *The Star of Redemption* studies the notions of religious truth, figuration or figurative thought, and temporality as the dialectics of onto-existentially pertinent and continuously renewed sempiternity in contrast with the idealistic notion of divine eternity. The Rosenzweig essay may be taken as an analysis of what Ricoeur elsewhere describes as a religious claim for truth, distinct from those of logic, science, or poetics. The following essay is linked with the previous one in its analyses about testimony that it provides by a brief but attentive reading of Heidegger, Nabert, and Levinas. The notion of religious truth is further explored through testimony by asking about its "epistemic status"[8]—extending to that of religious discourse. As Ricoeur shows, there clearly are epistemic and semantic standards as well as practical extensions, albeit ones that diverge from the philosophical notion of truth.

It is clear from their contents and organization that the first two parts of the anthology form the theoretical background for the subsequent three parts of the work. In spite of their specific thematic approaches, the subsequent parts are not distinct or detachable from the six essays preceding them. As for the rest of the anthology, Ricoeur's essays on biblical discourse (part three), theological systematizations and problems (part four), and issues in practical theology (part five) apply and put in test his hermeneutics of reconfiguration. To provide but one example: even though using biblical material for pursuing the analysis, Part Three focuses on interpretation, imagination, temporality, and on what Ricoeur calls narrative articulation. Ricoeur, even in *Figuring the Sacred*, is not a theologian whereas he retains the position of a philosopher, whose interests cover and include the questions of religion and religious discourse or, rather, the question of an experience searching for an expression that, then, results in a discourse and the institution of a religion (which provide further means for the interpretation and identification of the self).[9] This is why for Ricoeur religious discourse can be approached as emergent (mythic-symbolic) expressions that accumulate into or give rise to semantically rich scriptural narratives, speculative theorization at the level of theological discipline, and as practical action in need of both conceptual and phronetic thought: "The sacred does not reveal itself just in signs that are to be contemplated, but also in significant behavior."[10] The inclusion of practical action stands in spite of Ricoeur's distinction between the phenomenology of manifestation and the hermeneutic of proclamation; a polarity Ricoeur attributes to the Judeo-Christian tradition in particular.

What distinguishes Ricoeur from many theologians is his philosophical insistence to not lose sight of the semantic polyphony at the origins of discourse. Theological reflection and speculation tend to systematize, harmonize, and "univocize" whereas originating expressivity is polysemic, elastic, and therefore surprising. The notion that the originating expressivity not only speaks up (in finding an expression for an experience) but also speaks to (the person finding an expression verbalizing this particular novel aspect in his or her being-in-the-world) results in an existentially and hermeneutically informed stance that Ricoeur willfully holds. The "theology" Ricoeur indicates to argue for takes place in a living summons to become a responsive (individual or communal) self who has in some manner begun—amidst of encountering evil[11]—to articulate for himself or herself the hope-retaining and hope-generating onto-existential structure of being called by the other. This sets up Ricoeur's interest in issues in practical theology, or in suffering and pastoral care, theological ethics, and the dialectic of (self-giving) love and (distributive) justice. Again, the issue of life's multivalence and its complexity is underscored and cherished—in similar fashion as biblical polysemy.

The pains of becoming a self are soothed in the meeting of the self through the (structures of) care of another. Just as justice is "the necessary medium of love,"[12] semantic innovation extending to symbolic and narrative creativity is the necessary medium of hermeneutic action seeking meaning.[13] Parts three, four, and five therefore form a kind of sub-cycle in *Figuring the Sacred*. Part three, however, serves as a starting point for the cycle that in a way returns back to its origins in terms of meaningful and suitable action. In the end, Ricoeur's stance is that the most meaningful action is the creation or redescription of meaning through innovation and interpretation. Biblical hermeneutics is an example of "an interpretation *in* the text and *through* the text."[14] We should therefore be extremely clear about the manner of Ricoeur's approach. In his own words:

> If the Bible can be said to be revealed, this ought to be said of the "issue" that it speaks of—the new being that is displayed there. I would go as far as to say that the Bible is revealed to the extent that the new being unfolded there is itself revelatory with respect to the world, to all of reality, including my existence and my history. In other words, revelation, if the expression is meaningful, is a trait of the biblical *world*.[15]

Ricoeur's interest is in figuration, the imaginative-intellectual creation of meaningful worlds within which the existence of the one(s) figuring discovers a dwelling place. Exploring this in their own respective ways, the four essays under the heading of biblical discourses bid for a move from the use of exegetical methods (i.e., an analytical reading by way of interrelated genetic and structural approaches) to interpretation, allowed by the imagination in its power of redescription.

It is these steps that lead the discussion to the questions of narrative temporality and articulation that culminate in the observation that a narrativized kerygma is already interpretive even before any particular interpretation of that very narrative. In other words, biblical texts and passages such as passion narratives bring to light that a narrative can have "an interpretive function in relation to its own kerygmatic intention."[16] But the application of this function results in the notion that there is no "pure" kerygma, devoid of its interpretive handling; just consider the Creation myth (Gen. 1:1–2:4a) that Ricoeur takes as exemplary in this regard. Given the already standing interpretive character of narratives, it becomes evident at the outset that "without a doubt there is not such thing as an innocent interpretation."[17] The narrative itself articulates—that is, interprets—kerygma by verbalizing, accentuating, and structuring it, and its interpretation is likewise guided by introducing the narrative "into a speculative space that is no longer that of the text but that of our culture as a whole."[18] Ricoeur means that textual appropriation is always facilitated by the cultural, as is all understanding. In short, there is no conceptual or cultural innocence in interpretation. This also pertains to biblical narratives that are subjected to interpretations *of* or *about* them but which also carry non-innocent and yet revelatory interpretations *in* and *through* them.

A key analysis that distinguishes interpretations in the text from those about the text is focused on intertextually produced extension of meaning in biblical narratives. The same analysis explores the role of productive imagination as both rule-governed and redescriptive; Ricoeur's point is that reading biblical narratives and especially narrative-parables exemplify that productive imagination is "at work in the text itself" as well as in "recontextualizing it in today's *Sitz-im-Leben*."[19] The demonstration takes three steps in customary Ricoeurian fashion:

1) An analysis of parables such as the wicked husbandmen and the sower, "narratives within a narrative,"[20] brings it to light that their metaphorization, or the collision of semantic fields or codes, relies on intertextuality between the encompassing and embedded narratives;

2) The intertextual operation, an extension to metaphorization, can be shown to be not merely restricted but general as the case of Old and New Testaments makes evident;

3) Such general character of narratives, intertextuality that exposes "the interpretive dynamism of the text itself,"[21] stands for and indicates the rule-governed imagination that, we should note, is also in redescriptive play in the act of reading.

The fact of productive imagination is brought to light in intertextuality. Ricoeur's focus here though is in the observation that there is a kind of "texture" of the text generated by intertextuality as "the text interprets before having been interpreted."[22] But the internal dynamism that results in "narrative's extravagance on the narrative plane"—meaning that "the narrative metaphorizes itself by transgressing its own narrative structure"[23]—is turned into a real transgression when taken as an invitation for interpretation in the act of reading. Such interpretation is first of all transgressive in the sense that it exceeds the limits of the narrative and applies the resources offered by the reader's culture. This, however, results in yet another transgression in form of providing a possibility for the redescription of those very cultural elements applied and used in the act of reading. The "passage from text to life" is both enabled and facilitated by "the text's horizon of structuration."[24] Such is the origin of the shift from the rule-governed imagination or the work of the interpretation *in* the text to that of redescriptive imagination or the interpretation *about* the text.

As it then comes to asking about the re-figuration of the con-figured "enigma-expressions," or about that "passage from the text to life,"[25] we enter into the territory of existentially pertinent mode of interpretation. Such move can be emphasized as well as explored by way of asking about temporality. What Ricoeur in his essays calls the semantic phase of interpretation—meaning the configurative phase of the recurring hermeneutical cycle—has no need for acknowledging the temporal structure, whereas in the existential phase or in refiguration the world of the interpreter or the reader is reconfigured in such manner that it is also temporally (re)structured. Interpretation itself gives or "donates" time for the interpreter. This is exemplified in Ricoeur's analysis on biblical time. In short, he attempts to "disengage the temporality implied by, or in a way brought about by, the Bible as Scripture."[26] Again, as is easy to see, the Bible serves in the role of material support for his more general philosophical pursuit. His specific interest lies in showing that each type of discourse results in or brings about a type of temporality corresponding to its respective discourse; support for this thesis is drawn from historically recounting narration (e.g., the Yahwist) and its accompanying legislation (the Torah), eschatologically future-oriented and re-evaluative prophecy (from Amos to Zechariah), the transitory immemorial of wisdom texts (e.g., Proverbs or Ecclesiastes), and the reactualization and renewal in hymn (the Psalms). Moreover, Ricoeur also attempts to point out a certain "interweaving" between these narrative and non-narrative types of discourse in the interpretative act of reading that "contemporalizes" or "synchronizes" all scriptural texts—also disregarding their specific historical background—with one another. This intertextual interweaving between discourse-specific temporalities in the act of reading provides an understanding of "biblical time" that makes manifest the role and work of "reconstructive imagination" relying on the productive capacity of the imagination.[27]

THE POLYPHONY OF BIBLICAL DISCOURSES

A specific question that caught Ricoeur's attention concerns the interpretive function of narrative configuration. In brief, narrative itself with its structure is a "major hermeneutical mode"[28] for theology or, even more fundamentally, the kerygma that seeks literary expression. Here narrative configuration—that Ricoeur in this context calls kerygmatic narrativization—relies on the task and act of articulation that is (1) facilitated by semiotic constraints, (2) in-formed by an instantiation of discourse, and (3) addressed to the listener or reader through the narrative voice or "the speaking in the writing, the narration of the narrative."[29] As Ricoeur shows analyzing the passion narrative in the Gospel of Mark, these three are some of the main resources that constitute a kerygmatic narrative in its peculiar interpretive character and give an opportunity to argue for its articulation to be the very interpretation of the kerygma.[30]

This exploration into a narrative's interpretive function can be expanded to concern the whole collection of texts with their unique interpretive aspects. In Ricoeur's thought this relates to his astute observation that there is no one sacred text—untouchable and uneditable because of being sacred and holy in itself—whereas the Judeo-Christian tradition has a history of the canon with its multiple genres and narrative voices. Much as with individual texts, the constellation of the collection of texts itself is therefore a product of critical interpretation, reception, and organization. What is striking is that the end product, the canon, allowed for "a certain equivocity of the texts,"[31] or that the collection is not a harmonious or harmonized constellation. The Bible is not a literal or a narrative monolith but a multifaceted collection of texts and genres that, in their own ways, intend to testify about encountering the sacred. In Protestantism in particular this led to the adoption of a hermeneutical principle that serves in the acquisition of the gore kerygma or the gospel, the good tidings. Even though each and every text is about the divine encountered in some shape, form, or mode, a fuller understanding can be gained only by reaching beyond each individual text and by drawing the meaning from the wider collection of these canonical texts.[32] That *"scriptura sui ipsius interpres"* or that the canon interprets itself by itself brings about the notion that there is a possibility for interpretative unity in spite of the diversity of the textual body known as the canon.[33] This interpretive-homiletic approach to the Bible seems to find a close resemblance or at least a strong analogy in Ricoeur's insistence of interpretive confluence: "[In addition to narration and prophecy] all the other genres of discourse in which biblical faith has found expression must be brought together, not just in an enumeration that would juxtapose them, but in a living dialectic that will display their interferences with one another."[34] Such statements, philosophically intended and hermeneutically inclined perhaps, propose an outlook deviant from the mainstream exegetical work concerning the Bible.

That Ricoeur was not foreign using the Bible as both Scripture and exemplary cultural material for pursuing philosophy is well clear for us already. This is evident on the basis of *Figuring the Sacred*, let alone Ricoeur's other works, some of which refer to biblical texts in detail: *The Symbolism of Evil* stands as an example of this openness.[35] More than simply using the Bible, however, Ricoeur was also not foreign to an analytical approach to biblical material in a scholarly sense. I mean that Ricoeur's considerations about the potential narrative coherence in the Bible somewhat stand out in that they are being made in the context of having the knowledge that exegetes, or Bible scholars, have long concluded that the very issue of the diversity included in the canon cannot fundamentally be resolved by any eisegetical approach. Ricoeur himself openly admitted in the preface to *Thinking Biblically*—a thematic dialogue with André LaCocque, a Bible scholar—that:

> The philosopher [i.e. Ricoeur] does not ignore the specificity of the texts found within the biblical *corpus*, any more than he denies the originality of the Hebrew, then the Christian way of thinking. He is so aware of this, in fact, that the very concept of a Christian philosophy, or even of a "biblical metaphysics," once put forward by Etienne Gilson, appear completely inadequate to him.[36]

As the authors further explain it, the very composition of *Thinking Biblically* testifies to the fact that neither approach is about to be ruled by the other but that they both open up toward each other. From Ricoeur's side, this means that the "philosopher" acknowledges the inherent value of exegetical or historical-critical analysis. More strongly, the joint statement that Ricoeur also signs as his own is that "it is the apparent antinomy between retrospection and prospection, between the text and its reception, that we want to refute."[37] For Ricoeur's part, this means that he subjects himself to the exegetical mode of analytical thought, puts himself "in the school of exegesis," and "becomes a reader of exegesis."[38] Without abolishing or removing the philosophical and hermeneutical attitude, Ricoeur opens up an avenue of thought toward exegesis with the intention to understand as broadly and deeply as possible. In a way, this is nothing but a continuation of Ricoeur's critical hermeneutics that grows from the conviction that to explain more is to understand better—or that each methodological approach is a potential medium for a broader and clearer understanding.

This is why we now also make a jump from hermeneutics to exegetics. In his work *The Old Testament: Canon, Literature and Theology*, John Barton (the Emeritus Oriel and Laing Professor of the Interpretation of Holy Scripture at the University of Oxford) makes a strong case that at the same time both aligns and stands in contrast with Ricoeur's notion of dialectical-hermeneutical unity we saw him to make in *Figuring the Sacred*. In Barton's words: "That the biblical canon contains diversity is obvious to most readers; that it is nevertheless a unity is the conviction those for whom it functions as Holy Scripture."[39] Exploring diversity as both a problem and a virtue, Barton highlights the aspect of interpretive unity that stands out when the collection of variegated texts of the canon are examined as they are in their respective literary compositions. This, as Barton points out, is already clear due to the need to conform the scriptural teaching with *Halakhah* as well as the creative interpretation techniques needed in matters of Christian ethics that bases itself on the whole of the Bible. Moreover, for Christianity the Bible as a whole would have to express the promise-fulfillment theology so that the scheme of salvation is made clear and it forms a coherent narration. In short, the need for these interpretations results in the observation that "it is difficult to read either the Old or the New Testament carefully without becoming aware of the presence of diversity and inconsistency."[40]

The various means for maintaining the interpretive unity in spite of the textual diversity include deletion, alteration, reconciliation, and synthetization. The first of these could well be called selective interpretation, and they include omitting passages and even whole texts as well as "reading only under special terms and conditions."[41] Admitting that such an approach is actually rather common—as "most people who read the Bible have an "effective" canon which is smaller than the theoretical [or the actual] one"[42]—Barton holds that the theoreticians do not widely see the canon from such an angle anymore. This is not to say that it hadn't been historically approached precisely so: "we might list Marcion, Tatian, Luther, Bultmann and Käsemann."[43] This tendency to select or prioritize, however, is already present in the canon. Barton's examples include the Chronicle versus the Samuel-Kings version of the history of Israel and Luke the Evangelist versus other Gospel writers. Also, the Gospel according to John would fit well to this in its clearly theologizing interpretation and constellation of events regarding Jesus of Nazareth as "the theory that there is a 'canon within canon' represents the 'deletion' approach in a more nuanced form."[44] This tendency to omit and alter is also continued in attempts at reading the included texts so that the inconsistencies between them are apparent but not substantial. This "reconciliation" approach pertains, for example, to reading the Pentateuch as theologically coherent (i.e., by setting aside the tensions arising from different sources representing differing theologies) and the four Gospels as presenting a coherent passion narration. Again, the Gospel according to John stands out in comparison between the Synoptic Gospels that, in spite of sharing much of the same narrative, have themselves differing storylines as also seen in Andreas Osiander's attempt at harmonization.

But beyond this reconciliation approach, Barton introduces a more sophisticated manner to harmonize. Not denying the diversity and inconsistency in and between the texts, a claim can nevertheless be made for a "higher unity" or "a unified truth"[45] that brings meaning and purposefulness to the whole without abolishing the apparent tensions. Barton takes an example of this from attempts at reconstructing or distilling a biblical theology; such approach can be taken in both *textually* as in the case of taking covenant as the lens through which everything else should be read and *doctrinally* as in the case of adopting the "hermeneutical imperative which flows from the Church's recognition of it as Holy Scripture."[46] Both of these, textual and doctrinal, follow the idea of a higher unity or purpose, but in Barton's opinion the second is detached from the texts in the sense of approaching them "as Scripture" that by default is an integrated whole serving theological appropriation. Here we find Barton's critique of interpretation: "The important point here is that the 'canonical' approach is a hermeneutic of the text—and one that chimes in with the perceptions of most Christians—rather than a critical observation about it; it is issued in the imperative, not the indicative mood."[47]

Up to this point Barton has discussed diversity as a burdening problem, but would there be a way to view inter- and intratextual non-coherence from a neutral or even positive angle? Even after having provided patristic and modern reasons for seeing that this can be the case, Barton's stance on this point remains ambiguous. For example, whether the four variant versions of the life and teachings of Jesus allow for keeping authoritarianism in check or that diversity serves the purpose of indicating that a reader or believer may explore scriptures and the world of which they testify in the spirit of freedom seem to remain precisely for Barton within the confines of reading the canonical texts "as Scriptures." In other words, Barton seemingly detaches himself of the manner of approach that would grant some unity—albeit not necessarily a narrative one—that runs through the whole collection of texts known as the canon. Even though such stance is feasible for a historical-critically attuned scholar, it somehow feels quite one-sided and narrow. Surely it cannot be the case that we would merely have to accept the fact of literary diversity without also taking into account that the canon quite possibly still contains some kind of unity or at least a sense of it. The fact of the canon itself gives rise to a thought that the collection has at least a unitary function that binds together its parts. Moreover, it is worthwhile to be tested whether such unity could be found beyond reducing all potential unity to "the conviction of those for whom it functions as Holy Scripture" as Barton does.[48]

Barton's observations are not to be sidelined but to be taken seriously. The challenge of the canon is evident, particularly if we were to look for some narrative or interpretive unity that has some credence or legitimation. Instead of the whole of the canon, the question can be entertained by examining the New Testament as James Dunn has done in his widely read *Unity and Diversity in the New Testament*. Not handling the challenge of kerygmatic coherence as that between orthodoxy and heresy, however, Dunn (Professor Emeritus of New Testament in the Department of Theology at the University of Durham) points out that a formulation that is able to avoid additional problems relating to the terminology around these particular terms can simply be about unity and diversity: "In short, what was the unity, the unifying element, the unifying force in earliest Christianity? And what breadth of diversity existed in Christianity from the first?"[49] Taking the undeniable diversity as his starting point, Dunn explores the traditions leading up to the collection known to us as the New Testament.

Beginning with the oral traditions and preaching, Dunn's first examination concerns whether those traditions had one kerygma, one gospel, or rather the plurality of kerygmata or "expressions of the gospel."[50] At least in terms of post-Easter accounts of Acts, Paul, and John the Evangelist, there actually seems to be a three-sided "core kerygma"[51] that binds the otherwise variegated texts together: proclamation about the resurrection, the request of faith, and the aspect of promise relating to faith. Dunn is compelled to draw the overall conclusion that such core kerygma is merely an abstraction that cannot be found as such in any of the NT texts, reduced to these three elements. The diversity and even disagreement of kerygmata are simply a given for Dunn after the initial examination. Moreover, such diversity is even more pertinent in the case of Jesus the proclaimer and Jesus that is proclaimed. This becomes quickly evident by comparing the post-Easter accounts to that of Jesus who "proclaimed the kingdom," "called for repentance and faith," and "held out the offer of God's forgiveness and acceptance" instead of proclaiming himself as the early believers did.[52] This leads Dunn to note that the post-Easter kerygma has a more central role; the experience of resurrection draws a defining difference between the historical Jesus and early Christianity. Even so, "any attempt to find a single, once-for-all, unifying kerygma is bound to fail."[53]

But should it not be acknowledged and even perhaps admitted that in terms of the post-Easter kerygma it is the early confessional formulae—such as "the Son of Man," "You are the Christ, the Son of God," "Jesus is the Christ," "Jesus is Lord," and so on—that provide the unifying interpretive lens for the whole of New Testament? Is it not the case that without such understanding or confession there would not be any Gospel to be shared? In spite of what he has observed, Dunn seems to allow room for this kind of thinking that springs from the *present* exalted role of historical Jesus as Lord. Given the evangelists interest in the sayings of Jesus, it is somewhat surprising (and yet again not) that "it is not the faith *of* Jesus which here comes to expression but faith *in* Jesus."[54] Jesus both was and is. But again, no single confessional formula was universally used, and nuances if not outright differences between the expressed understanding of who or what this Jesus was remain. This also relates to the varying interpretive contexts the Palestinian or Hellenistic Jewish Christians or, then again, Gentile Christians had. A derived point is an important one for us. The need to come up with new formulations, Dunn theorizes, did not cease with the early Christians as different cultural contexts invite different confessional formulae not only synchronically but also diachronically. This, however, is not yet what Dunn has in mind as his ultimate criticism regarding the impression of a unified kerygma or understanding. The most difficult challenge that all formulae share is that "any slogan is an *over*simplification."[55] That, is clear to us now, that such a challenge, in particular confines the specific contexts that are produced.

These considerations lead Dunn to examine tradition as a potential provider of unity. That all denominations or historical-cultural social groupings

have a tradition is not in dispute whereas Dunn takes it as a point of departure for his exploration. The ways different churches or denominations have
not merely theorized but practiced faith results in a functional outlook and
understanding that passes these practices on or transmits the living tradition
into the future generations. But the question of the tradition that should be
passed on has remained in constant discussion. Dunn brings it up that Phari-
sees and Sadducees disputed over the exclusivity of scriptural tradition over
the oral one, and Jesus seems to have contested upholding the ritualistic
tradition dictated by Halakah. The first generation of disciples had con-
frontations of their own over these issues; Dunn refers to the conflict Peter
and Paul had on whether the Gentile converts are to observe the Mosaic
Law. The early Christian communities, however, both relied on the oral
tradition on Jesus and needed Paul's guidance in matters of community life
and rituals—such as the eucharist—as several letters included in the New
Testament evince. The pastoral epistles addressed to Timothy and to Titus
provide a slightly different view to the question of having and upholding a
tradition as they refer to "the teaching" that is quite simply to be kept (see
Dunn, 74). For what it is worth, it is nevertheless the kerygmatic tradition
on Jesus that provided a sense of unity for the early Christians that we
can still detect in the scriptures preserved from that period. Quite unsur-
prisingly, then, Dunn concludes that "[the kerygmatic] tradition [and the
traditions about Jesus] formed a unifying strand of some importance within
the diversity of earliest Christianity." And still, "there are several marked
features of diversity."[56] As is well known, the interpretive richness and the
processes of reinterpreting the kerygmatic tradition have not diminished but
grown and expanded.

The central problem, it appears, considers the continuity between the
historical Jesus and what Dunn calls the kerygmatic Jesus. Even though the
two aspects are firmly linked with one another, it is not possible to deny the
discontinuity between them, especially in light of the various and differing
accounts on them both. Still, "there are sufficiently clear foreshadowings of
the centrality of the kerygmatic Christ in the self-understanding of Jesus during his ministry for us to recognize the kerygmata of the early churches as a
development from Jesus' own proclamation in the light of his resurrection."[57]
Recognizing the various post-Easter kerygmatic accounts in the same line
of development will, however, once again bring it to light that the christologies that began to develop of the resurrected and exalted Jesus are differing
in nature. This is clear not only when the early kerygmata is considered but
also of the soteriologically, ontologically, and conceptually more developed
christologies that followed the initial kerygmatic formulations of the historical Jesus as Lord. Scriptural descriptions of the exalted Jesus soon began to
include notions of pre-existence, incarnation, divine Wisdom or Logos, and

so on. These, in turn, lead to the development of the theologies of Christ—or christologies proper—in the coming centuries.

The notion of the kerygmatic Christ is therefore essentially split into a broad variety of Christs as can already be seen in the respective theological outlooks of Jewish Christianity, Hellenistic Christianity, Apocalyptic Christianity, Early Catholicism, and so on. Even though Dunn's exploration "has shown the surprising extent to which the different unifying factors in the first-century Christianity focus again and again on Christ, on the unity between Jesus the man and Jesus the exalted one,"[58] he is nevertheless compelled to admit that "there was no single normative form of Christianity in the first century"[59] or the centuries that followed. In spite of the undeniable unifying strand of thought focusing on Christ, it is not possible to deny the remarkable diversity of types of Christology that took place at the same time. All in all, then, in their respective manners "all Christians have operated with a canon within the canon"[60] both in terms of the New Testament and also concerning the whole of the Bible. In the end, this might be the most eye-opening outcome; that the canon brings about and affirms a "canonical diversity."[61] This turns our thoughts back to the direction of potential understandings regarding the Scriptures. The key question, it seems, was always about a variety of narratives that themselves serve as kerygmatic interpretations—and the very same pertains to the canonical collection of such texts known to us as the Bible.

IN THE MIRROR OF THE SCRIPTURES?

Barton and Dunn lead us to the brink of thinking about the processes of interpretation at both collective and individual levels. As we have seen, however, their attention is textually oriented. Here Ricoeur's hermeneutic approach well complements the exegetical or the analytical, methodological, or the critical way of considering the canon. In particular, Ricoeur's work on narrative figuration brings it to light that a narrative—or even a collection of texts—can be viewed as a "concordant discordance" as he phrases it in *Time and Narrative 1*.[62] This is the result of reconfiguration or the continuous interpretive process that enables meaning by using cultural mechanisms such as textualization and social institutions such as natural languages, the collective systems of values and justice, and so on. The so-called threefold *mimesis* or the threefold process of this interpretive activity is grounded in the prefiguration or the "preunderstanding of the world of action" that includes the meaningful structure of action, symbolic structures, and the temporal character of that world of action.[63] In other words, prefiguration concerns the preunderstanding of the cultural world of action. For its part, configuration concerns the world of the "text," that is, cultural schematization. Refiguration, or *mimesis₃*, then marks "the intersection of the world of the text and the world of the hearer or reader."[64] This description of the threefold interpretive process is not to be read as an arc, however, but as a spiral instead. When internalized, the enriched world of the reader becomes integrated in the preunderstanding and thereby also in prefiguration; the cycle of reconfiguration is unceasing.

A connection to considering the canon is established under these premises of reconfiguration. Ricoeur's understanding is that instead of being sacred, the canon could be called authoritative, meaning that the canon gains its proper production process and its interpretation only in connection to a community that considers the collection to be in some sense foundational for it. Here, thanks to the unceasing process of reconfiguration, also the possibility of self-identification comes to the fore. In Ricoeur's words: "There is a reciprocity between the reading and the existing self-identification of the identity of the community. There is a kind of reciprocity between the community and the text."[65] This, as Ricoeur notes, becomes especially clear in the act of preaching or in the continuous grounding reinterpretation within the community.

Such an approach to the canon is in crosshairs with Barton and Dunn as we have seen. After the review of their key arguments, these questions present themselves immediately in relation to Ricoeur's thought that emphasizes the interpreting community: Which Bible are we then discussing about? The Hebrew Bible, the New Testament, or perhaps a collection inclusive of the Apocrypha? What is the canon discussed? Are we to make use of the old manuscripts that have been found? Should the unemended text be strictly safeguarded or do we allow emendations when there is a perfectly obvious reading in place for a clearly corrupted nonsensical one? And what about the question concerning languages: should we not take into consideration the fact of Hebrew, Greek, or Latin texts as well as the plethora of vernacular versions? Furthermore, which translations should be considered authoritative? Surely not all of them? Barton, in particular, remains critical of the mere applicative approach to the canon as this again sidelines the text as a historical cultural artifact with its own production process; approached with theological or faith-based lenses *exe*-gesis is in danger of being replaced by *eise*-gesis. Moreover, such approach easily sets aside the very question of discordance and variegation and takes the canon merely and uncritically in its "final form" without asking about its historical origins or the trajectory of its variants.

Being critical of the conventions of his own discipline, Barton also represents a different stance compared to Ricoeur whose hermeneutics is always about remaining "in front of the text":

In the English-speaking world, there has been in the last twenty years or so a clear drift in the direction of exegesis of the "final form" of the text as the preferred style for biblical interpretation. There are at least two different conceptual bases for this shift. One is theological and is associated with so-called 'canonical criticism'; the other is literary, and rests on the argument that the interpreter of any text, biblical or not, has a primary duty to interpret the text that lies before us, before (or instead of) being concerned with putative earlier stages underlying that text. Where we are told in the Gospels that the disciples, as they go out on their preaching mission, are to eat what is set before them, the motto of current biblical studies might be "Read what is set before you".[66]

For Barton, the "final form exegesis" or "reading the text in its final form as an aesthetic or communicative unity" makes the mistake of not understanding the *Sitz im Leben* or the context in which the particular text first carried and received its meaning.[67] Barton's concern is that the "final form" approach gives license for neglecting the text's historical background as well as the variegation and even confusion that lies in the text itself: "To take a now familiar example, Robert Alter has tried to show how Genesis 38, the story of Tamar and Judah, is not the erratic block within the Joseph story that generations of commentators have believed, but can be read as perfectly well integrated into its narrative context."[68] Barton's correlating thesis is that not every literary constellation reads as a coherent and unitary narrative whole. Still, there is a way to appreciate the "final form" of the text without needing to resort to unwarranted holism: "My own belief is that 'final form' exegesis can just as well lead towards a recognition of disjunctions and inconcinnities in the text, and thence back to something more like what we have come to call historical criticism."[69] Put differently, Barton argues for critical reception or reading that may well need or spring from textual wholeness, but which is able to recognize inconsistencies in it as well as try to understand why these exist in the first place. It is only on such basis that a "hermeneutical" approach may be allowed, that is, when the idea of discordance in any perceived concordance is fully retained.[70]

Here Barton indirectly criticizes the Ricoeurian way of phrasing the issue by being more Ricoeurian than Ricoeur himself. The point is that one cannot merely "read" a text whereas any "text" is always read by some manner of approach or by resorting to some particular method. In Barton's words: "On the face of it it sounds simple and almost obvious to say to the interpreter: Read what is before you in the text, instead of delving into all kinds of hypothetical queries about it. Just read *what is there*. But as soon as we begin to unpack this proposal, it turns out to be far from simple."[71] Barton's emphasis is very much a Ricoeurian one; there is no pure or complete hermeneutics but only limited and necessarily critical ones because of the very reason that some manner of approach is always adopted—and these can be contrasted with each other. There is no approach to a text that would not be of some kind. This, however, does not mean that the particular manner of approach, or the method used, would fully determine the meaning of the text. For this reason Barton also ventures into discussing reader-response criticism. The idea that "the reader has the leading role ('is privileged') over the author and indeed over the text, and uses the text as a vehicle for meaning which ultimately derives from elsewhere"[72] does not sit well with him. If that were the case, there is no exegesis but merely "readings" that have no fixed meaning. In that case all possible and permissible meaning is constructed and not discovered; the text is a mere platform for the meaning generated by the individual or the collective "reader." In this view, "the interpreter is a creator."[73] The text, in other words, does not constrain the interpretation or reading of it in any way—this, of course, also applies to the Bible as well as reading reader-response theories themselves, rendering them obsolete! Contrary to such views, Barton points out that the idea that a text—the canon, for example—has some authority leads us to think that the possibility of some determinate meaning of a text must be allowed. Not thinking "authority" in ecclesiastical or applicative such as homiletic terms (which he remains critical about) but in the context of exegetical analysis, Barton's thesis is that the text has a role in determining its meaning. His stance is that "texts have definite [albeit by no means simple or obvious] meanings, which it is the business of the critic to discover."[74] Following Wolfgang Iser—just as Ricoeur does in *Time and Narrative 1* when introducing the theory of threefold mimesis or reconfiguration[75]—Barton argues that "texts and readers are in *dialogue*."[76] The only possible model of reader-response approach that Barton could consider espousing is of such kind which acknowledges the role of the text itself at least in the sense of "this" text that gives rise to, or results in, some further avenues of thought.

Acknowledging that Ricoeur's hermeneutics stands in sharp contrast with romantic models of interpretation (Schleiermacher, Dilthey), it is still possible to consider that, at least in some respect, Barton's anti-solipsistic, historical-critically open, and dialogical reader-response approach finds its relatively close corollary in Ricoeur's critical hermeneutics in a more substantial manner than merely in the sense of them both having been influenced by Iser's theory of reading. Here we need to be mindful of the critical nuances of Ricoeur's philosophical stance, however, as he carefully positions himself in the post-Kantian reflexive and phenomenological traditions as well as between Gadamer and Habermas in terms of his hermeneutics. In contrast with Gadamer's notions of belongingness and historically effected consciousness, it is correct to maintain that Ricoeur holds the reader to have a preunderstanding that has a determining role in the process of interpretation, but this only to the extent that it serves as the prefigurative phase in the whole process of reconfiguration. Revisiting Habermas' main criticism against Gadamer, the fusion of horizons cannot, therefore, be of such kind that the reader/interpreter is wholly lost or consumed by the tradition or the historical—or the limited set of permissible interpretations dictated by the space of experience that results in the horizon of expectation. That such horizon is there is not a point of dispute but the extent to which the horizon allows the reader or interpreter to stand in front of the text that has its own standing. The reader-response theories in some ways seem to parallel the Gadamerian hermeneutical model, whereas Barton's view parallels that of Ricoeur in that a role for the text is retained.

Even though it would be wrong to describe Ricoeur's hermeneutics as one granting a text a wholly objective meaning that is completely independent from its readers, Ricoeur—and Barton alike—nevertheless maintains that the text (that represents cultural schematization) is involved in the whole process of interpretation, and that it may open avenues of thought previously uncharted by the reader. This is how Ricoeur phrases this in his essay "Philosophical Hermeneutics and Biblical Hermeneutics":

> Our general hermeneutics invites us to say that the necessary stage between structural explanation and self-understanding is the unfolding of the world of the text; it is the latter that finally forms and transforms the reader's being-a-self in accordance with his or her intention. The theological implication of this is considerable: the primary task of a hermeneutics is not to bring about a decision in the reader but first to allow the world of being that is the "thing" of the biblical text to unfold. In this way, above feelings, dispositions, belief, or unbelief is placed the proposal of a world, which, in the language of the Bible, is called a new world, a new covenant, the kingdom of God, a new birth. These are realities that unfold before the text, unfolding to be sure for us, but based upon the text. This is what can be called the "objectivity" of the new being projected by the text.[77]

The biblical texts as well as the canon provide an opportunity for an enriched understanding of the world by proposing a different or a variant world for the reader to consider. The "new birth" serves as a metaphor for such enrichment or an enlargement of the reader's world of life and action; the text stands for the opportunity to understand better and in novel ways.

It is then clear that both Barton and Ricoeur repudiate the thought that interpretation does not involve any potential for discovery—or a creation of meaning as seen in semantic innovation—but merely validation of the historically or experientially limited or the permissible. On this, their thoughts are aligned. Still, it is perhaps the case that Ricoeur is more open to consider the aspect of collective application than Barton. In spite of analyzing the individual reader and the dialogical aspect of being engaged with a text, Ricoeur also ponders the collective that is involved in the whole process and in each aspect of interpretation. This seems to set Ricoeur on a different path compared to Barton. In this sense, it would be a mischaracterization to claim that Ricoeur is all about the meaning received from the text as he seems to maintain: "to understand is to understand oneself in front of the text. It is not a question of imposing upon the text our finite capacity for understanding, but of exposing ourselves to the text and receiving from it an enlarged self."[78] In short, Ricoeur's stance is that the text *mediates* self-understanding, and that being in front of the text means to be open about the potential meanings initiated by the text that are then taken as aspects of the thereby enriched world of life and action that itself has been granted to exist at the outset. Here the Habermasian aspect of Ricoeur's thought stands out: "we can no longer oppose hermeneutics and the critique of ideology. The critique of ideology is the necessary detour that self-understanding must take if the latter is to be formed by the matter of the text and not by the prejudices of the reader."[79] Still, Ricoeur's critical hermeneutics is more open to the collective and the horizon of expectation than that of Barton.

To be sure, Ricoeur's hermeneutic model of reconfiguration should be further discussed, but the notion of an "enlarged self" necessitates that we now fully understand the coupling between this hermeneutics and self-identity. In short, the process through and with which self-understanding may be gained is precisely that of reconfiguration. When discussing the "reader," this applies to all subjects potentially having an understanding of the self. Here a crucial extension should be noted. Ricoeur extends the scope of narrative identities from the level of individuals to that of social collectives. As individuals, human collectives also require the support of narrative identities that maintain social coherence. In Ricoeur's words in *Time and Narrative 3*:

> Self-constancy refers to a self-instructed by the works of a culture that it has applied to itself. The notion of narrative identity also indicates its fruitfulness in that it can be applied to a community as well as to an individual. We can speak of the self-constancy of a community, just as we spoke of it as applied to an individual subject. Individual and community are constituted in their identity by taking up narratives that become for them their actual history.[80]

Both an individual and a community, Ricoeur argues, gain an understanding of their respective identities by taking a detour through culture in which their identities are manifested and objectified in such a way that a person's or a community's existence can be appropriated in reflecting upon those cultural works that narrate the mute but experienced life. The self, both individual and communal, is formed "in front of the text" or by the cultural means that allow for their "reading" in such a manner that the self can be identified in the very act and process of reading.

This also means that Ricoeur's hermeneutics is not purely a personalist kind and his commentary on the canon is an exemplary for the very point that could well be made of any other literary composition that in some manner has served and serves some human community: "The biblical world has aspects that are cosmic (it is a creation), communal (it involves a people), historico-cultural (in concerns Israel, the kingdom of God), as well as personal."[81] As it comes to "biblical Israel," Ricoeur considers it to be a primary example of communal narrative self-identification: "This example is especially applicative because no other people has been so overwhelmingly impassioned by the narratives it has told about itself. (. . .) The relation is circular—the historical community called the Jewish people has drawn its identity from the reception of those texts that it had produced."[82] To be in the mirror of the Scriptures is to recognize being part of a narratively in-formed people and to recognize the self as one instructed in the perennial process of reconfiguration. A reader is one who responds "to a call in the sense of conforming to the conception of existence it proposes."[83] As Ricoeur explains it, "this call does not come from philosophy but from the Word, harbored in scripture and transmitted by the tradition and interpretive traditions issuing from these writings."[84] Furthermore, the response he has in mind "is not that of theology, considered as a more or less systematic discourse, but that of the self, which moves from being a self that is called to being a responsive self."[85] This is how the Bible is literally revelatory in the world of the reader.

NOTES

1. Mark Wallace, "Introduction" in Paul Ricoeur: *Figuring the Sacred: Religion, Narrative, and Imagination* (Minneapolis: Fortress Press, 1995), 15.

2. See Paul Ricoeur, "Manifestation and Proclamation" in Paul Ricoeur: *Figuring the Sacred: Religion, Narrative, and Imagination* (Minneapolis: Fortress Press, 1995), 63–67.

3. See Paul Ricoeur, "Philosophy and Religious Language" in Paul Ricoeur: *Figuring the Sacred: Religion, Narrative, and Imagination* (Minneapolis: Fortress Press, 1995), 45; Paul Ricoeur, "The Bible and the Imagination" in Paul Ricoeur: *Figuring the Sacred: Religion, Narrative, and Imagination* (Minneapolis: Fortress Press, 1995), 164–66.

4. Paul Ricoeur, "Toward a Narrative Theology" in Paul Ricoeur: *Figuring the Sacred: Religion, Narrative, and Imagination* (Minneapolis: Fortress Press, 1995), 240–41.

5. Ricoeur, "Philosophy and Religious Language," 39.

6. Paul Ricoeur, "A Philosophical Hermeneutics of Religion: Kant" in Paul Ricoeur: *Figuring the Sacred: Religion, Narrative, and Imagination* (Minneapolis: Fortress Press, 1995), 75.

7. See Paul Ricoeur, "Hope and the Structure of Philosophical Systems" in Paul Ricoeur: *Figuring the Sacred: Religion, Narrative, and Imagination* (Minneapolis: Fortress Press, 1995), 207–16.

8. Paul Ricoeur, "Emmanuel Levinas: Thinker of Testimony" in Paul Ricoeur: *Figuring the Sacred: Religion, Narrative, and Imagination* (Minneapolis: Fortress Press, 1995), 124.

9. Ricoeur, "Hope and the Structure," 205: "Now I am not a theologian, but a philosopher."

10. Ricoeur, "Manifestation and Proclamation," 50–51. Also consider Ricoeur's basic thesis in *From Text to Action*.

11. Paul Ricoeur, "Evil, a Challenge to Philosophy and Theology" in Paul Ricoeur: *Figuring the Sacred: Religion, Narrative, and Imagination* (Minneapolis: Fortress Press, 1995), 258–61.

12. Paul Ricoeur, "Love and Justice" in Paul Ricoeur: *Figuring the Sacred: Religion, Narrative, and Imagination* (Minneapolis: Fortress Press, 1995), 329.

13. Cf. Paul Ricoeur, "On the Exegesis of Genesis 1:1—2:4a" in Paul Ricoeur: *Figuring the Sacred: Religion, Narrative, and Imagination* (Minneapolis: Fortress Press, 1995), 140–3.

14. Ricoeur, "On the Exegesis," 140.

15. Ricoeur, "Philosophy and Religious Language," 44.

16. Paul Ricoeur, "Interpretive Narrative" in Paul Ricoeur: *Figuring the Sacred: Religion, Narrative, and Imagination* (Minneapolis: Fortress Press, 1995), 181.

17. Ricoeur, "On the Exegesis," 139.

18. Ibid., 140.

19. Ricoeur, "The Bible and the Imagination," 145.

20. Ibid., 149.

21. Ibid., 161.

22. Ibid., 161–2.

23. Ibid., 165.

24. Ibid., 166.

25. Ibid., 166.

26. Paul Ricoeur, "Biblical Time" in Paul Ricoeur: *Figuring the Sacred: Religion, Narrative, and Imagination* (Minneapolis: Fortress Press, 1995), 170.

27. Ibid., 171.

28. Ricoeur, "Interpretive Narrative," 182.

29. Ibid., 191.

30. Ibid., 191–9.

31. Paul Ricoeur, "The "Sacred" Text and the Community" in Paul Ricoeur: *Figuring the Sacred: Religion, Narrative, and Imagination* (Minneapolis: Fortress Press, 1995), 69.

32. See Paul Ricoeur, "Naming God" in Paul Ricoeur: *Figuring the Sacred: Religion, Narrative, and Imagination* (Minneapolis: Fortress Press, 1995), 224.

33. See Ricoeur, "The 'Sacred' Text," 70–1.

34. Ricoeur, "Naming God," 226.

35. See Paul Ricoeur, *The Symbolism of Evil*. Translated by Emerson Buchanan (Boston, MA: Beacon Press, 1967), 6–7.

36. André LaCocque & Paul Ricoeur, *Thinking Biblically: Exegetical and Hermeneutical Studies*. Translated by David Pellauer (Chicago and London: The University of Chicago Press, 1998), x.

37. Ibid., x.

38. Ibid., xv.

39. John Barton, *The Old Testament: Canon, Literature and Theology* (Routledge: London and New York, 2016), 53.

40. Ibid., 55.

41. Ibid., 55.

42. Ibid., 57.

43. Ibid., 55.

44. Ibid., 57.

45. Ibid., 59–60.

46. Ibid., 61.

47. Ibid., 62.

48. Ibid., 53.

49. James Dunn, *Unity and Diversity in the New Testament: An Inquiry into the Character of Earliest Christianity* (SCM Press: London, 2006), 7.

50. Ibid., 11.

51. Ibid., 30.

52. Ibid., 31–2.

53. Ibid., 33.

54. Ibid., 60.

55. Ibid., 63.

56. Ibid., 82.

57. Ibid., 232.

58. Ibid., 405.

59. Ibid., 407.

60. Ibid., 409.

61. Ibid., 415.

62. Paul Ricoeur, *Time and Narrative 1*. Translated by Kathleen McLaughlin and David Pellauer (Chicago and London: The University of Chicago Press, 1984), 70. Cf. ibid., 38–45.

63. Ibid., 54, 64.

64. Ibid., 71.

65. Ricoeur, "The 'Sacred' Text," 69.

66. Barton, *The Old Testament*, 181.

67. Ibid., 181.

68. Ibid., 182.

69. Ibid., 183.

70. See ibid., 183–4.

71. Ibid., 191.

72. Ibid., 194.

73. Ibid., 194.

74. Ibid., 197.

75. Ricoeur, *Time and Narrative 1*, 64, 77.

76. Barton, *The Old Testament*, 198.

77. Paul Ricoeur, *From Text to Action: Essays in Hermeneutics II*. Translated by Kathleen Blamey and John B. Thompson (Evanston, IL: Northwestern University Press, 1991), 95–6.

78. Ibid., 88.

79. Ibid., 88.

80. Paul Ricoeur, *Time and Narrative 3*. Translated by Kathleen McLaughlin and David Pellauer (Chicago and London: The University of Chicago Press, 1988), 247.

81. Ricoeur, *From Text to Action*, 96.

82. Ricoeur, *Time and Narrative 3three*, 247–8.

83. Paul Ricoeur, "The Self in the Mirror of the Scriptures," in *The Whole and Divided Self*. Eds. David E. Aune and John McCarthy (New York: Crossroad Publishing Company, 1997), 201–2.

84. Ibid., 202.

85. Ibid., 202.

BIBLIOGRAPHY

Barton, John. *The Old Testament: Canon, Literature and Theology* (London and New York: Routledge, 2016).

Dunn, James. *Unity and Diversity in the New Testament: An Inquiry into the Character of Earliest Christianity*. Third edition (London: SCM Press, 2006).

LaCocque, André & Ricoeur, Paul. *Thinking Biblically: Exegetical and Hermeneutical Studies*. Translated by David Pellauer (Chicago and London: The University of Chicago Press, 1998).

Ricoeur, Paul. "The Bible and the Imagination" in *Figuring the Sacred: Religion, Narrative, and Imagination*. Edited by Mark I. Wallace, translated by David Pellauer (Minneapolis: Fortress Press, 1995), 144–66.

———. "Biblical Time" in *Figuring the Sacred: Religion, Narrative, and Imagination*. Edited by Mark I. Wallace, translated by David Pellauer (Minneapolis: Fortress Press, 1995), 167–80.

———. "Emmanuel Levinas: Thinker of Testimony" in *Figuring the Sacred: Religion, Narrative, and Imagination*. Edited by Mark I. Wallace, translated by David Pellauer (Minneapolis: Fortress Press, 1995), 108–26.

———. "Evil, a Challenge to Philosophy and Theology" in *Figuring the Sacred: Religion, Narrative, and Imagination*. Edited by Mark I. Wallace, translated by David Pellauer (Minneapolis: Fortress Press, 1995), 249–61.

———. "Interpretive Narrative" in *Figuring the Sacred: Religion, Narrative, and Imagination*. Edited by Mark I. Wallace, translated by David Pellauer (Minneapolis: Fortress Press, 1995), 188

————. "Love and Justice" in *Figuring the Sacred: Religion, Narrative, and Imagination*. Edited by Mark I. Wallace, translated by David Pellauer (Minneapolis: Fortress Press, 1995), 315–29.

————. "Manifestation and Proclamation" in *Figuring the Sacred: Religion, Narrative, and Imagination*. Edited by Mark I. Wallace, translated by David Pellauer (Minneapolis: Fortress Press, 1995), 48–67.

————. "On the Exegesis of Genesis 1:1—2:4a" in *Figuring the Sacred: Religion, Narrative, and Imagination*. Edited by Mark I. Wallace, translated by David Pellauer (Minneapolis: Fortress Press, 1995), 129–43.

————. "A Philosophical Hermeneutics of Religion: Kant" in *Figuring the Sacred: Religion, Narrative, and Imagination*. Edited by Mark I. Wallace, translated by David Pellauer (Minneapolis: Fortress Press, 1995), 75–92.

————. "Philosophy and Religious Language" in *Figuring the Sacred: Religion, Narrative, and Imagination*. Edited by Mark I. Wallace, translated by David Pellauer (Minneapolis: Fortress Press, 1995), 35–47.

————. "The "Sacred" Text and the Community" in *Figuring the Sacred: Religion, Narrative, and Imagination*. Edited by Mark I. Wallace, translated by David Pellauer (Minneapolis: Fortress Press, 1995), 68–72.

————. "The Self in the Mirror of the Scriptures" in *The Whole and Divided Self*. Edited by David E. Aune and John McCarthy (New York: Crossroad Publishing Company, 1997), 201–220.

————. *The Symbolism of Evil*. Translated by Emerson Buchanan (Boston, MA: Beacon Press, 1967).

————. *From Text to Action: Essays in Hermeneutics II*. Translated by Kathleen Blamey and John B. Thompson (Evanston, IL: Northwestern University Press, 1991).

————. *Time and Narrative 1*. Translated by Kathleen McLaughlin and David Pellauer (Chicago and London: The University of Chicago Press, 1984).

————. *Time and Narrative 3*. Translated by Kathleen McLaughlin and David Pellauer (Chicago and London: The University of Chicago Press, 1988).

————. "Toward a Narrative Theology" in *Figuring the Sacred: Religion, Narrative, and Imagination*. Edited by Mark I. Wallace, translated by David Pellauer (Minneapolis: Fortress Press, 1995), 236–48.

Wallace, Mark. "Introduction," in Ricoeur, Paul. *Figuring the Sacred: Religion, Narrative, and Imagination*, 1–32 (Minneapolis: Fortress Press, 1995).

Chapter 4

Ricoeur and Hope

Living after Rupture

Stephanie Arel

In *Freedom and Nature* (1950),[1] Ricoeur discusses hope as a decision and an effort that incorporates both a theory of fault and a poetics of the will, neglecting neither the cogito nor the body. His reflections emerge from five years in German prisoner of war camps wrestling with the themes of constraint and freedom. *Figuring the Sacred*, the collection of essays published nearly fifty years later, echoes Ricoeur's early work on the conflict between freedom of will in the face of forces manifested in radical evil that attempt to constrain the will.[2] A large part of my presentation revolves around one essay in the collection, "Hope and the Structure of Philosophical Systems,"[3] published in 1970, which underscores the dynamic between the poles of freedom and constraint. Hope intertwines with the dialectic here implicated with good and evil, openings and closings, possibility and impossibility. Ricoeur presents each term or idea to his reader from a theoretical point of view yet saturated in the practical reality of a history filled with traumatic incidents.

I begin by considering hope in Ricoeur's work from its function as an action to its power and effect as regeneration. Within that trajectory, I underscore how Ricoeur counters the idea that hope assuages or eliminates suffering. Ricoeur departs from notions of hope that offer an ultimate solution—or ultimate knowledge, manifested in the granting of salvation in some Christian frameworks. Instead, he affirms that despair—in its theoretical and practical dimensions—already indicates hope. In fact, nothing can save humanity from despair—as a process of acknowledging limits or as recognizing the existence of evil. Having enough hope or having the right hope does not stave off evil or dire circumstances. Thinking with Ricoeur that despair evidences hope exposes an opening, a rupture of constraints, and a possibility for a surplus of meaning.

Processing Ricoeur's work on hope includes recognizing—conceptually and practically—that the disruption of constraint is a necessary step to freedom. Constraint restricts the will as "a dead weight on consciousness."[4] In the face of radical evil, inciting consciousness becomes integral to hope as an impulse or action that does not close interpretation but opens to possibility. Not relying on absolute knowledge or believing in the accessibility of absolute knowledge—or an absolute fix—constitutes this openness. Being open is being vulnerable and conscious; it is accepting anguish,[5] pain, and despair as part of hope. In Ricoeurean terms, considering the function of the rupture that leads to openness which neither refutes nor glorifies suffering, begs self-examination, in front of the text and in an engagement with the world. This leads to envisioning hope as regeneration, not as a solution or an answer but as a process that motivates human agency and freedom. Thus, Ricoeur grounds hope in praxis. Hope cannot stay in the realm of the theoretical if it is to help anyone at all. This goal emerges in all my work on trauma and shame, and in this chapter, I attempt to enhance my understanding through Ricoeur's theory.

"HOPE" THE PASSION FOR THE POSSIBLE

In "Hope and the Structure of Philosophical Systems," Ricoeur raises up the concept of hope, rather than faith or love, to change the nature of the confrontation between philosophy and religion. Hope, he says, points to a required change in the structure of philosophical systems. He seeks, as he puts it, "a relation that has its expression in the movement and in the impulse of the discourse."[6] Ricoeur underscores that philosophy must recognize the dimension of hope as a "theological virtue." Yet Ricoeur emphasizes two important concepts—that theology be resituated on the idea of a cosmological vision and that the theology of history be governed by "the tension between promise and fulfillment."[7]

Neglecting the differences between promise and fulfillment leads to complications. In Judeo/Christian cultures, a Christian pattern—assuring concordance over discordance or privileging fulfillment over multiple (superabundant) meanings—characterizes the problem. To further explain this, Ricoeur adopts Ulrich Simon's diagnosis in *Theology of Auschwitz* of a "cultic pattern" that expects grace after suffering, the transformation of murder and sacrifice into an offering to God to make sacrifice meaningful, to integrate death into redemption, and ultimately to dissolve death through eternal salvation.[8]

This "post canonical 'history of salvation'" embeds itself in language and behavior, in theology and in secular society. The idea that Christ saves humanity from pain and suffering transmutes into an expectation of salvation from suffering; the expectation manifests in the words "I deserve"—pervasive in Western society in general as a need and desire for relief. If relief isn't provided, the need surfaces in other ways: incessant streaming, obsession with sports, drug and alcohol abuse. Society supports addictive behavior and the hope assured through a controlled manipulation of power[9] (what Julia Kristeva labels as totalitarianism, through social media for instance) that grants an illusion of individual freedom but fails to lead to liberation. Addiction constrains.

Christianity itself is not to blame, Ricoeur asserts. "Won over," he states in "Freedom in the Light of Hope,"[10] by Moltmann's interpretation of the Christian kerygma, he refutes hope's location in a historical figure because it fails to account for hope in the whole of history. Ricoeur turns to Moltmann—and by default Moltmann's influence by Martin Buber—to define hope theologically.[11] Moltmann discloses this connection in his situation of the Resurrection story within a Jewish theology of promise and outside of a Hellenistic framework of epiphany. The framework facilitates Ricoeur's analysis and adjudication that theology must be resituated on the tension between the two poles—promise and fulfillment—in lieu of a reliance on one or the other. Reliance on fulfillment as an epiphany manifests finally in a pattern that is not exclusive to Christianity but easily perceived in its theology. This pattern interprets resurrection as a fulfillment that translates too often in contemporary daily life into privileging concordance, purity, and perfection. In trauma, the privileging emerges in damaging expectations of healing, or in fragmentation (as the damaged parts of myself that do not easily accommodate purity and perfection are split off from the rest of myself, repressed, and denied.)

But harmony, perfection, and quick fixes sell. Anything that rebukes suffering and death outweighs the wrestling with suffering and death saturated with conflict and ambiguity. The other side of the pendulum—the interpretation of suffering as a way to fulfill the promise—promotes its glorification. Both sides of the pendulum lead to a logic that cannot tolerate the ambiguity, conflict, and tension which open the pathway to consciousness.

Hope that abnegates suffering sells (in some circles, hope mired in suffering also sells). Thus, hope has become a marketable commodity. A commodified hope offers solutions to problems, resolved storylines, and quick-fixes that can be easily substituted by others of its kind—alternate narratives, a new face, a swing on the pendulum. This hope is Nietzsche's conception of Zeus's last "gift" emerging from Pandora's box: the greatest of evils because it prolongs torment.[12] This sellable hope does not accompany despair, as Ricoeur would have it, but instead attempts to ignore despair, to veil its existence, or to promise despair will disappear. Torment ensues because this hope attempts to stop something that cannot be stopped: pain as a normal human experience, not an aberrant one. To be so tormented by a hope that renounces suffering leads to the denial of pain, the minimization of pain, and the attempt to erase pain—even our own. Grief met with the message that "this is how things were meant to be" exemplifies the residue of this hope.

Within certain religious frameworks, commodified hope is a path out of suffering and death into eternal life. Wikipedia reflects contemporary consciousness and reports simply: "Hope is a key concept in most major world religions, often signifying the 'hoper' believes an individual or a collective group will reach a concept of heaven."[13] In some Christian frameworks, rhetoric reflects that God comes to save. A similar message within a philosophical or secular framework provides a pathway to a utopian or final vision. The sales pitch works subconsciously through language that promises something: the fulfillment of a goal, a dream, an escape, even a fantasy—of strength, beauty, and happiness—that repudiates ordinary life or struggle.

For Ricoeur, hope sold in this religious framework is a hope that requires no working with, conjoining with, action, or discourse; it entails an interpretation of resurrection only as a *fulfillment* of the promise characteristic of Jewish theology, rather than a *confirmation* of that promise—or, to draw on Ricoeur's conception of superabundance, an *adding to* that promise.

Turning again to Moltmann, Ricoeur supports an assertion of confirming hope (hope's promise) not as fulfillment, the attainment of perfection, but as a testimony, as consent. Thus, resurrection shifts; it is not an event that closes or completes itself but opens. Resurrection is a "sign . . . that meaning abides in the future, in the death of death, in the resurrection of all from the dead"; it is thus a symbol, that, and he repeats his famous phrase, "gives rise to thought."[14]

Resurrection confirms a promise when it gives rise to such thought. Ricoeur does not claim that the hermeneutic of resurrection (the promise that God is the one that comes) is either valid or orthodox but rather that it opens discourse and refocuses theology on the consciousness encapsulated by the phrase "I hope in order to understand." The encounter with resurrection from this lens portrays the term as a symbol of potentiality; in the future, the symbolic dimension engages the realm of the irrational even as potentiality grounds hope in the rational.

Thus, aligned with resurrection, hope gives rise to "the irrationality of hope itself"[15] further clarified through Kierkegaard's idea of absurd logic.[16] That existence is absurd imposes a set of limits: hope is rational but paradoxically irrational. The authentic rationality of hope emerges only with acceptance of the paradox that ultimately expresses itself in the logic of superabundance. An expression of absurd logic is the antinomic anthropology expressed by Paul in Romans articulating the parallel between Adam and Jesus—the trajectory from sin to grace or abundance or to "much, much more."[17] The story of the resurrection creates the pathway for a similar trajectory in humans—a movement that leads to possibility, to the superabundance of meaning, to hope in spite of death that gives hope its "lucidity, its seriousness, its determination."[18]

Hope, for Ricoeur, is practical engagement on the path toward the good "which is not something to be grasped intellectually, nor is it a static goal or achievement" but manifests in one's temporal existence.[19] Ricoeur further draws on Kierkegaard: "hope makes of freedom the passion for the possible against the sad mediation of the irrevocable."[20] Hope implies no illusion; life is not the contrary of death, but its denial, superabundance or the excess of sense exceeds non-sense. In this latter construction, Ricoeur unites, "the logical, the ethical, the existential, and the religious aspects of meaning and meaninglessness in life."[21]

Like Ricoeur's idea of utopia in its most positive interpretation and unlike the utopian vision for perfection,[22] hope conceived outside of the intellectual legacy of an epiphany but within a conception of superabundance never completes but instigates more—more meaning, more action, more opportunities. Hope does not uncover the final gratification that alleviates all our woes, and it is not a final opportunity. Instead, hope opens to the impossible possibility.

Dan Stiver's words in *Theology after Ricoeur* help articulate the connections of resurrection and hope.

> In this life, we are encouraged not to succumb to the despairing spirit of skepticism, but to make affirmations of truth. These are in a sense wagers, however, in which we can say, "I hope, that I am within the bounds of truth." We hope that the future, and perhaps even the eschaton, will bear us out. In the meantime, we live in risk and in hope. This is why truth claims are a kind of testimony that we back with our lives, even our sacrifices and sufferings. . . . The promise of Christian hope relates psychologically, he says, to a passion for the possible which arises from our productive imagination in the ways we have discussed, such as metaphor, emplotment and utopia. It relates ethically to a mission that should not be understood in existential terms, in terms of the individual and the eternal present, but with communitarian, political and even cosmic implications. The twofold dynamic of the Christian hope is hope, in spite of offering how much more. Then we get to the logic of surplus.[23]

Life brings risk and hope. The passion of the possible—as hope—arises from the productive imagination. Productivity arises as a result at least of a receptivity to symbol, interpretation, and thought, each of which open to more, much more.

HOPE OPENS

Let me focus on the concept of opening—that leads to more—and its converse, the horizon of the philosophical discourse which Ricoeur calls the "closing point." In "Hope and the Structure of Philosophical Systems," Ricoeur delineates Hegel's closing point: absolute knowledge. He argues that Hegel develops a system that is contrary to hope[24] one that fails to account for the irrationality of evil (the something broken in the very heart of human action).[25] In accounting for this irrationality, Ricoeur refers to Kant's philosophy of limits. The limits apply to those in humankind—in action and in knowledge. Limits relate to hope, pulling hope back from a conception tied to *the* or *an* absolute: completion, perfection, conclusion. A philosophy of limits refutes such absolutes but leads to possibility:

> In that way, we may understand that a philosophy of the limits does not close the philosophical discourse but breaks the claim of objective knowledge to close it at the level of spatio-temporal objects. The limit is an act which opens, because it is an act which breaks the closure. In that sense, it already belongs to hope, in spite of the fact that it is merely negative, as the destruction of an illusion and of a claim.[26]

In his rejection of absolute knowledge, Ricoeur defines hope as neither canon nor a proclamation of fact. Nor does it arise from certainty of salvation. Ricoeur introduces the first step of the philosophy of hope—an act of renunciation of reason's ability to offer an absolute claim or absolute knowledge. Atheism is an example Ricoeur uses to show a critique of transcendental illusion through a philosophy of limits. The problem is that atheism creates its own illusion and puts humankind at the center creating a new absolute. Hope can never bestow absolute knowledge or fullness of being. Thus, Ricoeur writes, "hope is not a theme that comes after other themes, an idea that closes the system, but an impulse that opens the system, that breaks the closure of the system; it is a way of reopening what was unduly closed."[27]

Interpretations or allocations of meaning[28] evolve fostered by "a mature openness to the symbolic world."[29] Such openness is a risk because openness connects to a state of emptiness.[30] "Unlike absolute knowledge," Ricoeur writes, "primary affirmation, secretly armed with hope, brings about no reassuring *Aufhebung* [sublation]; it does not 'surmount,' but 'affronts;' it does not 'reconcile' but 'consoles'; this is why anguish will accompany hope until the last day."[31] The consolation leads to two directions. First, like a promise, consolation opens to a sense of being with (God for instance), and second, consolation implies that anguish, despair, and even evil accompany hope.

The incomplete opening, to meaning, discourse, and interpretation, that Ricoeur stands before, requires a *response* from humanity. For Ricoeur, the response manifests in an attitude that allows human reason to relate to those questions which cannot be answered by experience. In the *Critique of Pure Reason*, Kant poses the question "For what may I hope?" Building from Kant, Ricoeur draws on the practical and theoretical implications of this question, asserting, "I must hope in order to believe that I am able to act."[32] Kristeva says something similar in a piece entitled *Jerusalem*; she looks to Jewish theology reflected in Psalm 116, "I believe and therefore I spoke."[33] Hope thus assumes a starting place in his philosophical system connecting to agency and freedom—the ability/power to act, to be efficient, and to endure in time.

Ricoeur appreciates the temporal location, asserted also by Moltmann, encompassed by the idea that encountering God is always ahead of the present time. In *Conflict of Interpretations*, this divine trajectory parallels myth read by Ricoeur as directing experience from a beginning to an end, from memory to hope.[34] This hope is the actionable quality of a goal, the encounter that lies ahead of present time. Hope, an actionable component, is a goal for freedom[35] setting a pathway for action and opening possibility. Ricoeur repeats himself in several works[36] speaking of (1) the goal that hope gives, as it (2) hangs between morality and happiness, and (3) functions as a part of religion itself in Kant's question "for what may I hope?"

BY WAY OF RUPTURE

The question turns us toward possibilities. But possibility, in Ricoeur's lexicon, necessitates a "rupture."[37] The concept of a rupture—the break in the unity of a thing—affiliates with other terms in Ricoeur's body of work. In "Quest of Hope: Paul Ricoeur and Jürgen Moltmann," David Stewart connects Ricoeur's use of the term "fault" (to describe the condition of humanity) with the geological sense of "rift" or "fracture." Ricoeur links fractures and ruptures to openings. He does this most frequently in *Memory, History, Forgetting*. With rupture, Ricoeur tells readers, "a finger is pointed in the direction of a fault-line fissuring from within the presumed encompassing, totalizing idea of world history."[38] For instance, a rupture between the Greeks and the Romans occurs as a result of the triumph of Christianity.[39] Both the French Revolution and the Reformation create historical ruptures in political and religious development respectively.[40]

When Ricoeur speaks of hope for attending to fractures in human existence, he echoes Moltmann. This existence can be summarized as temporally located between ambiguity and future possibilities. Moltmann explains ambiguity in terms of the divine promise, while Ricoeur refers to the conflict between being (human nature) and the imagination of what is possible, or freedom in the light of hope (in psychological terms).[41]

But ruptures occur on the individual level as well. A rupture breaks up human existence as a disruption, disturbing equilibrium, introducing unintelligibility, and mimicking conflict. Ricoeur refers to reflection as a rupture in *Freedom and Nature*:

> I am alive, I am my life. But the birth of reflection is the rupture of this initial intimate coordination of consciousness and the body; hereafter it is the very act of freedom assuming its reasons, its abilities, and its condition in a new practical conciliation.[42]

In *History and Truth*, Ricoeur employs an image to communicate the interplay I am describing, and how this further links to hope. In the text, Ricoeur refers to a broken mirror. The crack in the mirror imitates a rupture. Even with the rupture, seeing is possible, though the seeing is altered. Affectively, the reality of brokenness and the alteration such brokenness reveals about the reflection express anguish accompanying hope. Anguish rests alongside freedom the freedom to choose—an interpretation for instance—in the reflection. Reflection or new consciousness unveils new possibilities. Practically, the possibility promotes action. Movement results, arising from a rupture that creates an opening—for thinking, translation, and discernment. In contrast, a commodified hope engenders closure; a broken mirror provides no consolation or room for a new interpretation. This hope seeks, instead, a complete answer in line with absolute knowledge. Evil as something broken in the very heart of human action has no place in this hope.

Yet, brokenness is a human reality constituting a rupture in the framework of hope. Ricoeur mentions the rupture effect in an article on Levinas and later in *Memory, History, Forgetting*. This rupture effect or point of rupture at two levels of understanding—produced by novelty[43]—generates an opening for configuration.[44] Something new develops, leading to Ricoeur's use of innovation and rupture together, and thus consciousness.[45] This critical consciousness signifies disruption, a willingness to be disrupted by symbol for instance, demonstrating hope. But consciousness is also paradoxically a bond. Ricoeur writes,

> Consciousness is always in some degree both a disruption and a bond. This is why the structures which connect the voluntary and the involuntary are structures of rupture as well as of union. Behind these structures lies the paradox which culminates in the paradox of freedom and nature.[46]

The bond is one to the other, temporality to incarnation, passion to emotion, or word to act, joining subjective power and the creative act in the way of Jasper's cipher, a metaphysical symbol that indicates the impossibility of absolute knowledge while alluding to it. In the face of the impossible, in the heart of disruption and instability, the possibility for action and agency exists. Even this unity of the will is unstable—the unconscious, character, life, and the body are all broken, and fractured. But action is possible—even through the imagination.

Turning again to essays in *Figuring the Sacred* facilitates a link between ruptures and hope. I refer again to the notion of the Christian pattern and its constraints; Ricoeur presses a liberation from such restraints that he envisions emerging from the tasks of narrative theology. This liberation signifies the end of a privileged status of absolute knowledge. "Then memory and hope would be delivered from the visible narrative" (what we may call absolute) "that hides that which we may call, with Johann B Metz, 'dangerous memories' and the challenging expectations that together constitute the unresolved dialectic of memory and of hope."[47] Dangerous memories bring to the fore the reality of injustice and innocent suffering; they challenge the hegemony of Western knowledge that inferiorizes other forms of knowledge (i.e., indigenous), undermining agency and imposing shame: to be outside of this form of knowledge is to be marginalized.

Hope in Ricoeur allows for other forms of knowledge as it resists compliance with, and thus finds the rupture within, dominant narratives that secure an absolute. He exemplifies resistance through narrative theory, a method that facilitates the loosening/opening of resources, and thus the imagination, within the Bible as a text. The Bible offers a model of narration, has teaching potential resonant of Aristotle's practical wisdom, and facilitates mediation and understanding. This mediation takes place between humankind and the world, among humans themselves, and between the human being and the self.[48] Possibilities for understanding the world, the other, and the self, amidst the reality of human suffering, open discourse and the path to hope.

Hope enters in the simple will to live, in human freedom, in spite of evil. "In spite of evil" is a form or category of hope for possibility that aligns with Kant's insight into seduction, that despite the capacity for seduction by evil, goodness exists. The presence of the word and the condition indicates hope. In theology, such hope is engendered by the "symbol of God"—of unknown possibilities;[49] philosophically, such hope emerges after rupture in the idea of regeneration or in the establishment of a new character, the liberation of the power of free choice and the emancipation of goodness.[50] Ricoeur writes in *History and Truth* "That 'it is good' . . . this I do not see: in the darkness, I hope it is."[51]

REGENERATION OF THE WILL

In "Hope and the Structure of Philosophical Systems," Ricoeur raises up the concept of hope, rather than faith or love, to change the nature of the confrontation between philosophy and religion.[52] Hope, he says, points to a required change. He seeks, as he puts it, "a relation that has its expression in the movement and in the impulse of the discourse."[53] I underscore the words—change, movement, and impulse in this assertion.

He continues in the text to consider two dialectics—a conclusive one (257) and a broken one. Hegel's absolute knowledge constitutes the first. Karl Barth's conception of humankind being completely dissociated from God or transcendence constitutes the second. Ricoeur asks if the latter does better justice to the phenomenon of victimization? The answer is yes—"up to the point of acknowledging the broken condition as irretrievable." The irretrievability of the broken condition makes healing or complete healing impossible; brokenness can never be eliminated. Two presuppositions follow that ground the practical. (1) We are broken; we cannot completely eliminate this brokenness (hoping we can already diverge from hope), and (2) the capacity to do evil and to do good resides within us; hope exists in spite of evil and opens to a meaning where we have a choice.

Ricoeur brings readers to a second approximation by reason of the philosophical meaning of hope: "It is the anticipation, the expectation, of a connection between the purity of heart and satisfaction of our most intimate desire."[54] This expression situates hope with the good. With this philosophical framing, Ricoeur addresses the breaking open of hope to its practical requirement, that of fulfillment of the will. But as is characteristic with Ricoeur, the opposing viewpoint or challenge appears: returning to Kant's limits, Ricoeur presents the problem of evil, which existentially and philosophically makes freedom an "impossible possibility."[55]

I want to pause here and note that my concern is the ability to access hope in the face of despair, amidst trauma, and in trauma's aftermath. Ricoeur's theory begs interpretation before a child who watches horror or endures wounding daily, not statistically an exceptional situation. In one sense, his words more likely apply to a survivor who assumes a state of self-reliance to which the child has little access. I will return to the dilemma of the child. In situations of human betrayal, or human evil, the survivor develops or carries a sense of worthlessness. This sense, undergirded by shame, results from the double-edged sword of trauma which inspires terror and helplessness. Recovery from these includes action—agency. However, to act, I must believe I can act.

A sense of worth enables belief in agency. Agency includes an ability to extract oneself from a traumatic situation, and to subsequently bring it into view to wrestle with its effects and meaning. Judith Herman calls this the process of recovery from trauma. The process attempts to alter the sense of helplessness and terror that define trauma and distinguish trauma from human suffering. Though agency plays a significant role in the response to suffering and the process of recovery, representing a key feature of hope: as action and as accompanying despair.

Recall that the broken condition is irreparable to Ricoeur. The process of hope includes acknowledging this condition. We have limits. Every action in or as hope, or every effort to recover, to respond, and to work through trauma and suffering unveils limits. We can neither eliminate suffering nor eradicate the wounds of suffering. The word "heal" falls short and aligns itself with the marketable hope. However, hope as an act aligns with anything we can do in our ethical responsibility to the world, to the other, and to ourselves.

In trauma, responsibility emerges as an attendance to pain and suffering that refutes the original sense of helplessness and terror. Doing something is key here. Victims of rape who fight their attackers suffer fewer PTSD symptoms and a reduction of self-worth than those who react passively or who attempt to negotiate.[56] The same is true for children. Children who react actively in the face of violence suffer to a lesser degree from PTSD than children who respond passively.[57] Children press an in-depth understanding of agency as those who are suffering or abused challenge any conception of an ability to act or to be ethically responsible. They press theorists to conceive of agency as less active than we might expect.

Ricoeur guides the understanding through his explication of hope. In hope, we are open to being disrupted, not closed. The rupture reveals the opening. Hope signifies this "openness to the symbolic world" (irrationality) and potentiality (the rational). Symbol and potentiality point to the facility of the imagination. The imagination provides children access to agency, the reflection and response that follow Ricoeur's sense of rupture.

Imagination is key to recovery for children. Children with greater literary capacities—and the ability to imagine a future different than what they are experiencing—develop stronger resilience in the face of trauma.[58] The imagination exists as the tool children have at their disposal. Exercising the imagination—through play, for instance—creates a means for enduring trauma. Imaginative activities offer momentary divergence from traumatic circumstances, serve as containers for enhanced affect (as in a drawing), and allow for the formulation of more appealing narratives.[59] Imagination leads to freedom and hope. In the process of recovery, imagination enables the ability to see potential, to name trauma, and to place the trauma outside of the self. Through play, for instance, a child can enact what happened, using play to speak, and employ play to enact other alternative endings thus building coping and resilience.

The recovery process echoes Ricoeur's envisioning of freedom passing through powerlessness—a trajectory that resembles the Christian kerygma even in the philosophical interpretation of hope, and one that defines along with helplessness the condition of trauma—a hope of resurrection among the dead. Ricoeur tells readers, "evil requires a nonethical and nonpolitical transformation of our will, which Kant calls regeneration."[60] Regeneration is essentially the emancipation of goodness set out in *Philosophical Anthropology* and discussed extensively in *Figuring the Sacred*. "The good principle," Ricoeur writes, "stems from a distinct problematic, that of the regeneration of the will, which itself has its origin in the enigma of radical evil."[61] On the one hand, in the face of absolute evil, humanity can do nothing, but on the other hand, regeneration exists in the establishment of a new possibility or new interpretation that leads to the surplus of meaning.[62] The imagination and play can be understood as features of regeneration.

For Ricoeur, the interweaving of the recognition of radical evil and the responsibility of regeneration is constitutive of the motif of hope in Kant's hermeneutics of religion. Hope is its object. "Concrete, effective freedom thus becomes an object of hope."[63] The project of regeneration is the liberation of the power of free choice; the liberation necessitates an appropriate institution to guard the symbolic grounds of such freedom. Ricoeur uses, for example, representation through Christ of divine aid; the historical vehicle for the adhesion of faith contributes, he writes, to the efficacy of this symbolism.

For Kant, the task of religion within the limits of reason is "to elaborate the condition of possibility of this regeneration, without alienating freedom either to a magical conception of grace and salvation or to an authoritarian organization of the religious community."[64] Memory is an inner truth,[65] and reflection is inner testimony that leads to the possibility of regeneration. Ricoeur supports the notion of regeneration that does not rely on God alone, or on something transcendental to itself for strength, but rather insists on autonomy: the individual must insist on capacity, not moral incapacity, to resist and regenerate the will.

Regeneration is the establishment of a new character;[66] it is the surplus of meaning, of goodness in hope. Regeneration situates agency, empowering people to choose—to enact what is in their capacity—and to even in the face of evil manifest goodness. "The good principal stems from a distinct problematic," Ricoeur writes, "that of the regeneration of the will, which itself has its origin in the enigma of radical evil."[67] The actuality of evil ties human freedom to Regeneration, which is the content of hope.[68]

Perhaps we need to understand that the way of consent does not lead only through admiration of marvelous nature, focused in the absolute involuntary, but through hope which awaits something else. Here the transcendence implied in the act of consent assumes an altogether new form. Admiration as possible because the world is an analogy of transcendence. Hope is necessary because the world is quite other than transcendence. Admiration sings of the day, reaches the visible miracle. Hope transcends in the night. Admiration says the world is good. It is the possible home of freedom. I can consent. Hope says the world is not the final home of freedom. I consent as much as possible, but hope to be delivered of the terrible, and at the end of time to enjoy a new body and a new nature granted to freedom.[69]

I would like to frame this in the construction of something called Karpman's drama triangle[70]—something used very little in academic literature, but which holds quite well with contemporary theories about trauma that envision human betrayal at its center. The triangle also elucidates hope as (1) a passion for the possible, (2) an opening rather than a closing, (3) something that grows out of rupture and acknowledges despair and the condition of brokenness, and (4) requires the will to act.

Three roles exist: perpetrator, victim, and rescuer. In the process of survival, those who have experienced trauma likely shift to one of these roles, almost in perpetuity, until the notion of victim is dispelled and the understanding of each role is both conceptualized and then resisted. And it takes resistance. It takes an ability to see the roles at play or to be conscious of them, to identify them and then to step outside of the triangle to be able to suspend engagement in any one role. This happens at greater or lesser degrees. Sometimes inhabiting the roles is useful; the victim must identify as a victim for instance. In the case of gross human violence, admitting that the trauma occurred—or acknowledging it includes understanding oneself as a victim. However, throughout the process of recovery, resistance is necessary. The resistance includes taking responsibility for the self (refuting the victim role), not lashing out at others (refuting the perpetrator role), and not rushing to save others—or to eradicate another's agency (refuting the rescuer role). While any of these roles are inhabited, the trauma—or to use Karpman's words the drama triangle is fully in play.

Building on these ideas, I summarize my vision of hope as a practical means for responding to tragedy. In that response, a demand is made on the human person—to resist absolutes and closings. The resistance occurs within religious and psychological frameworks. We must resist the expectation of the eradication of suffering emphasized by a viewpoint in some patterns of Christianity and adopted by contemporary culture that suffering is an aberration or that we are unbroken. We are broken.

To embody the response is to remain suspended in ambiguity. To respond is to reject absolute knowledge—remaining vulnerable—to understand that despair is a part of life and hope. In this posture, hope introduces an opening, an abundance of meaning, rather than a closure of meaning (i.e., in the structure of a Christian pattern that signifies completion and fulfillment). This hope must be dynamic, aware of suffering but significant of growth. Hope

liberates, as an active pattern, not absent of conflict, but unveiling possibilities in conflict.

Two, the nature of hope as impulse and action, awakens and unveils possibility rather than closing options—in any type of constraint, whether that is
ideological, political, or religious. Any promise that leads to fulfillment and
not to conjoining with in possibility (or which maintains an openness to additional change or regeneration), fails to indicate hope. This failure parallels a
closing of interpretation or meaning.

Three, embrace rupture, in time, in history, in new interpretations of narratives, in new understandings, in the body, and in the self. Discomfort with
change in ruptures reveals possibilities for openness. Discoveries happen this
way (the renaissance). Then we can start to see hope as regeneration, not sav-
ing, not an answer, but a process that leads to human agency and freedom.

NOTES

1. Paul Ricoeur, *Freedom and Nature*, trans. and ed. by Erazim V. Kohak (Evanston, IL: Northwestern University Press, 1966).

2. Paul Ricoeur, *Figuring the Sacred*, trans. by David Pellauer and ed. by Mark
I. Wallace (Minneapolis, MN: Augsburg Fortress, 1995).

3. "Theological Overtures: God, Self, Narrative, and Evil."

4. Ricoeur, *Freedom and Nature*, trans. and ed. by Erazim V. Kohak (Evanston,
IL: Northwestern University Press, 1966), 126.

5. Ricoeur underscores anguish in *History and Truth*, trans. and ed. by Charles
Kelbley (Evanston, IL: Northwestern University Press, 1965): "We shall learn from
anguish only if we try to understand it and if, by understanding it, we reestablish
contact with the fount of truth and of life, which nurtures our rejoinders to anguish"
(294).

6. Paul Ricoeur, "Hope and the Structure of Philosophical Systems," in *Figuring
the Sacred*, trans. by David Pellauer and ed. by Mark I. Wallace (Minneapolis, MN:
Augsburg Fortress, 1995), 203.

7. Paul Ricoeur, "Hope and the Structure of Philosophical Systems," in *Figuring
the Sacred*, trans. by David Pellauer and ed. by Mark I. Wallace (Minneapolis, MN:
Augsburg Fortress, 1995), 203.

8. Ulrich E. Simon, *A Theology of Auschwitz* (London: SPCK, 1978).

9. See Ulrich E. Simon, *A Theology of Auschwitz* (London: SPCK, 1978), 134.

10. Paul Ricoeur, "Freedom in the Light of Hope," in *Essays on Biblical Interpretations*, 215–34 (Minneapolis, MN: Fortress Press, 1980).

11. In his essay "In Quest of Hope: Paul Ricoeur and Jürgen Moltmann," *Restoration Quarterly* vol. 31, no. 1 (1970), David Stewart references a movement in
theology. He groups Moltmann with other theorists in this category including the
originator of the term "The Hope Tendency." Walter Capps (see Walter H. Capps,

"The Hope Tendency," *Cross Currents* vol. 18, no. 3 (1968): 257–272), Wolfhart Pannenberg, Johannes Metz, Ernst Bloch, and Nikolai Berdyaev.

12. Friedrich Nietzsche, *Human all too Human*, trans. by Marion Faber and Stephen Lehmann (Lincoln, NE: University of Nebraska Press, 1984), 58.

13. "Hope," Wikipedia, accessed October 7, 2023, https://en.wikipedia.org/wiki /Hope.

14. Paul Ricoeur, "Hope and the Structure of Philosophical Systems," in *Figuring the Sacred*, trans. by David Pellauer and ed. by Mark I. Wallace (Minneapolis, MN: Augsburg Fortress, 1995), 205.

15. Paul Ricoeur, "Hope and the Structure of Philosophical Systems," in *Figuring the Sacred*, trans. by David Pellauer and ed. by Mark I. Wallace (Minneapolis, MN: Augsburg Fortress, 1995), 205.

16. Paul Ricoeur, "Hope and the Structure of Philosophical Systems," in *Figuring the Sacred*, trans. by David Pellauer and ed. by Mark I. Wallace (Minneapolis, MN: Augsburg Fortress, 1995), 205.

17. Paul Ricoeur, "Hope and the Structure of Philosophical Systems," in *Figuring the Sacred*, trans. by David Pellauer and ed. by Mark I. Wallace (Minneapolis, MN: Augsburg Fortress, 1995), 206.

18. Paul Ricoeur, "Hope and the Structure of Philosophical Systems," in *Figuring the Sacred*, trans. by David Pellauer and ed. by Mark I. Wallace (Minneapolis, MN: Augsburg Fortress, 1995), 207.

19. Ruby Guyatt, "Kierkegaard in the Anthropocene: Hope, Philosophy, and the Climate Crisis," *Religions* vol. 11, no. 6 (2020): 279.

20. Paul Ricoeur, "Hope and the Structure of Philosophical Systems," in *Figuring the Sacred*, trans. by David Pellauer and ed. by Mark I. Wallace (Minneapolis, MN: Augsburg Fortress, 1995), 206.

21. Paul Ricoeur, "Hope and the Structure of Philosophical Systems," in *Figuring the Sacred*, trans. by David Pellauer and ed. by Mark I. Wallace (Minneapolis, MN: Augsburg Fortress, 1995), 207, footnote. Also see Dan Stiver, *Theology after Ricoeur* (Louisville, KY: Westminster John Knox Press, 2001), 119 . . . his discussion of surplus in the idea of the gift as opposed to hope as absolute knowledge or secured through something we can see.

22. Consciousness provokes thought but can never be complete. The politics of hope recognizes the incompleteness of discourse and action (xiv). Ricoeur's work on ideology and utopia helps here. In his foreword, to Dauenhauer's *Politics of Hope* (London: Routledge and Kegan Paul, 1986)*,* Ricoeur writes, "Religious hope and utopia seem to share a common presupposition, namely that a complete resolution of historical contradictions are possible above or beyond history." While utopia—in its most positive interpretation—"extends to the boundary line between the possible and the impossible," it never completes but is a dynamic with ideology. Ideology invests in "an imaginary relation that expresses hope or nostalgia rather than describing reality," *Ideology and Utopia*, 136. This imaginary relation, for Ricoeur, might culminate in full mutual recognition—a utopian element.

23. Dan Stiver, *Theology after Ricoeur* (Louisville, KY: Westminster John Knox Press, 2001), 222.

24. Paul Ricoeur, "Hope and the Structure of Philosophical Systems," in *Figuring the Sacred*, trans. by David Pellauer and ed. by Mark I. Wallace (Minneapolis, MN: Augsburg Fortress, 1995), 208. Ricoeur writes that Hegel's system is a philosophy of reminiscence, where rationality belongs to the present.

25. Paul Ricoeur, "Hope and the Structure of Philosophical Systems," in *Figuring the Sacred*, trans. by David Pellauer and ed. by Mark I. Wallace (Minneapolis, MN: Augsburg Fortress, 1995), 211.

26. Paul Ricoeur, "Hope and the Structure of Philosophical Systems," in *Figuring the Sacred*, trans. by David Pellauer and ed. by Mark I. Wallace (Minneapolis, MN: Augsburg Fortress, 1995), 213.

27. Paul Ricoeur, "Hope and the Structure of Philosophical Systems," in *Figuring the Sacred*, trans. by David Pellauer and ed. by Mark I. Wallace (Minneapolis, MN: Augsburg Fortress, 1995), 211.

28. Paul Ricoeur, "Foreword," in Bernard Dauenhauer, *Politics of Hope* (London: Routledge and Kegan Paul, 1986).

29. Paul Ricoeur, Mark I. Wallace's Introduction, *Figuring the Sacred* (Minneapolis, MN: Augsburg Fortress, 1995), 6.

30. Paul Ricoeur, "The Demythization of Accusation," in *Conflict of Interpretations*, trans. by Peter McCormick and ed. by Don Ihde (Evanston, IL: Northwestern University Press, 1974), 349.

31. Paul Ricoeur, *History and Truth*, trans. and ed. by Charles Kelbley (Evanston, IL: Northwestern University Press, 1965), 303–304.

32. Paul Ricoeur, *History and Truth*, trans. and ed. by Charles Kelbley (Evanston, IL: Northwestern University Press, 1965), xv.

33. Julia Kristeva, "Jerusalem," Public Lecture, Forum International des Religions, November 2008.

34. Paul Ricoeur, "The Hermeneutics of Symbols and Philosophical Reflection: II," in *Conflict of Interpretations*, trans. by Charles Freilich and ed. by Don Ihde (Evanston, IL: Northwestern University Press, 1974), 316.

35. A conception formulated in *Essays on Biblical Interpretation*, and *Conflict of Interpretations*.

36. See *Conflict of Interpretations* (Evanston, IL: Northwestern University Press, 1974), *Essays on Biblical Interpretations* (Minneapolis, MN: Fortress Press, 1980), *Figuring the Sacred* (Minneapolis, MN: Augsburg Fortress, 1995), *Philosophical Anthropology* (Malden, MA: Polity, 2015).

37. In French, the same word "rupture" functions as both a noun, a fissure, and a verb, to break or split apart. In English translations of his work, the noun "rupture" stands apart from its use as a verb; the verb "rupture" is replaced by other terms maintaining the linguistic and philosophical cohesiveness of "rupture" used as a noun—as a break or a breach in the unity of a thing or a relationship.

38. Paul Ricoeur, *Memory, History, Forgetting* (Chicago: University of Chicago Press, 2004), 301.

39. Paul Ricoeur, *Memory, History, Forgetting* (Chicago: University of Chicago Press, 2004), 231.

40. Paul Ricoeur, *Memory, History, Forgetting* (Chicago: University of Chicago Press, 2004), 302.

41. Paul Ricoeur, *Essays on Biblical Interpretations* (Minneapolis, MN: Fortress Press, 1980), 22.

42. Paul Ricoeur, *Freedom and Nature*, trans. and ed. By Erazim V. Kohak (Evanston, IL: Northwestern University Press, 1966), 353.

43. Paul Ricoeur, *Memory, History, Forgetting* (Chicago: University of Chicago Press, 2004), 307.

44. Paul Ricoeur, *Memory, History, Forgetting* (Chicago: University of Chicago Press, 2004), 150.

45. Paul Ricoeur, *Memory, History, Forgetting* (Chicago: University of Chicago Press, 2004), 309.

46. Paul Ricoeur, *Freedom and Nature*, trans. and ed. By Erazim V. Kohak (Evanston, IL: Northwestern University Press, 1966), 18–19.

47. Paul Ricoeur, "Toward a Narrative Theology: Its Necessity, Its Resources, Its Difficulties," in *Figuring the Sacred*, trans. by David Pellauer and ed. by Mark I. Wallace (Minneapolis, MN: Augsburg Fortress, 1995), 238.

48. Paul Ricoeur, "Toward a Narrative Theology: Its Necessity, Its Resources, Its Difficulties," in *Figuring the Sacred*, trans. by David Pellauer and ed. by Mark I. Wallace (Minneapolis, MN: Augsburg Fortress, 1995), 239–241.

49. Paul Ricoeur, "Ethical and Theological Considerations on the Golden Rule," in *Figuring the Sacred*, trans. by David Pellauer and ed. by Mark I. Wallace (Minneapolis, MN: Augsburg Fortress, 1995), 299.

50. Paul Ricoeur, *Philosophical Anthropology* (Malden, MA: Polity, 2015), 284.

51. Paul Ricoeur, *History and Truth,* trans. and ed. by Charles Kelbley (Evanston, IL: Northwestern University Press, 1965).

52. Ricoeur's first asserts that philosophy must recognize the dimension of hope as a "theological virtue." Ricoeur turns to Moltmann to define hope theologically, asserting that Moltmann is helped in his theories by Martin Buber. In his essay "In Quest of Hope: Paul Ricoeur and Jürgen Moltmann," *Restoration Quarterly* vol. 31, no. 1 (1970), David Stewart references a movement in theology. He groups Moltmann with other theorists in this category, including the originator of the term "The Hope Tendency" Walter Capps (see Walter H. Capps, "The Hope Tendency," *Cross Currents* vol. 18, no. 3 (1968): 257–272), Wolfhart Pannenberg, Johannes Metz, Ernst Bloch, and Nikolai Berdyaev.

53. Paul Ricoeur, "Hope and the Structure of Philosophical Systems," in *Figuring the Sacred*, trans. by David Pellauer and ed. by Mark I. Wallace (Minneapolis, MN: Augsburg Fortress, 1995), 203.

54. Paul Ricoeur, "Hope and the Structure of Philosophical Systems," in *Figuring the Sacred*, trans. by David Pellauer and ed. by Mark I. Wallace (Minneapolis, MN: Augsburg Fortress, 1995), 214.

55. Paul Ricoeur, "Hope and the Structure of Philosophical Systems," in *Figuring the Sacred*, trans. by David Pellauer and ed. by Mark I. Wallace (Minneapolis, MN: Augsburg Fortress, 1995), 215.

56. Judith Herman, *Trauma and Recovery* (New York City: Basic Books, 1992).

57. Raija-Leena Punamäki, Samir Qouta, and Eyad El-Sarraj, "Resiliency Factors Predicting Psychological Adjustment After Political Violence Among Palestinian

Children," *International Journal of Behavioral Development* vol. 25, no. 3 (2001): 256–267.

58. See Lenore Terr, *Too Scared to Cry* (New York City: Basic Books, 1990).

59. Cathy Malchlodi, "Ethics, Evidence, Trauma-Informed Practice, and Cultural Sensitivity," in *Creative Interventions with Traumatized Children*, ed. Cathy Malchlodi (UK: Guilford Publications, 2014).

60. Paul Ricoeur, "Hope and the Structure of Philosophical Systems," in *Figuring the Sacred*, trans. by David Pellauer and ed. by Mark I. Wallace (Minneapolis, MN: Augsburg Fortress, 1995), 215.

61. Paul Ricoeur, "A Philosophical Hermeneutics of Religion: Kant," in *Figuring the Sacred*, trans. by David Pellauer and ed. by Mark I. Wallace (Minneapolis, MN: Augsburg Fortress, 1995), 89.

62. Aux frontières de la philosophie. 32.

63. Paul Ricoeur, "Ethical and Theological Considerations on the Golden Rule," in *Figuring the Sacred*, trans. by David Pellauer and ed. by Mark I. Wallace (Minneapolis, MN: Augsburg Fortress, 1995), 297.

64. Paul Ricoeur, "Hope and the Structure of Philosophical Systems," in *Figuring the Sacred*, trans. by David Pellauer and ed. by Mark I. Wallace (Minneapolis, MN: Augsburg Fortress, 1995), 215.

65. Paul Ricoeur, "The Summoned Subject in the School of the Narratives of Prophetic Vocation," in *Figuring the Sacred*, trans. by David Pellauer and ed. by Mark I. Wallace (Minneapolis, MN: Augsburg Fortress, 1995), 269.

66. Paul Ricoeur, "A Philosophical Hermeneutics of Religion: Kant," in *Figuring the Sacred*, trans. by David Pellauer and ed. by Mark I. Wallace (Minneapolis, MN: Augsburg Fortress, 1995), 85.

67. Paul Ricoeur, "A Philosophical Hermeneutics of Religion: Kant," in *Figuring the Sacred*, trans. by David Pellauer and ed. by Mark I. Wallace (Minneapolis, MN: Augsburg Fortress, 1995), 89.

68. Paul Ricoeur, *Essays on Biblical Interpretations* (Minneapolis, MN: Fortress Press, 1980), 117.

69. Paul Ricoeur, *Freedom and Nature,* trans. and ed. By Erazim V. Kohak (Evanston, IL: Northwestern University Press, 1966), 480.

70. Karpman, Stephen B. "Fairy Tales and Script Drama Analysis." *Transactional Analysis Bulletin,* vol. 7 (1968): 39–43.

BIBLIOGRAPHY

Capps, Walter H. "The Hope Tendency." *Cross Currents* vol. 18, no. 3 (1968): 257–272.

Dauenhauer, Bernard. *Politics of Hope*. London: Routledge and Kegan Paul, 1986.

Guyatt, Ruby "Kierkegaard in the Anthropocene: Hope, Philosophy, and the Climate Crisis," *Religions vol.* 11, no. 6 (2020): 279.

Herman, Judith. *Trauma and Recovery.* New York City: Basic Books, 1992.

Karpman, Stephen B. "Fairy Tales and Script Drama Analysis." *Transactional Analysis Bulletin,* vol. 7 (1968): 39–43.

Kristeva, Julia. "Jerusalem." Public Lecture. Forum International des Religions. November 2008.

Malchlodi, Cathy. "Ethics, Evidence, Trauma-Informed Practice, and Cultural Sensitivity," in *Creative Interventions with Traumatized Children,* 24–44. Edited by Cathy Malchlodi. London, UK: Guilford Publications, 2014.

Nietzsche, Friedrich. *Human all too Human.* Translated by Marion Faber and Stephen Lehmann. Lincoln, NE: University of Nebraska Press, 1984.

Punamäki, Raija-Leena, Samir Qouta, and Eyad El-Sarraj. "Resiliency Factors Predicting Psychological Adjustment After Political Violence Among Palestinian Children." *International Journal of Behavioral Development* vol. 25, no. 3 (2001): 256–267.

Ricoeur, Paul. *Conflict of Interpretations.* Translated by Peter McCormick and edited by Don Ihde. Evanston, IL: Northwestern University Press, 1974.

———. *Essays on Biblical Interpretations.* Minneapolis, MN: Fortress Press, 1980.

———. *Figuring the Sacred.* Translated by David Pellauer and edited by Mark I. Wallace. Minneapolis, MN: Augsburg Fortress, 1995.

———. *Freedom and Nature.* Translated and edited by Erazim V. Kohak. Evanston, IL: Northwestern University Press, 1966.

———. *History and Truth.* Translated and edited by Charles Kelbley. Evanston, IL: Northwestern University Press, 1965.

———. *Memory, History, Forgetting.* Chicago: University of Chicago Press, 2004.

———. *Philosophical Anthropology.* Malden, MA: Polity, 2015.

Simon, Ulrich E. *A Theology of Auschwitz.* London: SPCK, 1978.

Stewart, David. "In Quest of Hope: Paul Ricoeur and Jürgen Moltmann." *Restoration Quarterly* vol. 31, no. 1 (1970): 31–52.

Stiver, Dan. *Theology after Ricoeur.* Louisville, KY: Westminster John Knox Press, 2001.

Terr, Lenore. *Too Scared to Cry.* New York City: Basic Books, 1990.

Chapter 5

Practical Theology as Practical Poetics

Building a Bridge between Prose, Poetics, and Praxis[1]

Dan R. Stiver

An explication of Ricoeur on practical theology initially seems like a misnomer in that Ricoeur seemed relatively uninterested in theology in general, not to mention the subfield of practical theology. And yet that is the heading for the last section in the collection of essays in *Figuring the Sacred*.[2] Ricoeur was of course interested in biblical interpretation and, of course, practical philosophy in his interest in ethics and in the final moment of "appropriation" or "application" in his noted hermeneutical arc.[3] As he remarked in one of these essays in the last section of *Figuring the Sacred* on hermeneutics in general, the most important thing to say in "the current peril facing hermeneutics" is to remember "that application is not some supplement to hermeneutics."[4]

I and others have long seen Ricoeur's significance for theology, whether or not how personally interested he was or what his personal specific theology was.[5] My purpose here is to reflect on this provocative last section of *Figuring the Sacred* to bring out that indeed Ricoeur has something to say, even transformatively, concerning practical theology. Although he does not himself draw out the implications of his general philosophy for practical theology, they are embedded in these essays, and they also show how his reflections on these theological issues impact his general philosophy, a to-and-fro movement that one can detect throughout his work, however hidden and in the background this movement may be. For instance, his critique of Immanuel Kant and John Rawls on love and justice for a moral and political philosophy is rooted in Ricoeur's interpretation of the Love Commandments and the Golden Rule in Scripture, not to mention the parables of Jesus.[6] One can draw from these reflections a corrective to a tendency in practical theology toward a logical formalism, deriving moral application in a logical inference, largely in prosaic language, from systematic theology or even abstract

125

moral principles. Rather, Ricoeur rejects a subordination of practice to theory and moreover highlights a complex interweaving of poetics and prosaics in an embodied practical wisdom irreducible to universal principles or precepts. He implies a creative practical, figurative wisdom presupposing embodied practice even to judge practice. His approach to the capable self recognizes both the capacity to act and the limitations of action, from creativity to tragedy.[7] Much as in Aristotle, he finds resolution of theoretical tensions in practical judgment, and perhaps beyond Aristotle, in practical action. Such a reconfiguration in Ricoeur, exemplified in these essays, promises to reconfigure practical theology.

In fact, Ricoeur gives a remarkably humble introduction to an essay on "ministry," where he declined the attempt to synthesize the conference on ministry with his own work, which one can relate to what he would say about practical theology:

> I saw one more reason not to attempt such a synthesis in the fact that the field of ministry, while not foreign to me, was not my profession. Rather it was familiar to me as a listener to the word and therefore as one of the actors in this practical field. Being one of these actors, I have no claim to give a survey of it from some higher point of view. Therefore, I shall set aside any concern for "synthesis" and take up "return," and I shall do so in several different senses. This will come down, as you shall see, principally to a return to oneself, a return to myself: What happened to me in participating in this conference?[8]

One could in fact ask this about participation in theology, "What happened to me?" It is reminiscent of Martin Luther saying, "Yet experience alone can make the theologian,"[9] that theology is about God *pro nobis*, God for us, with us, and relating to us. While systematic theology can seem far removed from such existential roots, and thus separate from practical theology, Ricoeur's hermeneutics helps us see that it should not.

In that vein, a *first* thing to emphasize is that, like hermeneutics, one cannot separate practice from theology, even systematic or philosophical theology. A long tradition has been to separate these three, but I would argue that all theology is practical, so the separation is at best artificial. Ricoeur follows Gadamer in seeing application as not a third and optional aspect of hermeneutics or exegesis but one with "understanding" itself.[10] Ricoeur explains his emphasis on practice in general in terms of being at that time "beyond the linguistic turn."[11] One of the great dangers of hermeneutics, he says, is that it becomes just talk about talk, "discourse about discourse."[12] Rather, the need, in a good phenomenological manner, is a return "to the things themselves," which involves life, action, and praxis. Ricoeur expresses the fundamental dimension of action in his overall ontology of the self in *Oneself as Another* in this way, "There is no world without a self who finds itself in it and acts in it; there is no self without a world that is practicable in some fashion."[13] Even for hermeneutics, we have to recognize both "that discourse is an action . . . and in a contrary sense, the recognition that human action is a speaking action."[14] This emphasis works against the idea that Ricoeur left embodiment behind in his hermeneutical turn, which Richard Kearney has suggested in his proposal of a "carnal hermeneutics."[15] Ricoeur's continuing emphasis on praxis and action implicitly at least assumed embodiment. Kearney, however, does an excellent job of showing how Ricoeur returned later to a more explicit emphasis on embodiment—and also Kearney himself develops this turn, especially in his work on "touch."[16] These *Figuring the Sacred* essays reveal the "incarnational" aspect of Ricoeur's philosophy, which one can see in other later work in terms of the capable and suffering self, which I will treat more later. By incarnational, I refer both to the way that French philosophers in the twentieth century such as Gabriel Marcel, Maurice Merleau-Ponty, and Ricoeur were called incarnational philosophers,[17] referring not to religion as much as to their emphasis on embodiment, and to the religious sense in which incarnation refers to Jesus Christ being fully human, being fully flesh (John 1:14).

Perhaps too optimistically, Ricoeur observes that "we are no longer caught in the quarrel between praxis and discourse."[18] This "escape" is not true in the realm of theology. Thus, part of the value of Ricoeur's remarks here involves a corrective to the split between systematic theology and practical theology. Perhaps there is a place for a relative distinction in terms of focus and specialization, but in the end, both systematic and practical theology suffer from a sharp division. I recall, for example, a prominent evangelical summarizing the way he thought evangelicals worked, namely, that systematic theology gives the meaning of the Bible, and then action or practical theology is logically inferred from systematic theology—a position that incredibly manages to subordinate both Scripture and praxis to high-level conceptual, prosaic thought.

This observation brings up the *second* point where Ricoeur is helpful, namely, to highlight that there is not a straight, one-way, discursive line between prosaic theological or even ethical "explanation" and praxis. In between, or perhaps better, interwoven, is poetics. When speaking of "love," he talks of the "logic of God"[19] and "the strangeness or oddness of the discourse of love."[20] Interestingly, he connects the poetry of love in Scripture with hymnic praise, a heartfelt extravagance not at home in the univocal logic of prosaic positions.[21] In his last essay, "Love and Justice," he in fact over and over provides an artful critique of this linear, prosaic, logical approach to practical theology. It bursts the bonds of such "analysis."[22] Ricoeur criticizes the tendency to reduce the commandment to love to a "moral principle."[23]

He follows Franz Rosenzweig in connecting the "command" to the Song of Solomon.[24] This "'poetic use of the imperative,' Love me, subordinates the command, strikingly, to 'the amorous invitation.'"[25] This inviting appeal is an "economy of the gift" that transcends strict logical analysis.[26] It is, he said, linked to the "power of metaphorization."[27] This moves the ethical aspect of practical theology to the "hyperethical,"[28] which explodes the traditional discursive approach to practical theology and Christian ethics. Such a move requires poetics to express. So one cannot do practical theology without it.

Ricoeur calls upon his insightful work on metaphor applied to the parables of Jesus that "reorient by disorienting."[29] The parables of Jesus have a special power to disorient or deconstruct. Yet Ricoeur also insists upon the capacity to reorient,[30] perhaps only a pointer in the parables, but in the dialectic of love and justice this reorientation gains concretion. He allows for poetics *and* prose; moreover, the touch that allows for a productive use of both requires practical wisdom or discernment. A key to his approach is expressed in the challenge "to build a bridge between the poetics of love and what we might now call the prose of justice, between the hymn and the formal rule."[31] Poetics, however, has not been prominent in practical theology, not to mention the hymn!

A profound illustration is Ricoeur's remarkable only sermon in a synagogue, invited by Rabbi Joseph Edelheit in 1989, which is chapter 18 in *Figuring the Sacred*, "The Memory of Suffering," in this last section on practical theology.[32] It is an exercise in the interweaving of prosaics, poetics, and praxis. There is factual re-telling, as Ricoeur says, paying a debt to the past. There is also creative exploration, all with a practical imperative to remember and not to forget—already looking forward, it seems, almost as a basis, for his later and last great work, the monumental *History, Remembering, Forgetting*.[33] In Ricoeur's technical terms, in fact, he warns against the Holocaust/Shoah being leveled down by "explanation," in other words, prosaics.[34] Rather, it needs understanding and then a second understanding again and again, to be sure, amplified by careful critique or "explanation," but moving beyond it to a post-critical appropriation or application. This is always a timely word but especially crucial at a time when hate crimes against Jews are increasing rather than decreasing.[35]

Ricoeur says against a tendency in mythical thought (especially in Christian theology such as in Augustine) to find the cause of present suffering in the past, making it somehow deserved, "The Torah is above all a forward-oriented instruction, an ethical call addressed to the action to be done tomorrow or right now. This is beyond doubt."[36] The move then is toward reconciliation and repentance in the sense of change for the future and not just focused on the past, involving forgiveness but not forgetting in the sense of learning from the past.

In Ricoeur's remarkable last section in *Memory, History, Forgetting* on "a difficult forgiveness," he amplifies the theme of how love goes beyond and qualifies justice.[37] He shows there that one can hardly avoid recourse to poetics in dealing with the extravagance of forgiveness, which involves a difficult forgetting as well as remembering. He refers to what he calls the hymn of love in 1 Corinthians 13 in relation to the excess of forgiveness. He says, "There is forgiveness as there is joy, as there is wisdom, extravagance, love. Love, precisely. Forgiveness belongs to the same family."[38] Such a phenomenon requires the prodigality of poetic language, which then would be crucial in practical theology, as crucial as love is to practical theology.

How do we do this? The *third* point, then, is the inherent role of imagination. One cannot require a poetics of practical theology without imagination. We could borrow here Ricoeur's work on the utopian imagination in the seventies that appeals to the productive imagination over against the reproductive imagination.[39] One could say that in the past, practical theology has been seen more in line with the reproductive imagination as a fairly straightforward extrapolation from philosophical and systematic theology. If one sees the movement not as linear but as circular in the way that both Gadamer and Ricoeur see practice as implicated all the way along, then more creativity is involved at all stages. Especially if the application needs to be a novel yet wise, practically wise, elaboration of a theologically fitting treatment of a complex ethical issue, then that imaginative creativity must be at play at every point: in exegesis, systematic theology, and practical theology. And certainly if "application" is poetic, metaphorical, narrative, and, in other words, figurative, then often a metaphorical, imaginative leap is required, to the hyperethical beyond the prosaic ethical. This can be seen in the case of forgiveness that goes beyond what can be expected, that astonishes as it moves beyond reciprocity or even justice toward reconciliation and transformation. It is an economy of the gift beyond an economy of equivalence. It reflects the phrases that Ricoeur loved to derive from the parables, namely, "how much more" and "superabundance."[40]

As mentioned, Ricoeur saw an indispensable role for the utopian imagination as a critical perspective on ideology. Utopia represents the capacity to imagine what is not, an alternative, perhaps a radical alternative, to a dysfunctional status quo. He did not develop very much the following particular point, but he sometimes indicates that there can be renewal of an original utopian vision *within* an ideology as critique and as transformation.[41] It is not difficult to see this at work in church history where over and over groups appeal to Jesus or to the early church as a source of renewal, from the Reformation to restorationist groups like the Baptists and the Christian churches to the Civil Rights movement of Martin Luther King, Jr. King's famous "Letter from Birmingham Jail" is an appeal to ministers to be true to their calling.[42]

Ricoeur deals with this insightful creativity in a later work in terms of critical remembering,

> In the moral order, the past leaves not only inert traces, or residues, but also dormant energies, unexplored sources which we might assimilate to something like unkept promises. . . . This dormant character of as-yet-unfolded potentialities is what allows for resumptions, rebirths, reawakenings, through which the new gets connected with the old. . . . It is always after the fact that one discerns in the past what did not reach maturity in its own time.[43]

Practical theology obviously is not going to leave the tradition wholly behind, but it is constantly in need of this kind of rebirth and reawakening of "as-yet-unfolded potentialities."

The need for creativity can also be seen in the *fourth* point, which is that the judgments in practical theology, as in ethics in Aristotle, involve practical wisdom (*phronesis*), or as Ricoeur called it, "phronetic judgment."[44] This perhaps seems obvious, but it is not always so obvious in the assumption of a direct logical inference from systematic theology to practical theology. Practice cannot simply be inferred from theory, as Aristotle saw. Ricoeur states in his discussions of love and justice that there is no straight line between them. Rather, the mediations "are always fragile and provisory."[45] Ricoeur says, "It is the task of both philosophy and theology to discern, beneath the reflective equilibrium expressed in these compromise formulas, the secret discordance between the logic of superabundance and the logic of equivalence. It is also their task to say that it is only in the moral judgment made within some particular situation that this unstable equilibrium can be assured and protected."[46]

This point chimes in with practical theologians who see practical hermeneutical and ethical judgments as inherently improvisations.[47] Ricoeur specifically criticizes the tendency of analytic philosophy to move toward a logical extrapolation from a ruling category such as love in practical theology, in other words, relying on an ethical calculus.[48] Is there a place for logic and analysis? Yes, but it involves complex discernment. It involves bringing together the poetics of love and the prose of justice. As he points out, "love does not argue," but "justice does argue."[49] He recognizes that the formalism of judicial practice can be seen "not as a fault, but as a sign of force."[50] Yet as Ricoeur pointed out, however, drawing on Aristotle again, making judgments about "proportional equality" in distributive justice (which we can place within an ecclesial setting just as in a secular setting) is not the same as "mathematical equality."[51] Ultimately, hermeneutical, holistic practical wisdom (phronetic thinking) is needed in a situation to bring all of the elements together. Building the bridge of judgment between the poetics of love and the prose of justice thus requires a high level of creativity, imagination, and wisdom.

One can add to the need for practical wisdom the dynamics of Ricoeur's later emphasis on the self as both capable and limited, as faced with possibility and yet constraints, as creative but also suffering. He adds the category of tragedy in his "little ethic" in *Oneself as Another*[52] as a common category in practical decisions, as in the case of Antigone. Tragedy strikes still as people of faith face decisions where they risk their jobs, their careers, and sometimes their lives. In the case of ministers per se over the last few years in light of the Covid challenge, they have had need of creativity in the face of constraints. They have faced unwinnable decisions about whether their churches would meet in person or manage to meet online. Such decisions became highly politicized, so they often faced fire no matter what decision they made. In any case, the predictable outcome was the loss of some of the congregation, and it is not clear how many will come back.[53] Many ministers themselves are leaving.[54] Moreover, there were no simple guidelines, no adages from the past, no reservoir of maxims to follow in such situations. It was new, it required creativity, it involved ineradicable limitations, and sometimes it involved tragedy, as when family and ministers could not visit in person their dying relatives and church members. Ricoeur's earlier phenomenology of the will added to aspects of action the recognition that willing inevitably involves "consent" to the prevailing conditions, to that over which one does not have control. Practical acts of the will always take place within the limits of a situation and even the limits on the "capable self." Some pastors lost their jobs. Many have just given up and left the ministry. These pastors would probably relate not only to Ricoeur's notion of a tragic wisdom but also to Ricoeur's language of practical judgment being a wager, a risk, a decision made without certainty, one that can only be "a question of our whole life. No one can escape this."[55] The aporias of philosophy that he thought one could not escape are matched by aporias in practical theology.[56]

In many ways, the challenge of Covid involved changing not just the concepts but the metaphors of what it meant to be "church," to worship together, to be a community of faith. Just as some people dropped away, sometimes in isolation that involved higher degrees of anxiety and depression, others joined in from afar off via the possibilities enabled by videoconferencing or streaming. We actually joined a church during the Covid summer of 2020 when the church was not meeting in person but streaming a service attended by a few people in an empty sanctuary. We were interviewed ahead of time with the interview being streamed on Sunday morning, the most extensive introduction my wife and I have ever had in joining a church. We participated in this new church in an adult Sunday School class for a year via videoconference before we met anyone in person. Yet we came to be quite close, and the fellowship was an oasis in the desert of isolation of having moved to a new city about the time that Covid began. Several people participated from far away, and it was somewhat disappointing to lose them when we started meeting again in person. Again, what does it mean to be a part of a church? To be a community? To be a part of a local body of Christ, to use the Apostle Paul's metaphor? We still use videoconference for many church meetings. And one can see here how practice feeds back into theology in terms of ecclesiology and soteriology. How does one decide what to do? How does one relate the mission of the church in a new context that is not always face to face? How does one now negotiate the fault lines of church and politics? The systematic theology helps, but it does not decide what is to be done in so many cases. That requires improvisatory, poetic, and phonetic thinking.

The *final* point is that such thinking is always embodied. It involves not only acute analysis but the intelligence of emotions, of the body. As mentioned, Ricoeur has been called an incarnational philosopher, along with Gabriel Marcel and Maurice Merleau-Ponty (and now we could add Richard Kearney), due to his emphasis on the body, on the involuntary, in his phenomenology of the will. His later attention to the active and passive body underscores it. The move to virtue ethics fits here, where the whole formation of the self, including the emotions and the body, is crucial to ethical judgments. And the capacity for such practical judgments involves training and practice over time, the development of insight and finesse. Ricoeur's drawing on Alasdair MacIntyre in terms of habits and virtues points to embodied practical theology.[57] I would add here that it is not just the capable body and emotions that are significant here, but also the wounds of the body and the emotions, not to mention the mind. The tragedy that Ricoeur mentions is often part and parcel with trauma. Just as ideology affects judgments in unconscious ways, so does trauma affect judgments in unconscious ways. Bessel van der Kolk, a leading trauma expert, indicates in *The Body Keeps the Score* that cognitive treatments, while helpful and necessary, also need to be accompanied by treatment of the body and the emotions.[58] When one considers scholars who underscore the role of everyday trauma and inherited trauma where ongoing trauma to some extent affects judgments, often unconsciously, the complexity of practical theology increases.[59] Practical, ethical, theological judgments about difficult decisions cannot ignore the imprint of the body and the emotions. Western thought has had a long distrust of the body and the emotions in favor of the mind. However, we should not assume that the role of the body is negative. It can distort, but it can also illuminate as a source of guidance and wisdom that discursive thought cannot always capture. Practical theological judgments are, at best, holistic judgments. The training and preparation of which virtue ethics (and virtue epistemology) speaks is consequently not just training of the mind but training of the whole self.

The practical wisdom that thus founds the development of a practical theology is a practical poetics but one also haunted by the specters of embodied ideology, trauma, and tragedy. This wisdom is a religious bridge between prose, poetics, and praxis, but one where repairs are often made while in traffic, swaying in the wind. In the end, it must be backed up by one's whole life of faith. No one can escape this.

NOTES

1. An earlier version of this paper was given at the Fall 2022 Society for Ricoeur Studies conference in Los Angeles, California. I express appreciation to that ongoing source of rich dialogue and to feedback specifically on this paper.

2. Paul Ricoeur, *Figuring the Sacred: Religion, Narrative, and Imagination*, ed. Mark I. Wallace, trans. David Pellauer (Minneapolis: Fortress Press, 1995).

3. See Paul Ricoeur, "What Is a Text? Explanation and Understanding," in *Hermeneutics and the Human Sciences: Essays on Language, Action, and Interpretation*, ed. and trans. John B. Thompson (Cambridge: Cambridge University Press, 1981), 164; Paul Ricoeur, "The Model of the Text: Meaningful Action Considered as a Text," in *Hermeneutics and the Human Sciences: Essays on Language, Action, and Interpretation*, ed. and trans. John B. Thompson (Cambridge: Cambridge University Press, 1981), 219–21.

4. Ricoeur, *Figuring the Sacred*, 304.

5. For example, see Boyd Blundell, *Paul Ricoeur between Theology and Philosophy: Detour and Return* (Bloomington, IN: Indiana University Press, 2010); Dan R. Stiver, *Theology After Ricoeur: New Directions in Hermeneutical Theology* (Louisville: Westminster John Knox Press, 2001); Dan R. Stiver, *Ricoeur and Theology*, Philosophy and Theology (New York: T & T Clark International, 2012); Kenneth A. Reynhout, *Interdisciplinary Interpretation: Paul Ricoeur and the Hermeneutics of Theology and Science*, Studies in the Thought of Paul Ricoeur (Lanham, MD: Lexington Books, 2013).

6. Ricoeur, *Figuring the Sacred*, 315–29.

7. Paul Ricoeur, "Asserting Personal Capacities and Pleading for Mutual Recognition," in *A Passion for the Possible: Thinking with Paul Ricoeur*, ed. Brian Treanor and Henry Isaac Venema, Perspectives in Continental Philosophy (New York: Fordham University Press, 2010), 22–26; Richard Kearney, "Capable Man, Capable God," in *A Passion for the Possible: Thinking with Paul Ricoeur*, ed. Brian Treanor and Henry Isaac Venema, Perspectives in Continental Philosophy (New York: Fordham University Press, 2010), 49–61.

8. Ricoeur, *Figuring the Sacred*, 303.

9. Elisabeth Parmentier, "The Paradoxical Way of Experiencing Faith through Spiritual Attack (Anfechtung—Tentatio)," in *Theological Anthropology, 500 Years after Martin Luther* (Boston, MA: Brill, 2021), 255–69, https://doi.org/10.1163/9789004461253_015.

10. Hans-Georg Gadamer, *Truth and Method*, trans. Joel Weinsheimer and Donald G. Marshall, 2d ed. (New York: Crossroad, 1991), 307; Ricoeur, *Figuring the Sacred*, 304.

11. Ricoeur, *Figuring the Sacred*, 305.

12. Ricoeur, 304.

13. Paul Ricoeur, *Oneself as Another*, trans. Kathleen Blamey (Chicago: University of Chicago Press, 1992), 311.

14. Ricoeur, *Figuring the Sacred*, 305.

15. Richard Kearney, "The Wager of Carnal Hermeneutics," in *Carnal Hermeneutics*, ed. Richard Kearney and Brian Treanor, Kindle, Perspectives in Continental Philosophy (New York: Fordham University Press, 2015), 15–56.

16. Richard Kearney, *Touch: Recovering Our Most Vital Sense* (New York, NY: Columbia University Press, 2021).

17. See, for example, Erazim Kohák's introduction in Paul Ricoeur, *Freedom and Nature: The Voluntary and the Involuntary*, trans. Erazim Kohák, Northwestern University Studies in Phenomenology & Existential Philosophy (Evanston, IL: Northwestern University Press, 1966), xii–xiii.

18. Ricoeur, *Figuring the Sacred*, 305.

19. Ricoeur, 279.

20. Ricoeur, 317.

21. Ricoeur, 317.

22. Ricoeur, 318.

23. Ricoeur, 318.

24. Ricoeur, 319.

25. Ricoeur, 320. See also Ricoeur's striking reflection on the Song of Solomon where he characteristically puts into play a dialectical reading between the Song and the prophets, "If the prophetic reading of the Song of Songs—conjoined, it is true, with the exegesis of Genesis 2—bring out the so-to-speak sacred innocence of the erotic bond, the reinterpretation of the prophetic texts [in light of the Song of Solomon] tends, in return, to inflect the Covenant relation in the direction of a mutual belonging of equal partners to each other." André LaCocque and Paul Ricoeur, *Thinking Biblically: Exegetical and Hermeneutical Studies*, trans. David Pellauer (Chicago: University of Chicago Press, 1998), 302.

26. Ricoeur, *Figuring the Sacred*, 320.

27. Ricoeur, 320.

28. Ricoeur, 325.

29. Ricoeur, 329. See also Paul Ricoeur, "Biblical Hermeneutics," *Semeia* 4 (1975): 27–138.

30. Ricoeur, *Figuring the Sacred*, 329.

31. Ricoeur, 325.

32. Ricoeur, 289–92.

33. Paul Ricoeur, *Memory, History, Forgetting*, trans. Kathleen Blamey and David Pellauer (Chicago: University of Chicago Press, 2004).

34. Ricoeur, *Figuring the Sacred*, 290.

35. The Anti-Defamation League reported that antisemitic incidents rose by 36 percent in 2022.

The report, released Thursday [3.23.23], tracked 3,697 incidents of harassment, vandalism and assault targeting Jewish people and communities last year. It is the third time in five years that the tally has been the highest number ever recorded since the ADL first began collecting data in 1979.

Vanessa Romo, "Antisemitic Incidents Are at an All-Time High, the Adl Reports," *NPR*, March 23, 2023, sec. National, https://www.npr.org/2023/03/23 /1165737405/antisemitism-statistics-report-2022-anti-defamation-league.

36. Ricoeur, *Figuring the Sacred*, 290–91.

37. Ricoeur, *Memory, History, Forgetting*, 457–506.

38. Ricoeur, 467.

39. Paul Ricoeur, *Lectures on Ideology and Utopia*, ed. George H. Taylor (New York: Columbia University Press, 1986).

40. See Ricoeur, *Figuring the Sacred*, 326; Ricoeur, "Biblical Hermeneutics," 121. See also George Taylor on Ricoeur's lectures on imagination, not yet published, that bring out the role of the productive imagination. George H. Taylor, "Ricoeur's Philosophy of Imagination," *Journal of French Philosophy* 16 (Spring/Fall 2006): 93–104.

41. For more development of this point, see Dan R. Stiver, "Renewing the "Period of Effervescence": Utopia as Ideology Critique," in *Ideology and Utopia in the Twenty-First Century: The Surplus of Meaning in Ricoeur's Conception of the Dialectical Relationship of Ideology and Utopia*, ed. Stephanie N. Arel and Dan R. Stiver, Studies in the Thought of Paul Ricoeur (Lanham, MD: Lexington Books, 2021), 53–71.

42. Martin Luther King, Jr., *Why We Can't Wait*, reissue ed. (Boston, MA: Beacon Press, 2011), chap. 5.

43. Paul Ricoeur, *Reflections on the Just*, trans. David Pellauer (Chicago: University Of Chicago Press, 2007), 181–82.

44. Paul Ricoeur, *The Just*, trans. David Pellauer (Chicago: University of Chicago Press, 2000), xxii.

45. Ricoeur, *Figuring the Sacred*, 315.

46. Ricoeur, 329. See also the parallel issue in legal studies in an article appropriating Ricoeur. As Taylor says, "Despite often its pretenses, the law does not invoke an ineluctable logic leading to one true form of justice." George H. Taylor, "Ricoeur, Narrative, and Legal Contingency," in *Reading Ricoeur through Law*, ed. Marc de Leeuw, George H. Taylor, and Eileen Brennan (Lanham, MD: Lexington Books, 2022), 135. Walter Salles argues that love and justice can be brought more closely together in the legal system than Ricoeur seems to think, making the practical, creative reconciliation less discordant. Walter Salles, "The Interaction between Love and Justice in the Legal System," in *Reading Ricoeur through Law*, ed. Marc de Leeuw, George H. Taylor, and Eileen Brennan (Lanham, MD: Lexington Books, 2022), 252–67.

47. Kevin J. Vanhoozer, *The Drama of Doctrine: A Canonical-Linguistic Approach to Christian Theology* (Louisville: Westminster John Knox Press, 2005); Samuel Wells, *Improvisation: The Drama of Christian Ethics* (Grand Rapids, MI: Brazos Press, 2004).

48. Ricoeur, *Figuring the Sacred*, 315. Ricoeur refers to "theology" here, but the context implies practical theology.

49. Ricoeur, 321.
50. Ricoeur, 322.
51. Ricoeur, 323.
52. Found in Studies 7–9 of Ricoeur, *Oneself as Another*.
53. Justin Nortey and Michael Rotolo, "How the Pandemic Has Affected Attendance at U.S. Religious Services," *Pew Research Center's Religion & Public Life Project* (blog), March 28, 2023, https://www.pewresearch.org/religion/2023/03/28/how-the-pandemic-has-affected-attendance-at-u-s-religious-services/.
54. Pam Durso and Carol McEntyre, "Leaving Church, Part 2: The Great Baptist Resignations and Covid," Baptist News Global, January 18, 2022, https://baptistnews.com/article/leaving-church-part-2-the-great-baptist-resignations-and-covid/.
55. Ricoeur says, "We cannot eliminate from a social ethics the element of risk. We wager on a certain set of values and then try to be consistent with them; verification is therefore a question of our whole life. No one can escape this." Ricoeur, *Lectures on Ideology and Utopia*, 312.
56. See, for example, the end of his three-volume Time and Narrative, Paul Ricoeur, *Time and Narrative*, trans. David Pellauer and Kathleen Blamey, vol. 3 (Chicago: University of Chicago Press, 1988), 241–74.
57. Ricoeur, *Oneself as Another*, 157–60; Alasdair C. MacIntyre, *After Virtue: A Study in Moral Theory*, 2nd ed. (Notre Dame: University of Notre Dame Press, 1984).
58. Bessel van der Kolk, *The Body Keeps the Score: Brain, Mind, and Body in the Healing of Trauma* (New York: Penguin Books, 2015).
59. See Mark Epstein, *The Trauma of Everyday Life* (New York: Penguin Books, 2014); Resmaa Menakem, *My Grandmother's Hands: Racialized Trauma and the Pathway to Mending Our Hearts and Bodies* (Las Vegas, NV: Central Recovery Press, 2017); Serene Jones, *Trauma and Grace: Theology in a Ruptured World* (Louisville, KY: Westminster John Knox Press, 2009).

BIBLIOGRAPHY

Blundell, Boyd. *Paul Ricoeur between Theology and Philosophy: Detour and Return.* Bloomington, IN: Indiana University Press, 2010.

Durso, Pam, and Carol McEntyre. "Leaving Church, Part 2: The Great Baptist Resignations and Covid." Baptist News Global, January 18, 2022. https://baptistnews.com/article/leaving-church-part-2-the-great-baptist-resignations-and-covid/.

Epstein, Mark. *The Trauma of Everyday Life.* New York: Penguin Books, 2014.

Gadamer, Hans-Georg. *Truth and Method.* Translated by Joel Weinsheimer and Donald G. Marshall. 2nd ed. New York: Crossroad, 1991.

Jones, Serene. *Trauma and Grace: Theology in a Ruptured World.* Louisville, KY: Westminster John Knox Press, 2009.

Kearney, Richard. "Capable Man, Capable God." In *A Passion for the Possible: Thinking with Paul Ricoeur*, edited by Brian Treanor and Henry Isaac Venema, 49–61. Perspectives in Continental Philosophy. New York: Fordham University Press, 2010.

———. "The Wager of Carnal Hermeneutics." In *Carnal Hermeneutics*, edited by Richard Kearney and Brian Treanor, Kindle., 15–56. Perspectives in Continental Philosophy. New York: Fordham University Press, 2015.

———. *Touch: Recovering Our Most Vital Sense*. New York: Columbia University Press, 2021.

King, Jr., Martin Luther. *Why We Can't Wait*. Reissue ed. Boston, MA: Beacon Press, 2011.

Kolk, Bessel van der. *The Body Keeps the Score: Brain, Mind, and Body in the Healing of Trauma*. New York: Penguin Books, 2015.

LaCocque, André, and Paul Ricoeur. *Thinking Biblically: Exegetical and Hermeneutical Studies*. Translated by David Pellauer. Chicago: University of Chicago Press, 1998.

MacIntyre, Alasdair C. *After Virtue: A Study in Moral Theory*. 2nd ed. Notre Dame: University of Notre Dame Press, 1984.

Menakem, Resmaa. *My Grandmother's Hands: Racialized Trauma and the Pathway to Mending Our Hearts and Bodies*. Las Vegas, NV: Central Recovery Press, 2017.

Nortey, Justin, and Michael Rotolo. "How the Pandemic Has Affected Attendance at U.S. Religious Services." *Pew Research Center's Religion & Public Life Project* (blog), March 28, 2023. https://www.pewresearch.org/religion/2023/03/28/how-the-pandemic-has-affected-attendance-at-u-s-religious-services/.

Parmentier, Elisabeth. "The Paradoxical Way of Experiencing Faith through Spiritual Attack (Anfechtung—Tentatio)." In *Theological Anthropology, 500 Years after Martin Luther*, 255–69. Boston, MA: Brill, 2021. https://doi.org/10.1163/9789004461253_015.

Reynhout, Kenneth A. *Interdisciplinary Interpretation: Paul Ricoeur and the Hermeneutics of Theology and Science*. Studies in the Thought of Paul Ricoeur. Lanham, MD: Lexington Books, 2013.

Ricoeur, Paul. "Asserting Personal Capacities and Pleading for Mutual Recognition." In *A Passion for the Possible: Thinking with Paul Ricoeur*, edited by Brian Treanor and Henry Isaac Venema, 22–26. Perspectives in Continental Philosophy. New York: Fordham University Press, 2010.

———. "Biblical Hermeneutics." *Semeia* 4 (1975): 27–138.

———. *Figuring the Sacred: Religion, Narrative, and Imagination*. Edited by Mark I. Wallace. Translated by David Pellauer. Minneapolis: Fortress Press, 1995.

———. *Freedom and Nature: The Voluntary and the Involuntary*. Translated by Erazim Kohák. Northwestern University Studies in Phenomenology & Existential Philosophy. Evanston, IL: Northwestern University Press, 1966.

———. *Lectures on Ideology and Utopia*. Edited by George H. Taylor. New York: Columbia University Press, 1986.

———. *Memory, History, Forgetting*. Translated by Kathleen Blamey and David Pellauer. Chicago: University of Chicago Press, 2004.

———. *Oneself as Another*. Translated by Kathleen Blamey. Chicago: University of Chicago Press, 1992.

———. *Reflections on the Just*. Translated by David Pellauer. Chicago: University Of Chicago Press, 2007.

———. *The Just*. Translated by David Pellauer. Chicago: University of Chicago Press, 2000.

———. "The Model of the Text: Meaningful Action Considered as a Text." In *Hermeneutics and the Human Sciences: Essays on Language, Action, and Interpretation*, edited and translated by John B. Thompson, 197–221. Cambridge: Cambridge University Press, 1981.

———. *Time and Narrative*. Translated by David Pellauer and Kathleen Blamey. Vol. 3. Chicago: University of Chicago Press, 1988.

———. "What Is a Text? Explanation and Understanding." In *Hermeneutics and the Human Sciences: Essays on Language, Action, and Interpretation*, edited and translated by John B. Thompson, 145–64. Cambridge: Cambridge University Press, 1981.

Romo, Vanessa. "Antisemitic Incidents Are at an All-Time High, the Adl Reports." *NPR*, March 23, 2023, sec. National. https://www.npr.org/2023/03/23/1165737405/antisemitism-statistics-report-2022-anti-defamation-league.

Salles, Walter. "The Interaction between Love and Justice in the Legal System." In *Reading Ricoeur through Law*, edited by Marc de Leeuw, George H. Taylor, and Eileen Brennan, 252–67. Lanham, MD: Lexington Books, 2022.

Stiver, Dan R. "Renewing the 'Period of Effervescence': Utopia as Ideology Critique." In *Ideology and Utopia in the Twenty-First Century: The Surplus of Meaning in Ricoeur's Conception of the Dialectical Relationship of Ideology and Utopia*, edited by Stephanie N. Arel and Dan R. Stiver, 53–71. Studies in the Thought of Paul Ricoeur. Lanham, MD: Lexington Books, 2021.

———. *Ricoeur and Theology*. Philosophy and Theology. New York: T & T Clark International, 2012.

———. *Theology After Ricoeur: New Directions in Hermeneutical Theology*. Louisville: Westminster John Knox Press, 2001.

Taylor, George H. "Ricoeur, Narrative, and Legal Contingency." In *Reading Ricoeur through Law*, edited by Marc de Leeuw, George H. Taylor, and Eileen Brennan, 126–44. Lanham, MD: Lexington Books, 2022.

———. "Ricoeur's Philosophy of Imagination." *Journal of French Philosophy* 16 (Spring/Fall 2006): 93–104.

Vanhoozer, Kevin J. *The Drama of Doctrine: A Canonical-Linguistic Approach to Christian Theology*. Louisville: Westminster John Knox Press, 2005.

Wells, Samuel. *Improvisation: The Drama of Christian Ethics*. Grand Rapids, MI: Brazos Press, 2004.

Part II

Part II

Introduction to Part II

The Crisis of Faith in a World Where God Is Not Yet God

Mark I. Wallace

In this chapter I want to take up an exposition of two of Paul Ricoeur's principal chapters that were not included in my original edited anthology of his religious writings, *Figuring the Sacred: Religion, Narrative, and Imagination.*[1] Both chapters are critical for understanding the scope and daring of Ricoeur's mature philosophy of religion. It is for this reason that they are featured in this volume's "refiguring" of his ongoing influence in the light of his collected works. Both chapters, however, were left on the cutting room floor as my collection moved from a working table of contents to a published volume with Fortress Press in 1995. In order to set the stage for my analysis of these chapters let me first say something about the origins of *Figuring the Sacred* and why this collection, then and now, continues to address a significant lacuna in the primary source anthologies of Ricoeur's thought.

The roots of *Figuring the Sacred* stem from my first introduction to Paul Ricoeur as a graduate student at the University of Chicago Divinity School in 1982. Before Chicago, I had read some of Ricoeur's philosophical essays and religious writings, but in those early years I did not know him personally nor his thought in any systematic sense. At the time of our meeting, Ricoeur was the John Nuveen Professor of Philosophical Theology at the University of Chicago, where he taught one or two quarters each year. His appointment positioned him at the nexus of three exciting scholarly programs at Chicago that were formative in my development: the Divinity School, the Department of Philosophy, and the Committee on Social Thought. The interdisciplinary character of these related programs, and the wide field-encompassing range of Ricoeur's interests, situated me within an intellectually convivial habitat where I could ask fundamental questions about the collaborative study of religion and philosophy within a broad-based liberal arts environment.

Looking back at these formative years in courses and during office hours with Ricoeur, I remember a humble and generous scholar-teacher who worked hard to adjudicate the claims of competing philosophical worldviews made by disparate thinkers with an eye toward promoting personal wellbeing and the common good. Today, Ricoeur is well known for putting down the marker that the proper aim of philosophy is "aiming at the 'good life' with and for others, in just institutions."[2] For Ricoeur, insofar as philosophy is fundamentally an ethical enterprise, it should model how to conduct constructive conversations with different interlocutors over a range of salient topics. Philosophy, then, is not a form of academic contestation in which warring opponents seek to crush one another in brutal games of one-upmanship. Prior to my Chicago studies, I was used to the Anglo-American analytic tradition in which intellectual life is regarded more as a winner-takes-all clash between combatants and less as a give-and-take dialogue between well-meaning discussants. Ricoeur's mediatorial approach to philosophical inquiry and debate, including the philosophy of religion, was a refreshing change of pace for me. In this regard, I found Ricoeur to be an approachable thinker in his published work and an affable teacher and dialogue-partner in his interpersonal relations with me and other students and faculty at the University of Chicago.

RICOEUR'S 1984 CHICAGO LECTURE ON THE PROBLEM OF EVIL

During my time in Chicago, I was fortunate to attend a talk by Ricoeur that both cemented my understanding of the distinctive significance of his philosophy of religion and, eventually, led me to anthologize his religious writings in the book that became *Figuring the Sacred*. On December 10, 1984, Ricoeur gave an insightful lecture that offered a fresh solution to the so-called "problem of evil" at the seventy-fifth annual meeting of the American Academy of Religion in Chicago.[3] Simply put, the problem of evil arises for religious adherents who confront the incorrigible reality of persistent malevolence in a world purportedly under the wise governance of a loving God. Attempts to render coherent the seeming irreconcilability of global suffering vis-à-vis divine providence and omnipotence are called "theodicy" in the classical philosophical lexicon. Glossing this term in Greek (*theos* means God and *dike* is justice), theodicy signifies forms of philosophical argument that seek to make rational sense of, or to justify, God's ways before humankind in the light of massive, unjust evil. Such arguments struggle to offer a compelling response to the time-honored anguish articulated by the Prophet Jeremiah some 2,600 years ago, "O Lord, why do the wicked prosper (Jeremiah 12:1)?" This *cri de coeur* continues to ring true to the incoherent pathos many of us still feel today: If God were all-good, then God would want to eradicate evil; and if God were all-powerful, then God would have the ability to do so; but evil, persistently and stubbornly, continues to flourish. Why, then, does evil perdure in the light of God's purported goodness and power?

In his 1984 lecture, Ricoeur surveys the wide range of answers to this perennial question and asks whether any of the standard academic theodicies in the history of Western thought are compelling to the rational philosopher or the heart-stricken believer. He concludes that the neat-and-tidy solutions theodicists employ to render logically compatible three irreconcilable propositions—God's benevolence, God's power, and the tenacity of evil—are, ultimately, intellectually unsound and spiritually unsatisfying. In the absence of a clear solution to this philosophical and existential contradiction, according to Ricoeur, we are left with the wreckage of classical philosophy's besetting failure to solve one of its most pressing quandaries, namely, if there is a God, whence evil? Philosophically speaking, Ricoeur calls the irresolvable paradox of the problem of evil a "speculative aporia,"[4] and I recall being embarrassed during his lecture that I did not know what the word *aporia* meant. (Indeed, I had to look up and ponder the definition of this term in a philosophical dictionary after returning home from his talk.) But even without knowing this key idea at the time, I understood the basic point of Ricoeur's argument: at the level of pure theory, there are no rationally sufficient reasons for explaining the origin and purpose of evil in a world ostensibly overseen by a good and powerful God.

At the time of this lecture, forty years ago, while I sensed something profound in Ricoeur's deconstruction of the enterprise of speculative theodicy, I became wary of his approach. I began to take stock of the wide-ranging implications of his thesis: the only path forward in addressing the mystery of evil, and perhaps other mysteries, begins with abandoning all hope of finding a philosophical solution to this and likely other enduring problems as well. At first, I resisted Ricoeur's thesis insofar as it degraded my trust in the value of philosophical theology to iron out one of the cardinal antinomies that arises from within the biblical worldview. But with this recognition my sense of despair about the whole operation of finely tuned philosophy of religion only deepened. I realized that if the problem of evil is unsolvable, how many other internal conflicts within the body of Christian belief are also devoid of rational solutions? If reason cannot solve this problem, then what other pairings of oppositional religious ideas will defeat any attempt at making sense of such ideas?

I puzzled over this conundrum. Is it rational, for example, to affirm that God's trinitarian manifestation of Godself in three distinct persons or forms is consistent with the unity and oneness of God? Or that the historical Jesus, as a singular flesh-and-blood human being, is both fully human and fully divine such that both natures are neither confused with nor separated from each other? Or that God is alternately transcendent, impassive, and wholly independent from creation and, at the same time, radically intimate with all beings and passionately committed to their wellbeing, even at great cost to Godself? Listening to Ricoeur's lecture that evening catapulted me into a vertiginous, liminal space where the commanding ideal of my young adult life—to discover an intellectual vocabulary by which I could make sense of the great mysteries of faith—was now destined, I painfully realized, to founder on the rocks of ambiguity, paradox and uncertainty.

And yet, as I listened to Ricoeur's lecture, and subsequently got to know him, I came to realize that his aim was not to *destroy* faith, including the rational articulation of faith, but to *render* faith more *intelligible*—and to render it more intelligible especially for those whose lives bear witness to the agony of irredeemable suffering. In this regard, Ricoeur's move away from theodicy contains the seeds of an approach to religion that eschews *faux intellectual solutions* to faith's insoluble mysteries in favor of mapping out *practical restorative pathways* in and through, but never around, the unmovable contradictions within formal expressions of faith. Thus, the rebuttal of philosophical theodicy serves as the mainspring of an innovative model of faith-based existence. Herein for Ricoeur, ironically, the *problem* of evil becomes the way forward to *confronting* evil: the stumbling block of existing in a world scarred by pain and loss becomes the cornerstone of a new form of belief and hope in spite of all the evidence to the contrary. At this juncture, philosophy falters for Ricoeur, and another form of rationality—a rationality, one might say, whose depths are deeper than reason itself—takes hold. At this juncture, philosophy goes beyond philosophy.

As his lecture progressed, alongside my own thinking then and in the months afterward, I understood that Ricoeur's refutation of philosophical theodicy was not simply an end in itself. Rather, his repudiation of intellectual formulas to explain seemingly irreconcilable religious ideas was only the beginning, not the culmination, of his argument against theodicy. As his talk moved forward, I better comprehended that his premise was the necessary condition for a groundbreaking solution to—or better, a dissolution of—the problem of evil. Rising up from the ashes of his deconstruction of all past attempts at theodicy—from Augustine's and Leibniz's to Hegel's and Barth's—Ricoeur concluded his talk by propounding a novel *antitheodicy* that embraces a robustly *therapeutic* approach to the problem of evil. Ironically, the frank avowal of the incorrigibly aporetic nature of persistent evil enables an edifying struggle with this problem through what he calls "the catharsis of lament."[5] By letting go of the need to *solve* the problem of evil in a theoretical register, one commits to "making the intellectual aporia productive"[6] by *confronting* the paradox of extreme evil through affective-existential *practice* rather than speculative-propositional *philosophy. While the inexplicable absurdity of unmerited pain and misfortune cannot be intellectually accounted for, the practice of expressing grief and sorrow over such loss can provide a measure of solace for the brokenhearted.*

RICOEUR'S POSITIONALITY: FAITH-BASED OR NOT?

Listening to Ricoeur's antitheodicy lecture in 1984 motivated me to read his work more broadly. But a review of his then-opus revealed a startling omission: though widely published at that time in the francophone philosophy of religion field, very little of Ricoeur's religious writings had come into English translation. As well, no definitive anthology of his primary religious essays and articles was available in English. While Ricoeur's 1967 book, *The Symbolism of Evil*—a masterful interpretation of ancient Hebrew and Greek mythologies of primitive chaos and tragic fate in order to understand the modern condition of human brokenness[7]—introduced him to anglophone audiences as a religious philosopher, very few of his primary essays in religious studies were available to English readers. With the exception of Lewis S. Mudge's *Essays on Biblical Interpretation* in 1980,[8] which comprised four of Ricoeur's theological and biblical articles, Ricoeur's primary religious papers were scattered in journals or general collections in which his religious thought was relegated to the margins of what editors deemed to be his primary philosophical contributions.

As I reviewed Ricoeur's original contributions to philosophy of religion, I realized that this lack of attention to his religious writings was a systemic mistake in the critical reception of his intellectual project. But to be fair, it wasn't just French and English philosophers, theologians, and editors who failed to grasp the significance of his religious thought; Ricoeur himself was also partly to blame for this oversight. Throughout his academic life, Ricoeur sought to drive a wedge between his public persona as a secular philosopher and his *sotto voce* identity as a religious thinker fundamentally shaped by Christian values and biblical ideas. He resisted being labeled as a Christian philosopher or philosophical theologian (in spite of the title of his University of Chicago John Nuveen chair) in order to avoid the charge that his philosophy was predetermined by *crypto theological* convictions that would undermine his appeals to reason and argument as the basis of his general thought.[9] His aim, in a nod to Kant's model of a non-aggression pact between philosophy and religion,[10] was to be able to say both that "I am agnostic on the plane of philosophy"[11] while still discreetly owning "the convictions that bind me to biblical faith."[12] In a remarkably revealing comment about his legitimation anxiety as a nonsectarian philosopher who wanted to be judged on the merits of his arguments, not his religious beliefs, Ricoeur says,

I perhaps had other reasons to protect myself from the intrusions, from the overly direct, too immediate infiltrations of the religious in the philosophical; there were cultural reasons, I would even say institutional reasons. It was very important to me to be recognized as a professor of philosophy, teaching philosophy in a public institution and speaking the common language, hence assuming the mental reservations that this entailed, even if it meant that I would periodically be accused of being a theologian in disguise who philosophizes, or a philosopher who make the religious sphere think or be thought. I take on all the difficulties of this situation, including the suspicion that, in actual fact, I would never be able to maintain this duality in watertight compartments.[13]

By Ricoeur himself laboring to maintain "this duality [between philosophy and theology] in watertight compartments,"[14] it is no wonder that his groundbreaking religious thought got short shrift in the compilations of his primary works. Over time, however, readers like myself became aware of how much the two compartments had leaked into each other. It was this recognition of the inseparability of Jerusalem and Athens in Ricoeur—the power and range of his theological vision inflected through a distinctive philosophical vocabulary—that became the impetus behind my inaugural conception of *Figuring the Sacred.*

WHAT WAS LEFT BEHIND

A year before his passing in 2005, Ricoeur writes of himself in a confessional tone as a "Christian: someone who professes a primordial adhesion to the life, the words, the death of Jesus" in his posthumous *Living Up to Death.*[15] In spite of the signal importance of his "primordial adhesion" to the Jesus tradition in his life and work, Ricoeur's deep-seated ambivalence about his dual identities as a public philosopher and a committed Christian shaped, I believe, his decision to truncate the final published version of his Gifford Lectures. While the stated purpose of the Gifford lectures is to "promote and diffuse the study of natural theology in the widest sense of the term—in other words, the knowledge of God,"[16] Ricoeur excised from *Oneself as Another,* the set of his Gifford Lectures first published in 1990, the two concluding theological essays that put the finishing touches on the ten purely philosophical papers comprising his overall series of lectures given at the University of Edinburgh in 1986.

In the early 1990s when I was collecting with David Pellauer Ricoeur's works for *Figuring the Sacred,* my intent was to include both of these theological chapters in this new anthology. Ricoeur's final Gifford chapter titled "The Summoned Subject," an analysis of how a divine mandate addressed to the conscience of the subject predetermines its journey to selfhood, had already appeared in French in 1988 and was expressly translated by Pellauer for inclusion in *Figuring the Sacred*.[17] But in my conversations with Ricoeur at that time, I felt that he wanted to embargo from publication, at least temporarily, his next-to-last Gifford essay, "The Self in the Mirror of the Scriptures," an exposition of the symbolic biblical grid by means of which the subject understands itself as a mandated self. While Ricoeur graciously granted to me permission to translate and bring into print other unpublished chapters for the *Figuring the Sacred* collection, his preference at that juncture was that "The Self in the Mirror of the Scriptures" not come into publication just yet (it did appear in English in 1997, though it is now out of print). Now with the publication of *Refiguring the Sacred*, this chapter is readily available again, and its appearance fills a notable gap in the original Table of Contents for *Figuring the Sacred*.

Not only this chapter, but I'd hope during this same period that a related paper titled "*Fides Quaerens Intellectum*: Biblical Antecedents?"[18] and two of Ricoeur's other writings from that time,[19] could be included along with the twenty-one articles that made up *Figuring the Sacred*. But Michael West, my then editor at Fortress Press, made it clear to me that the size of the anthology would need to be constrained by page number restrictions, and that I would have to cut a number of Ricoeur's works I wanted to include in the overall compendium. West was generous in all aspects of putting together *Figuring the Sacred*, and I bowed to his better judgment in order to stay within the limits of the press's production guidelines and to prevent the collection from becoming overly long and unwieldy. Today it gives me great pleasure to supply two of the chapters I had first wanted to incorporate into the previous collection. In order to make up for this original deficit, I will analyze in what follows the significance of "The Self in the Mirror of the Scriptures" and the corollary "*Fides Quaerens Intellectum*: Biblical Antecedents?" Both chapters are now included in this volume in the editors' efforts to round out a fuller understanding of Ricoeur's philosophy of religion than was possible for me when I edited *Figuring the Sacred* in 1995.

"THE SELF IN THE MIRROR OF THE SCRIPTURES"

As I have suggested, Ricoeur's penultimate Gifford lecture, "The Self in the Mirror of the Scriptures," forms a natural pairing with his final Gifford lecture, "The Summoned Subject." I have also noted that the joining together of both chapters and their exclusion from *Oneself as Another* represent Ricoeur's self-conscious attempt to split apart the rigorously philosophical and the faith-based Gifford lectures from each other. The understanding of the functional significance of this split in Ricoeur's *Oneself as Another* vis-à-vis his overall thought is crucially important. It signifies his commitment to analyzing the

phenomenon of the mandated self who practices self-care and care for others—the singular focus of his Gifford chapters *en toto*—through the optics
provided by two different but related universes of discourse: philosophy and
biblical faith. Each universe of discourse operates according to its own deeply
held assumptions and ways of understanding reality. Each universe proceeds
in accordance with its own canons of evidence and criteria for making truth-
claims. And neither universe can adjudicate the other's adequacy to formulat-
ing the right relationship between inner-directed and other-directed nurture
and solicitude.

Emerging from Ricoeur's *détente* between philosophical and faith-based
forms of expression, the obligated self envisioned by the biblical schema is
first and foremost constituted by its response to the divine Word. In the self's
deepest interiority, the one who is summoned—the prophet, the visionary, the
disciple, the acolyte—lives in ready openness to a possible mandate from God
to exercise solicitude toward others—and to do so, at times, even when such
solicitude requires great cost to oneself. In the Hebrew Bible, God issues the
divine call and the prophets reply, "here I am" (*hineni* in Hebrew), signaling
their willingness to chart a new path with and for others (Gen. 22:1 cf. Exod.
3:4); in the Christian scriptures, Jesus says "follow me" (*opiso* in Greek;
Mark 1:16-20), and his hearers immediately leave behind what they are doing
and follow him in ministry with and to others.[20] In the universe of biblical
discourse, this primordial Word anterior to all other words has its anarchist
origins in the ultimate referent toward which all scriptural language aims—
God in Godself—even though, according to Ricoeur, this Word now mediated through words can never fully approximate this referent. "The referent
God," he writes in "The Self in the Mirror of the Scriptures," "is also the sign
of the incompleteness of all the discourses of faith marked as they are by the
finitude of human understanding. It is thus both the common aim of all these
discourses and the vanishing point exterior to each and every one of them."[21]

Even as biblical discourse is not fully adequate to understanding the ultimate reference point toward which it aims so also is philosophy limited in
making sense of the origins and purpose of the divine call. In *Oneself as
Another*, Ricoeur is self-consciously agnostic about the derivation of this call,
the experience of being enjoined by the other:

> Perhaps the philosopher as philosopher has to admit that one does not know and
> cannot say whether . . . the source of the injunction, is another person . . . or my
> ancestors . . . or god—living God, absent God—or an empty place. With this
> aporia . . . philosophical discourse comes to an end.[22]

Nevertheless, while the basis of the call remains aporetic in philosophical
terms, I, as the mandated religious subject, can now make a wager of faith

about the *source* and *purpose* of this injunction. "[T]his call does not come from philosophy but from the Word, harbored in scripture and transmitted by the tradition and interpretive traditions issuing from these writings."[23] Not in the certainty of philosophical appeals to common human experience, but through the eyes and ears of faith passed on by generations of tradition, I can reasonably postulate a divine origin of this summons. Outside of my own willing and knowing, I find myself being addressed in a language that is both fundamentally proximate and, aporetically, abyssally exterior to me. Before I interpret this language it is already interpreting me. Paradoxically, this language is a language both internal and extrinsic to me—it is always-already *present* and discernible to me in my ownmost interiority, and it is *impossible* for me to imagine such a language in its radical depth, exteriority and otherness to me. *For Ricoeur, this is the model of the self in scripture's mirror: in myself and for others, I am called in an anterior language that is* deeper *to me than I am to myself and in a language* far removed *from my powers of control over this language.*

Ricoeur makes the point that this primitive word of address is self-referential: it centripetally sucks everything into its own internally coherent world of meaning. Sufficient unto itself and needing no external referents for establishing its veracity, the Word is essentially *kerygmatic* for me insofar as it urges me to conform to its demands by exercising personal responsibility for myself and others in particular situations.

> Precisely because the text aims at nothing outside itself, it only has us as its outside, we who, in receiving the text, assimilate ourselves to it and make the book a mirror. At this moment, the language which *in itself* is poetic becomes kerygmatic *for us.*[24]

In specific circumstances, I encounter a summons *pro me* that I can neither ignore nor make sense of apart from the internal text-world of the biblical witness. To *under-stand* this summons is to *stand-under* its overarching rhetorical canopy: the semantic *configuration* of this internal world definitively shapes the process of my own *refiguration* by subordinating my assumptions to its all-consuming solicitation.

Ricoeur analyzes the comprehensive force of the biblical text-world using literary critic Northrop Frye's category of the "great code." In *The Great Code: The Bible and Literature*, Frye argues that the Bible generates the "mythological universe" within which the reader comprehends their fundamental humanity. Read as a literary whole, the Bible provides the root metaphors and narrative structure for conceptualizing the meaning and truth of all facets of reality. Its orienting cognitive framework, according to Ricoeur, is animated by its "power to instill in listeners or readers the desire to understand themselves in light of this Great Code."[25]

Frye does not argue that this "great code" is scientifically accurate, historically factual, ethically praiseworthy, or even theologically sound. His case
for the centrality of the Bible in history and the present-day is descriptive
and analytical, not advocatory and evangelistic. "Clearly," Frye writes, "the
Bible is a violently partisan book: as with any other form of propaganda, what
is true is what the writer thinks ought to be true; and the sense of urgency in
the writing comes out much more freely by not being hampered by the clut-
ter of what may actually have occurred."[26] The Bible's dramatic narration of
the sweep of human history is the measure of its hold on the Western imagination—notwithstanding the disputed status of its scientific and historical
truth-claims, on the one hand, and the dubious character of some of its moral
and religious teachings, on the other. The point of the Bible, and its staying
power through the millennia, is its pitch-perfect capacity to describe with
poetic potency the significance of everyday events in relation to a Creator
who enlivens, sustains, and governs all things.

"FIDES QUAERENS INTELLECTUM: BIBLICAL ANTECEDENTS?"

At first glance, it may seem that Ricoeur's focus in "The Self in the Mirror of
the Scriptures" falls primarily on the Bible's narrative coherence as the "great
code" over and against its fractures and discontinuities. But it is his exposition
of the contrapuntal forms of naming God, and corresponding models of selfhood, that emerges as his culminating aim in this essay. Scripture's unity is
mediated through its polyphony of discourses. Ricoeur maintains that it is the
Bible's interplay of multiple literary genres—that is, narrative, prescription,
prophecy, hymns, wisdom, and parables—that generates its pluriform range
of meanings. His turn to biblical plurivocity in *"Fides Quaerens Intellectum"*
and related essays paves the way for his further analysis of contrasting modes
of scriptural discourses in his final Gifford lecture, "The Summoned Self."
As well, this turn frames his overall interpretive framework for understanding
Anselm's ontological argument for the existence of God in *"Fides Quaerens
Intellectum"*—one of the essays, as I said, that was regrettably omitted from
Figuring the Sacred, and that we can now turn to round out a more complete
understanding of his philosophy of religion.

In the eleventh century CE, English theologian St. Anselm penned a prayer
in which he sought to establish God's necessary existence based on a rational
comprehension of the nature of divinity. Predicated on the commonplace
definition of a supreme being (*ontos* in Greek, so the ontological argument),
Anselm argued that knowing the everyday concept of God logically entails
the proposition that God must exist. According to Anselm, for example, if

one rightly grasps that the concept of a triangle implies a three-sided figure, analogously, a clear understanding of the idea of God necessitates the judgment that such a being must necessarily exist. Embedded in the form of a prayer, Anselm's ontological argument can be distilled into a straightforward syllogism: by definition, God is a maximally great being, that is, a being than which nothing greater can be thought. Now it is assumed that a being that exists in reality is greater than a being that is merely a mental construct. Therefore, insofar as God is a maximally great being, it follows that God must exist in reality and not simply as an idea in the mind.[27]

While Ricoeur acknowledges that this line of philosophical reasoning can be abstracted from Anselm's prayer, what interests him about this proof of God is not its logical validity but its rootedness in the various biblical discourses that precede and envelop the argument in the first place (so the essay's subtitle, "Biblical Antecedents?"). Anselm doesn't simply write a series of theoretical propositions to prove God's existence; rather, he appeals to God to grant him the insight to better *understand* what he actually already knows to be true through *faith*, namely, God's necessary existence (so the essay's Anselmian-Latinate title, "*Fides Quaerens Intellectum*," that is, "Faith Seeking Understanding").

In particular, Ricoeur is intrigued by the literary-ecclesiastical form of Anselm's argument in the context of a prayer or *invocation*. He asks, "In other words, what dynamism drives the invocation to the argument?"[28] Religiously understood, an invocation is a summoning or calling upon the Absolute to become real: it is a rhetorical exercise in asking God to identify Godself—to become present to the supplicant and then expressing profound gratitude to God for becoming known accordingly. Initially, the biblical mode of discourse that generates such invocations is "principally narrative and prescriptive in form," as Ricoeur writes.[29] In the Hebrew Bible, when God's followers cry out for divine presence, God responds as the great "I am" to the liberator Moses and the prophets Isaiah and Jeremiah (Exod. 3:14, Isa. 44:6, Jer. 1:8), and in the New Testament, Jesus, in a tense-confusing statement of apotheosis, replies similarly when asked to identify who he is, "Before Abraham was, I am" (John 8:58). Classically understood, all such announcements create the impression of God (or God's son) revealing himself in autonomous, ontological terms. In this model, God *a se* is defined not as a relational being but as self-existent Being itself and fully independent from all others.

But this speculative understanding of God is wrong-headed. For Ricoeur, the Bible knows nothing of a God in and for himself. It only knows a God encountering human beings and even creation as a whole. The biblical God, as many have emphasized, is a relational God, which will justify Luther's subsequent thesis that the object of theology is not God, but God and humanity.[30]

Ricoeur's insight into the fundamentally intersubjective character of God cements his shift away from a secular philosophical understanding of Anselm's prayer as an "ontological argument" to a re-understanding of this prayer as a heartfelt plea for divine support of Anselm's search for better comprehending God's always-already presence in his life. God's (and Jesus') "I am" pronouncements in the Bible, therefore, are not speculative ontological statements but instead are expressions of God's interpersonal commitment to the wellbeing of the wider community. To put it bluntly, the point of the "I am" self-presentation statements is not *metaphysical* but *ethical:* in this modality, God is signaling divine fidelity to the covenant people for their care and protection. "The Bible," Ricoeur writes, "knows God only as related to his people, to humanity, to the whole of creation."[31]

At the end of "*Fides Quaerens Intellectum,*" Ricoeur's shift from a metaphysical to a communal model of God opens the door to his searching interrogation of divine fallibility. His abandonment of the classical definition of God as Being itself—and corresponding divine attributes of omnipotence and perfect goodness—paves the way for a deployment of his biblical hermeneutic of divine complicity with the chaos, even evil, at the heart of the creation God made.

> A *speculative theology*, claiming to speak of God in himself, "before" or "apart" from creation, may delay the confrontation with the problem posed by the persistence of evil and turn it into a separated chapter from any consideration of the divine perfections. A *relational approach*, on the contrary, has to think together and at the same time of creation and the persistence of evil.[32]

Instead of a seamless depiction of God's *aseity* as a self-sufficient supreme being divorced from the drama of ordinary life, the Bible portrays a God who is passionate, occasionally vindictive, and always ever-changing—a God who is never fully formed according to the canons of standard Western philosophy. Awash in the terror of history itself, the biblical God operates in a universe where "[e]verything happens as if God were not yet God."[33] Knocked off its pedestal as the *summom bonum* of classical thought, God is now fully implicated in the muck and mire of everyday existence.

In a world where misery abounds—in a world where God is not yet God—Ricoeur's theology of suffering begins with the principled renunciation of every philosophical system that claims to explain the purpose and necessity of systemic evil. This is the negative point he seeks to make. But positively, as we saw in Ricoeur's 1984 Chicago lecture, the question of evil can still be productively addressed through the piety of cultivating *anger* toward God alongside the ritual work of *mourning* one's losses. In this vein, he writes that the catharsis of the lament is to allow it to develop into a complaint against God. This is the way taken by the work of Elie Wiesel. The very relationship of the covenant, to the extent that it is a mutual action that God and human beings bring against one another, invites us to pursue this course, even to the point of articulating a "theology of protest."[34]

THE AGON BETWEEN WISDOM AND NARRATION

One of Ricoeur's signal contributions to contemporary religious thought is his retrieval of the Bible's wisdom literature as a needed counterpoint to the legal teachings within the polyphony of the scriptural texts. In *"Fides Quaerens Intellectum,"* that retrieval is central to the work of *lament*, even *anger*, directed against God for God's prima facie failure to abide by the terms of the covenant—a covenant, paradoxically, that God in Godself established for the wellbeing of the ancient Israelites. "The lament, in effect, is the cry that expresses the rending that affects every part of the creature as such, beyond the person of the covenant, beyond that of history, beyond even that of the *Heilsgeschichte* (salvation-history in German)."[35] In *"Fides Quaerens Intellectum" inter alia*, it is Ricoeur's unmediated juxtaposition of the agony of lament in biblical wisdom texts over and against the coherence of salvation-history in narrative texts that is the motive force behind his biblically modulated philosophy of religion.

In this contestation between wisdom and narration, what is the nature of the covenant obligation that the practice of lament, a theology of protest, stands opposed to? Throughout the Bible's historical, prescriptive, and prophetic texts, God promises to bless Israel insofar as the nation abides by the commandments (*mitzvot* in Hebrew) set forth in the first five books of the Bible (*Torah* in Hebrew, Pentateuch in Latin). "If you will only obey the Lord your God, by diligently observing all of the commandments that I am commanding you today . . . all of these blessings shall come upon you" (Deut. 28:1). God's obedience-blessings covenant formula with Israel ensures an endless flow of benefactions and gifts—agricultural wealth, material prosperity, biological fertility, even the godsend of a perfect climate—providing the chosen people maintain fidelity to their covenant relationship with God. From this perspective, it appears that the central message of the Bible is Deuteronomic and prescriptive at its core: God and Israel's binding agreement guarantees perpetual blessings of land, prosperity, and fecundity as long as the people of God remain faithful to divine teaching.

On further reflection, however, this longstanding assumption about the Bible's unshakable Deuteronomic foundation could not be further from the truth. In *"Fides Quaerens Intellectum,"* Ricoeur writes that the Israelites learn the bitter truth that it is impossible to reconcile their everyday praxis of affirming God's fidelity to the covenant alongside their protracted suffering: "An abyss exists that will never be closed between the liturgical affirmation of the sovereignty of God and the everyday experience of the persistence of evil."[36] So the exclamations and tears of despair, rage, and shattered hope in the wisdom books of Psalms, Proverbs, Job, Lamentations, and Ecclesiastes—alongside the channeling of these same emotions in the Christian scriptures where, for example, Jesus cries out at the moment of his crucifixion, "My God, my God, why have you forsaken me?" (Matt. 27:46; cf. Mark 15:34)—offer a spirited counter-testimony to the covenantal certainties of the Mosaic and prophetic books of the Bible. In the end, no matter how committed to following the *mitzvot* God's children aspire to, they continue to suffer the slings and arrows of a seemingly capricious and, at times, malevolent deity. Not only does God disproportionately punish Israel for its many shortcomings, but in some instances, God appears to relish exploiting faithful but fragile human beings as test cases or object lessons for communicating some sort of inhumane spiritual lesson about which no sane person can discern the meaning or rationale.

Arguably, the *locus classicus* for such absurdity is the book of Job. Ricoeur says,

> Job lays bare the scandal of unjust suffering, without which it is not possible to think about God, so long as we preserve the relational structure that binds together God, humanity, and the world, as seems to be the case throughout the Hebrew Bible.[37]

In *Job*, God is now in the dock and convicted of crimes against humanity for ignoring God's own self-professed covenantal obligations. In this archetypal narrative of divinely mandated evil and loss, we read that God acted out against his faithful servant Job by aiming intentionally to "*destroy [Job] for no reason*" (Job 2:3; my emphasis). In this case, and with no rational justification, God demolished Job's everyday existence—Job's family, home, livelihood, even his physical and emotional health—and appeared to take pride in providing no discernable explanation for such actions. This anti-covenantal counternarrative puts God on trial: Job's obliteration at God's hands once and for all undermines the promise of blessings concomitant of obedience to the covenant. "By laying bare the scandal of unjust suffering," as Ricoeur puts it, "the book of Job marks the extreme point of the crisis of the covenant."[38]

Ricoeur highlights how wisdom literature rises up against such instances of arbitrary divine cruelty in protest and fury. Far from justifying God's purposes—the raison d'etre of traditional theology, including classical theodicy—the wisdom writers find God to be an adversary who is hostile to humankind's best interests. With biting candor, biblical wisdom gives voice to a spirituality of defiance in opposition to what David Blumenthal calls "the abusing God."[39] In doing so, sapiential discourse has the potential of being soul-affirming and therapeutic for the innocent sufferer who seeks to hold God accountable for authorizing, or allowing, extreme acts of divine brutality. For God's covenant children, it might seem that no response other than abandonment of a life of Torah observance is the right response. But for those who have entered into a lifelong covenantal relationship with the God of the biblical witness, the best choice for deliverance from making sense of God's ways is not apostasy, but agonistic effort in the registries of lament and anger.

Aristotle argues that the point of good theater is to offer the spectator or reader imaginative opportunities for mimetically entering into a protagonist's struggles with debilitating emotions in order to purge oneself of being fully controlled by such emotions.[40] Such vicarious identification with a play's lead actor expands one's emotional range and can generate healthier responses to unbearable emotions (fear, shame, anxiety, and despair) than would otherwise be possible. As we saw in his 1984 Chicago lecture, Ricoeur writes that the injured targets of divine malice and caprice can render the "aporia" of living with incorrigible evil "productive" by therapeutically imitating the rhetoric and life-choices of the writers and protagonists of biblical wisdom. *This posture allows the religious adherent to maintain both the integrity of faith and to fully denounce the One who is the guarantor of faith.*[41] This seemingly contradictory disposition—what Ricoeur calls a "dialectic without resolution" in "*Fides Quaerens Intellectum*"[42]—makes it possible for the adherent to take up a unique position regarding religious commitment. For God's wounded followers, their focus falls not on atheism, but on protest theism. They learn to nurture not anger for its own sake, but righteous indignation toward God. And they find a new purpose in their conflicted religious vocation: not the renunciation of belief *per se*, but the preservation of faith in open defiance of God's militancy against the very conditions of hope and assurance that make religion possible in the life of the believer.

For Ricoeur, the praxis that accompanies faithful anger toward God—the scriptural catharsis of lament—is the work of mourning for the suffering devotee. It is not in the Pentateuch but in the wisdom writings that one is permitted, even encouraged, to give oneself over to expressions of loss and grief in the face of divine violence—and especially violence toward those whom God purports to love. Expressions of sorrow, lament and mourning, then, are the last steps in the process of maintaining the integrity of faith in spite of the persistence of recalcitrant evil in everyday existence. Summarizing Ricoeur's overall philosophy of religion, it is the work of lived catharsis, not theological speculation, that undergirds the possibility of faith in spite of all evidence to the contrary. In his 1984 lecture, Ricoeur writes that the final stage in the catharsis of the lament is to discover that the reasons for believing in God have nothing in common with the need to explain the origin of suffering. Suffering is only a scandal for the person who understands God to be the source of everything that is good in creation, including our indignation against evil, our courage to bear it, and our feeling of sympathy toward victims. In other words, we believe in God *in spite of* evil. To believe in God *in spite of . . .* is one of the ways in which we can integrate the speculative aporia into the work of mourning.[43]

MY OWN CONCLUSION: RICOEUR'S LEGACY

In taking this final step toward belief *in spite of*, I am reminded of Ricoeur's earlier reference to protest theology in "the way taken by the work of Elie Wiesel."[44] And here let me end my exposition of Ricoeur on a personal note by looking backward to his 1984 lecture and my then-reading of Wiesel's religious fiction. At the time of this lecture, I had also been reading Wiesel, fortuitously, and had encountered Wiesel's astonishing Hasidic spirituality of anger and elation in his holocaust novel *Gates of the Forest*.[45] In the immediate aftermath of the Shoah, a Rebbe appears at the novel's end with teary eyes and clenched fists and performs a strange sort of mad celebratory dance. He dances out of *fury* against God for God's abject abandonment of the chosen people in the Nazi period; and he dances out of *joy* for God having given to him the strength to endure this trial of genocidal terror, a trial in which God in Godself is implicated for crimes against God's own people. Addressing the Almighty directly in a spinning whirl of feverish indignation and rapturous bliss, the Rebbe shouts out,

> You don't want me to dance; too bad, I'll dance anyhow. You've taken away every reason for singing, but I shall sing. I shall sing of the deceit that walks by day and the truth that walks by night, yes, and of the silence of dusk as well. You didn't expect my joy, but here it is; yes, my joy will rise up; it will submerge you.[46]

On December 10, 1984, I left Ricoeur's Chicago lecture greatly moved by his adumbration of an original post-Shoah religious practice—the work of mourning for and against God—that offered a way beyond the impasse between naive belief and conventional atheism. Now remembering this lecture and reading again *"Fides Quaerens Intellectum,"* I see that his thought contains the seeds of a compelling post-Shoah theology of suffering—a wounded but still hopeful theology—that operates *in spite of* God's complicity with apocalyptic forces and *to spite* God for such complicity. In Wiesel's *Gates of the Forest*, the Rebbe doesn't give way to the deadly power of these toxic forces, nor does he blithely praise God for delivering him from the same. Rather, the Rebbe does what God was not willing or able to do during the period of Jewish extermination: he plunges himself into a kinetic delirium of mourning and loss, but also of joy and ecstasy, in order to realize emotionally, if not cognitively, some sort of purgative release beyond the madness of senseless mass death.

Much like Wiesel, Ricoeur's religious thought is an *aporia* of terror and belief, doubt and faithfulness, lament and catharsis, crisis and elation, suffering and God. *Coincidentia oppositorum.* In refusing to solve such paradoxes, Ricoeur, the antitheological philosopher writes, in my judgment, one of the most searching and honest theologies of divine pathos and human affliction for our time. Surveying Ricoeur's *oeuvre*, I stand in wonder at his lifelong attempt to hold together in an impossible tension the reality of suffering and the affirmation of religious belief—and it is this holding together, I believe, that offers to the reader the possibility of faith in our broken and now burning world.

NOTES

1. The two essays in question are "The Self in the Mirror of the Scriptures," in *The Whole and Divided Self: The Bible and Theological Anthropology*, trans. David Pellauer and ed. John McCarthy (New York: Crossroad, 1997), 201–20, and *"Fides Quaerens Intellectum*: Biblical Antecedents?" in *The Honeycomb of the Word: Interpreting the Primary Testament with André LaCocque*, trans. David Pellauer and ed. W. Dow Edgerton (Chicago: Exploration Press, 2001), 179–208.

2. Paul Ricoeur, *Oneself as Another*, trans. Kathleen Blamey (Chicago: University of Chicago Press, 1992), 172.

3. Paul Ricoeur, "Evil, a Challenge to Philosophy and Theology," *Journal of the American Academy of Religion* 53 (1985): 635–48. Reprinted in *Figuring the Sacred*, pages 249–61. Subsequent citations are from this edition.

4. Ricoeur, "Evil, a Challenge to Philosophy and Theology," 260.

5. Ibid.

6. Ibid., 258.

7. Paul Ricoeur, *The Symbolism of Evil*, trans. Emerson Buchanan (Boston: Beacon Press, 1967).

8. Lewis S. Mudge, *Essays on Biblical Interpretation* (Philadelphia: Fortress Press, 1980).

9. See the careful analysis of Ricoeur's personal and public conflict about whether he welcomed others' description of him as a Christian philosopher in François Dosse, *Paul Ricoeur: Les sens d'une vie (1913–2005)* (Paris: Le Découverte 2008), 554–81.

10. See Immanuel Kant, *The Conflict of the Faculties*, trans. Mary J. Gregor (Lincoln: University of Nebraska Press, 1992).

11. Paul Ricoeur, *Critique and Conviction: Conversations with François Azouvi and Marc de Launay*, trans. Kathleen Blamey (New York: Columbia University Press, 1998), 150.

12. Ricoeur, *Oneself as Another*, 24.

13. Ricoeur, *Critique and Conviction*, 150.

14. Ibid.

15. Paul Ricoeur, *Living Up to Death*, trans. David Pellauer (Chicago: University of Chicago Press, 2009), 69.

16. The Gifford Lectures. https://giffordlectures.org/

17. Paul Ricoeur, "The Summoned Subject in the School of the Narratives of the Prophetic Vocation," in *Figuring the Sacred: Religion, Narrative, and Imagination*. trans. David Pellauer and ed. Mark I. Wallace (Minneapolis: Fortress Press, 1995), 262–75.

18. Paul Ricoeur, "*Fides Quaerens Intellectum*: Biblical Antecedents?" in *The Honeycomb of the. Word: Interpreting the Primary Testament with André LaCocque*, ed. W. Dow Edgerton (Chicago: Exploration Press, 2001), 179–208.

19. The two other writings I was not able to add to the *Figuring the Sacred* collection were "Hegel aujourd'hui," *Études théologiques et philosophiques* 49 (1974), 335–55, a significant and nuanced critique of Hegel's appeal to absolute knowledge; and Ricoeur's unpublished Oxford University Sarum Lectures, 1980, which offer rich insight into his own developing narrative theology from that time but would have been too cumbersome to publish in their entirety in an essays-based anthology of his work.

20. All Biblical references are taken from *The New Revised Standard Version* (New York: Harper Collins, 1993).

21. Ricoeur, "The Self in the Mirror of the Scriptures," 213.

22. Ricoeur, *Oneself as Another*, 355.

23. Ricoeur, "The Self in the Mirror of the Scriptures," 202.

24. Ibid., 209–10.

25. Ibid., 209.

26. Northrop Frye, *The Great Code: The Bible and Literature* (New York: Harcourt Brace Jovanovich, 1981), 40.

27. Anselm, et al. *St. Anselm's Proslogion; With a Reply on Behalf of the Fool* (Norte Dame, Ind.: University of Notre Dame Press), 1980.

28. Ricoeur, "*Fides Quaerens Intellectum*," 185.

29. Ibid., 190.

30. Ibid., 193–94.

31. Ibid., 196.

32. Ibid., my emphasis.

33. Ibid., 199.

34. Ricoeur, "Evil, a Challenge to Philosophy and Theology," 260.

35. Ricoeur, "*Fides Quaerens Intellectum*," 196.

36. Ibid., 198.

37. Ibid., 200.

38. Ibid.

39. David R. Blumenthal, *Facing the Abusing God: A Theology of Protest* (Louisville: Westminster John Knox Press, 1993).

40. Aristotle. *Nicomachean Ethics*, trans. Roger Crisp (Cambridge, UK: Cambridge University Press), 2000.

41. Ricoeur, "Evil, a Challenge to Philosophy and Theology," 258–61.

42. Ricoeur, "*Fides Quaerens Intellectum*," 198.

43. Ricoeur, "Evil, a Challenge to Philosophy and Theology," 260.

44. Ibid.

45. Elie Wiesel, *Gates of the Forest*, trans. Frances Frenaye (New York: Shocken, 1982).

46. Ibid., 198.

BIBLIOGRAPHY

Anselm, et al. *St. Anselm's Proslogion; With a Reply on Behalf of the Fool.* Norte Dame, IN: University of Notre Dame Press, 1980.

Aristotle. *Nicomachean Ethics.* Trans. Roger Crisp. Cambridge, UK: Cambridge University Press, 2000.

Blumenthal, David R. *Facing the Abusing God: A Theology of Protest.* Louisville: Westminster John Knox Press, 1993.

Dosse, François. *Paul Ricoeur: Les sens d'une vie (1913–2005).* Paris: Le Découverte 2008.

Frye, Northrop. *The Great Code: The Bible and Literature.* New York: Harcourt Brace Jovanovich, 1981.

Ihde, Don. *Hermeneutic Phenomenology: The Philosophy of Paul Ricoeur.* Evanston, IL: Northwestern University Press, 1971.

Kant, Immanuel. *Critique of Pure Reason.* Trans. J. M. D. Meiklejohn. The Floating Press. ProQuest Ebook Central, 2009.

Mudge, Lewis S. *Essays on Biblical Interpretation.* Philadelphia, PA: Fortress Press, 1980.

Ricoeur, Paul. *Critique and Conviction: Conversations with François Azouvi and Marc de Launay.* Trans. Kathleen Blamey. New York: Columbia University Press, 1998.

———. "Evil, a Challenge to Philosophy and Theology," *Journal of the American Academy of Religion* 53 (1985): 635–48. Reprinted in *Figuring the Sacred: Religion, Narrative, and Imagination*, 249–61. Trans. David Pellauer and ed. Mark I. Wallace. Minneapolis: Fortress Press, 1995.

———. "Fides Quaerens Intellectum: Biblical Antecedents." In *The Honeycomb of the Word: Interpreting the Primary Testament with André LaCocque*, 179–208. Trans. David Pellauer and ed. W. Dow Edgerton. Chicago: Exploration Press, 2001.

———. The Gifford Lectures. https://giffordlectures.org/

———. *The Just.* Trans. David Pellauer. Chicago: University of Chicago Press, 2000.

———. *Living Up to Death.* Trans. David Pellauer. Chicago: University of Chicago Press, 2009.

———. *Memory, History, Forgetting.* Trans. David Pellauer. Chicago: University of Chicago Press, 2004.

———. *Oneself as Another.* Trans. Kathleen Blamey. Chicago: University of Chicago Press, 1992.

———. "The Self in the Mirror of the Scriptures." In *The Whole and Divided Self: The Bible and Theological Anthropology,* 201–20. Trans. David Pellauer and ed. John McCarthy. New York: Crossroad, 1997.

———. "The Summoned Subject in the School of the Narratives of the Prophetic Vocation." In *Figuring the Sacred: Religion, Narrative, and Imagination,* 262–75. Trans. David Pellauer and ed. Mark I. Wallace. Minneapolis, MN: Fortress Press, 1995.

———. *The Symbolism of Evil.* Trans. Emerson Buchanan. Boston, MA: Beacon Press, 1967.

Sohn, Michael. *The Good of Recognition Phenomenology, Ethics, and Religion in the Thought of Lévinas and Ricoeur.* Waco, TX: Baylor University Press, 2014.

Wallace, Mark I. *The Second Naiveté: Barth, Ricoeur, and the New Yale Theology.* Macon, GA: Mercer University Press, 1990.

Wiesel, Elie. *Gates of the Forest.* Trans. Frances Frenaye. New York: Shocken, 1982.

Chapter 6

The Self in the Mirror of the Scriptures

Paul Ricoeur, Translated by David Pellauer

My final two Gifford lectures form an inseparable whole.[1] In them, I discuss, on the one hand, how the self is instructed by the religious tradition that stems from the Judaic and Christian biblical scriptures and, on the other hand, the inner resources with which the self responds to this instruction, which determines it in the manner of a call that imposes no restraints.[2] The relation between call and response is thus the bond that holds these two lectures together. What is more, this relation also produces a gap between these concluding lectures and those that preceded them. This gap or break needs to be clarified, even if all the determinations of the self traced out in the earlier lectures, and worked out in *Oneself as Another*, are taken into consideration again here, where through this recapitulation they are both intensified and transformed.

I want to lay particular stress on this initial gap between these concluding lectures and what had gone before in order to dispel a possible error in interpretation that might appear to be fostered by the term "response." One might understand this term in the following way: to be a Jew or Christian is to possess the response (or answer) to the questions posed by philosophy but left without a response. Philosophy then would raise the question and theology would provide the answer. But this is not at all what I have in mind. In the first place, I do not set the response over against a question but rather a call. And this changes everything. It is one thing to respond to a question in the sense of resolving a problem that has been posed; it is something else again to respond to a call in the sense of conforming [correspondre] to the conception of existence it proposes. Next, this call does not come from philosophy but from the Word, harbored in scripture and transmitted by the tradition and interpretive traditions issuing from these writings. Finally, the response I have in mind is not that of theology, considered as a more or less systematic discourse, but that of the self, which moves from being a self that is called to being a responsive self.[3]

As for the relation between philosophy and faith, if we still want provisionally to use these problematic categories, this is not determined by the relation between question and answer, despite its apparent resemblance to the relation between call and response. First, we can apply the schema of question and answer only within a prior domain of understanding, which is exactly what is at issue if it is a question of the relation between philosophy and faith. Second, if we admit the existence of such a domain, it quickly becomes apparent that philosophy often gives the answer, and it is faith that poses the questions. But philosophy responds or answers in a way wholly other than does the believing self, that is, in the sense of resolving problems that it itself raises on the speculative plane that is proper to it. As for faith, it can pose questions as much about those mysteries that it refuses to transform into problems in need of resolution as about those solutions that philosophical speculation proposes out of its foundational and totalizing hubris. In short, for philosophy to respond by answering is to resolve a problem. Whereas to respond to the word of scripture is to conform to the proposed meaning that issues from what is given through the Bible, it follows that the relation between these two ways of responding or answering turns out to be immensely complex. It cannot be reduced to the handy schema of question and answer.

In order to give some account, however briefly, of this relation, which is not my real topic here, I shall limit myself to two assertions whose complementarity itself poses problems. On the one hand, the call to which faith responds in so many different ways, as I shall discuss in the following lecture, is born within a setting of human experience and language that has its own structures, whose internal coherence at a specific symbolic level I want to take up here. On the other hand, these originary structures of experience and language have come down to us only thanks to an uninterrupted process of transmission and interpretation that has always implied conceptual mediations that are foreign to the original expressions of the faith of Israel and of the early Christian church—those, for example, contributed successively by Hellenistic philosophy, by Neoplatonism, by scholasticism, and by Cartesian and post-Cartesian, Kantian, Hegelian, and post-Hegelian philosophy. As a result, neither Judaism nor Christianity can be thought about today in isolation, but only in relation to the rest of our theoretical and practical culture. This is not some kind of contamination that we ought to regret, even less does it represent a perversion. Rather it represents an unavoidable historical destiny that we have to take into account. I am not looking for any easy reconciliation of these two assertions. On the contrary, the tensions that result from this relation between the specific language of faith and the conceptual mediations that have been borrowed from its cultural milieu have animated many of the internal debates within Western thought, whether it accepts or rejects the biblical legacy.

If in this lecture I stress the specificity of the experience of the biblical human person and the coherence of the language at a symbolic level proper to this experience, I do not mean to lose sight of those cultural and conceptual mediations that were practically contemporary with the birth of this experience and its language. In fact, our recognition of the singular status of this experience and language is itself a characteristic of the hermeneutical era of Western reason.[4]

This restitution expresses a way of questioning backward—of *Rückfrage*, to use Husserl's terminology for his inquiry into the *Lebenswelt*, the life-world—that in no way means to restore the original immediacy of an originary experience and its language. What this questioning backward brings to light are, in fact, earlier interpretations whose interpretive import was incorporated into the oldest form of the texts that have come down to us and that are recognizable only within the framework of the self-critique of modern reason. In other words, the reconstitution of expressions taken to be the most original expressions of biblical faith is itself a modern phenomenon, which itself belongs to the history of interpretation. The use of historical-critical method, of structural analysis, of literary criticism, and especially the theory of symbolism all make evident the modern status of this reconstruction. I shall say nothing more here about the conflictual conjunction between the biblical background of experience and language and those cultural and philosophical mediations from which philosophy was born. If I believe I can abstract from these mediations—given the important reservations just indicated—it is because I am not concerned here with theology properly speaking, which consists of a discourse at a conceptual level that has its own rules and its own manner of incorporating philosophical concepts and ways of thinking. Instead, I mean to take up expressions of biblical faith that antedate formal theologies from the very point of view of their capacity to form the kind of responsive self whose phenomenological description I attempt to undertake in my final lecture.

This choice explains why I am placing the principal accent on the specificity of biblical experience and the language that gives it expression rather than on those cultural and philosophical mediations into which this specificity tends to disappear owing to a kind of compromise discourse. This stance also further explains my mistrust as regards the question-and-answer scheme when it is applied to the relationship between faith and philosophy, and even more my refusal of any apologetic attitude, whether it be intended to sing the praises of or to defend some profession of Jewish or Christian faith. I am well aware that my belonging to this particular field of experience and language is first of all a biological, geographical, and cultural contingency. However, I

also believe that it can be transformed into a freely assumed destiny by anyone who takes the path of a wager and a risk. The risk is that of responding
positively, in one way or another, to the nonconstraining call issuing from the
symbolic field determined by the biblical canon, whether Jewish or Christian,
in preference to any other classical canon.[5] The wager corresponding to this
risk involves a letting go of oneself, which calls for those different figures of
selfhood that I shall return to in the next lecture, that we wager will be compensated a hundredfold by a super-abundant increase in our understanding of
ourselves and of others. But I neither intend to impose nor to excuse myself
for introducing this wager. Certainly I must make sense of it (logondidonai),
but to do this is something other than to justify oneself—it means accepting and confronting one's own choice with the other choices made by one's
companions in life and thought, in that "loving struggle" for truth, as Karl
Jaspers so aptly put it.

I turn now to the theme of this next-to-last lecture. Its title is "The Self in
the Mirror of the Scriptures." To convey the sense of this title, I shall draw
on the vocabulary that governed the analyses in my work *Time and Narrative*. There I used the term "configuration" to refer to the internal organization of the type of discourse being examined—in that case, narrative—and I
called "refiguration" the effect of discovery and transformation this discourse
brings about in its hearer or reader through the process of receiving the text.
What I want to consider here is a relation similar to that between configuration and refiguration. The problem I want to pose is that of how the entirely
original configuration of the biblical scriptures can refigure the self, taken in
terms of all the determinations I have spelled out in *Oneself Another*. My title
places this relation under the guidance of one telling metaphor from Christian
hermeneutics: the metaphor of the Book and the Mirror. Liberet Speculum.
How does the self understand itself in contemplating itself in the mirror held
out to it by this book? For a mirror is never there just by accident. It is held
by an invisible hand. On its side, the book remains a dead letter so long as its
readers have not become, thanks to it, in Proust's phrase in *Time Regained*,
readers of themselves.

What I want to discuss is the internal dynamism that makes the book, made
up of the Hebrew Bible and the Christian New Testament, become a mirror
for a self who responds to the solicitation of this book.

I shall proceed as follows. In the first step, which is still a preliminary
one, I shall say in what sense Christian faith requires a linguistic mediation
in general and a "scriptural" one in particular. In a second step, I shall draw
upon a purely literary analysis of the Bible, influenced by the great Canadian
literary critic Northrop Frye, in order to emphasize both the originality and
internal coherence on the plane of verbal imagination of these writings, which
Frye, following William Blake, calls the great code.[6] From this follows an

initial approach, albeit still an external, extrinsic one, to the relation between book and mirror, or, using my own vocabulary, between configuration and refiguration. In a third step, one more marked by historical-critical exegesis but nevertheless directed toward biblical theology, I want to show how the theologoumena, bound to the various literary genres of the Bible, imply a human response that is an integral part of the meaning of these theological motifs. Finally, in a fourth, clearly hermeneutical step, I shall discuss how the dialectic between the manifestation of the Name and the withdrawal of the Name affects the constitution of the self, called at the same time to draw itself together and to disappear, in a decisive way.

THE LINGUISTIC AND SCRIPTURAL MEDIATION OF BIBLICAL FAITH

The reader will have noted how in my introductory comments I have repeatedly spoken about religious experience and its language, presupposing thereby an intimate union between them. It is time to justify my assertion regarding this inseparable relation. On the one hand, I willingly grant that there exists something like a "religious experience," whose "varieties" William James analyzed in his own well-known Gifford Lectures, published as *The Varieties of Religious Experience*. For my part, the formulations closest and most familiar to me are: a feeling of absolute dependence, in relation to a creation that precedes me; an ultimate concern at the horizon of all my preoccupations; an unconditional trust, which hopes despite everything. These are a few synonyms for what, in the contemporary period, has been termed "faith." And all the formulations we may give attest that faith, as such, is an act that cannot be reduced to any particular word or any piece of writing. In this respect, it marks the limit of any hermeneutics, because it is the origin of any interpretation. But the difficulty that is already evident that it is necessary to "name" this origin of interpretation indicates the necessity of providing a counterpart to the affirmation that faith is more primitive than any language or speech act. If the presupposition of hearing, for example, Christian preaching is that, in faith, everything is not language, it is as well that religious experience is always articulated in language, whether we understand this in a cognitive, practical, or emotional sense. The apparently naked formulations concerning faith given above are already phenomena of language, or, as much theology subsequent to Karl Barth likes to put it, word events. What is at stake in all these formulations is the possibility of "naming God." And however problematic this naming may be, as I shall say, it does constitute the originary linguistic structure of what we nevertheless call a lived faith.

But this is not all. What constitutes the specificity of biblical faith among all the possible linguistic configurations of religious experience is the scriptural mediation that served as an interpretive framework for the religious experience of the members of the Jewish and Christian communities. In these communities, naming God passes through the channel of the biblical writings. It is through them that religious experience attains not only expression, linguistic articulation, but those specific configurations delimited with more or less precision by the biblical canon, whether Jewish or Christian. As religious experience, biblical faith is instructed—in the sense of formed, enlightened, educated—within the framework of those texts that preaching brings back to living speech. This linguistic and textual presupposition of biblical faith precedes anything that may subsequently be said about the relation between the book and the mirror. The self, informed by scripture, will be able to be, as I shall say, a responding self, because, in a certain way, these texts precede life itself If I can name God, however imperfectly, it is because the texts that have been proclaimed to me have already done so. Or, to use another vocabulary, to which I have already referred above, we can say that biblical faith has its classics, which distinguish it among the cultural choices we make from all other classics. This difference is important for our investigation into the self insofar as the classics of Judaism and Christianity differ on one fundamental point from other classics from the ancient Greeks up to the present: Whereas these other classic texts speak to the readers one at a time, and with no other authority than what these readers choose to confer upon them, the classics that inform Jewish and Christian faith do so across the authority that they exercise over communities that place themselves under the rule—the canon—of these texts. In this way, these texts found the identity of the communities that receive and interpret them. It is against the background of this identity that a responsive self can stand out, following the modalities I shall consider in my final lecture.

THE IMAGINATIVE UNITY OF THE BIBLE

Let us now take up in more detail the configuration of scripture, a configuration that governs its power of refiguration. I shall begin by following the path traced out by Northrop Frye in his Great Code, relying solely on the resources of literary criticism applied to the Bible considered as literature. Without neglecting the achievements of the historical—critical method and setting aside the questions of authorship, sources, history of composition, and faithfulness to historical reality, let us simply ask how this text produces its meanings on the basis of its internal textual structures. I have become interested in this kind of reading, one that is foreign to the main currents of exegesis, because it protects the text from the claim that any subject whatever can govern its sense, by stressing, on the one hand, the foreignness of its language in relation to the one we speak today and, on the other hand, the internal coherence of its configuration in terms of its own meaning criteria. These two features have a decentering influence in relation to any effort to realize the self-constitution of the ego.

Frye begins by stressing the fact that biblical language is entirely foreign to our own in the sense that in order to join it we have to retrace the slope of language that went from being metaphorical in the age of Homer and the Greek tragic poets to becoming argumentative with Neo-platonic theologies and in particular with attempted proofs for the existence of God (from the scholastics to Hegel), finally to become demonstrative with modern mathematics and the empirical sciences. Today, in the midst of this third type of language, only poetry attests to the power of metaphorical language of the first type. This metaphorical language, in fact, says not "this is like that," but "this is that" It is by way of such poetry alone that we can move closer to the kerygmatic language of the Bible when it proclaims in a metaphorical mode "the Lord is my rock, my fortress," "I am the way, the truth, and the life," "this is my body . . .," and so on. By calling this language kerygmatic, we indicate that it is at least metaphorical, pre- or supra-metaphorical, so to speak. What is more, this language possesses complete internal coherence, but this coherence is precisely that of a language akin to that of metaphorical language. It results first of all from the extreme consistency of biblical imagery, which Frye sees organized in terms of two axes, the one paradisiacal or apocalyptic (where these two adjectives are typologically equivalent), the other demonic. We can traverse these two axes, along which are distributed the heavenly powers, heroes, human beings, animals, plants, and minerals, in either direction.

However, the imaginative-not the imaginary-unity of the Bible is assured in a much more decisive way through the thoroughgoing typological functioning of biblical significations. Indeed, Northrop Frye sees in the Bible a vast branching network of correspondences between types and antitypes, to use the language of Saint Paul, correspondences that produce an interconnection of meaning, for example, between the exodus of the ancient Hebrews and the resurrection of Christ, between the Law of Sinai and that of the Sermon on the Mount, between creation according to Genesis and the prologue of John's Gospel, even between the figures of Joshua and Jesus. This typological interpretation circulates not only between the Old and New Testaments for Christians, but within the Hebrew Bible itself, which puts into relation the series of covenants between God and Noah, Abraham, Moses, David, and so on. James Barr says something similar, without attributing such a large role to typological coherence, when he says that in the Bible events, characters, and institutions do not succeed one another in a linear way, where what comes next simply replaces what went before, but rather in a cumulative and

mutually reinforcing way. There is certainly a close tie between this cumulative process, which works principally on the narrative plane, and the typological process that is especially characteristic of the metaphorical language and
basic imagery of the Bible.

Frye sees this connection by starting precisely from the typological process,
particularly when it can be unfolded along the sequential and diachronic line
that goes from Genesis to the book of Revelation. In this way, he sees the Bible
as unfolding as a series of U-shaped figures, with highs and lows, summits and
abysses, all described in terms of the, by turns, apocalyptic or demonic overarching metaphor of the great code, and linked together by the typological rule
that assures its cumulative character. In this way, along the chain of summits
are placed the figures of Eden, then of the promised land, of the gift of the law,
of Zion, the second temple, the kingdom proclaimed by Jesus, the messiah
awaited by the Jews, and the second coming awaited by Christians. Along the
chain of abysses are the lost paradise and Cain, the captivity in Egypt, the Phi-
listines, Babylon, the profanation of the second temple, Rome and Nero, and
so on. The typological correspondence is thereby extended over a temporal
sequence, without the close connection broken between Eden, the promised
land, Jerusalem, Mount Zion, the kingdom of God, and the apocalypse.

If I have given Frye's notion of the Great Code so much importance in my
own presentation, it is to highlight the coherence of a symbolic field governed
by purely internal laws of organization and development—what Frye characterizes as the centripetal structure that the Bible shares with every great poetic
text This self-constitution and self-sufficiency of the Great Code constitutes
an important argument for our making sense of the self corresponding and
conforming to it If we place in parentheses any eventual representation of
real historical events, and with it the centrifugal and referential movement of
the text, which is characteristic of argumentative language and even more of
that demonstrative language that in our culture has largely covered over and
repressed metaphorical language, the only relation to reality that counts in a
poetic text is not nature, as in a book of cosmology, or the unfolding of events,
as in a history text,[7] but rather the power to instill in listeners or readers the
desire to understand themselves in light of this Great Code. Precisely because
the text aims at nothing outside itself, it only has us as its outside, we who, in
receiving the text, assimilate ourselves to it and make the book a mirror. At
this moment, the language which in itself is poetic becomes kerygmatic for us.[8]

THE BIBLE, A POLYPHONIC TEXT

In the third phase of my investigation I want not to oppose but to add
another vision of the biblical text with the intention of correcting the first one

somewhat. This new approach has important consequences for the passage from the internal configuration of the text to its refigurative effect on the self. This new vision of the text is still close to that of literary analysis in the sense that it places its emphasis on the genres to be found within biblical poetics: narrative discourse, prescriptive discourse, wisdom discourse, prophetic discourse, hymnic discourse, epistles, parables, and so on. But this approach differs from the preceding one on two important points. First, the main emphasis is placed on the variety of genres of discourse, rather than on the imaginative unity of the Bible, as with a typological reading. Without going so far as slicing apart the text, one begins, for example, by respecting the triadic structure of the Hebrew canon—Torah, Prophets, Writings—and then, with James Barr and Claus Westermann, stresses the absence of any single theological center to the Hebrew Bible, contrary to the claims of such respectable attempts at systematization as the theology of the covenant or even that of the Heilsgeschichte. If a unity can be recognized in the Bible, it is that of a polyphonic rather than a typological order.

The second feature by which this approach differs from the preceding one shows why they are not hostile to each other. Whereas typological unity is maintained on the pre- or hyper-metaphorical level of the text, here articulations in terms of genres are raised to the rank of theologoumena through a fortuitous conjunction of a historical-critical type of exegesis and biblical theology. Northrop Frye would perhaps say that this way of articulating the biblical domain belies the metaphorical style of biblical discourse. This is true. But, as I said in opening, it is by way of the many modes of modernity and with the language appropriate to this modernity that we attempt to recover something of the significance of biblical literature. However off-center this significance may be in relation to the modes of discourse appropriate to our age, this significance remains a significance for us, however modern we may be. And, in fact, our search for appropriate theologoumena is itself displaced and decentered in relation to past theological constructions imposed on the Bible by our way of asking questions, whether on the anthropological, cosmological, or theological plane. Theologoumena are what we shall articulate, but ones governed by language games that are no longer our own, even if they carry familiar names like narrative, prescriptive, and the like. Therefore these theologoumena do not resemble the speculations of theological discourse with an argumentative, or even demonstrative, claim, such as that God exists, is omnipotent, absolutely good, the first and last cause, and so forth.

The principal benefit of this new approach for our investigation into the self fashioned by scripture is that it places the eventual unity of the biblical canon beyond what I have above called its imaginative unity. At best, this unity will be a polyphonic unity. This kind of polysemy, which is complementary to the typological unity of the Bible, will be reflected in an equally polysemic production of the figures of the responsive self. However, it is initially in the work of naming God that this polyphony of theologoumena attached to the various literary genres finds expression, before finding an echo on the plane of the responsive self. The unity of this naming is what first carried over into the secret and silence of the fact that none of the literary genres taken one at a time fully captures this Name.

For example, for a purely narrative perspective, God is the metahero of a metahistory, which encompasses the myths of creation, the legends of the patriarchs, an epic of liberation, wandering, and conquest, a quasi-historiography of kings and reigns. God is spoken of here in the third person, as well as in the sense of a superagent or a supercharacter. This narrative naming gives rise to what Gerhard von Rad called a "theology of traditions," which he opposed globally to a "theology of prophecies." God is designated obliquely through the founding events in which the interpreting community recognizes itself inaugurated, instituted, and rooted. In this respect, for Christians the naming of God in the resurrection narratives of the New Testament agrees with that found in the narratives of deliverance in the Old Testament God is the one who recalled Christ from the dead. Here too God is designated by the transcendence of the founding events in relation to the ordinary course of history.

In the prophetic writings, on the contrary, God is signified as the voice of the Other, behind the voice of the prophet God is presented in the first person as the one who calls the prophet, who himself speaks in the first person. I return to this theme in my next closing lecture from the point of view of the mission that is implied here. Here I shall confine myself to emphasizing another aspect of the situation, namely, that God is named in a double first person, as the word of another in the prophet's word. It was this model that was, so to speak, hypostatized in those Christian theologies that identified inspiration and revelation, on the model of the double voice of prophecy. But in this way an essential dialectic between the narrative third person and the prophetic first person is overlooked. In this dialectic there is a constant interchange between the pronominal positions. On the one side, for example, narrators do not hesitate to place in God's mouth words taken as equivalent to God's thoughts. These "citations" are equivalent to the prophetic utterances. Conversely, the prophets refer to events, but in another way than the one used by narrators, the collectors of traditions. The prophets have a direct grasp on the imminence of catastrophic events that threaten the very existence of the community. Even more important, the announcement of these events undercuts from within the false security engendered by the recitation of the past. The tension between narration and prophecy engenders a paradoxical understanding of history, as founded on memory yet threatened by prophecy.

I would like to have more time to take up other tensions and other dialectics, such as between the Torah, on the one hand, and the pair narration or prophecy, on the other, both of which are concerned about past or coming events. Let me just note that the gift of the law is in its way a recounted event, while the law in turn gives every narrative an ethical color to the extent that they are narratives of obedience and disobedience. In relation to prophecy, the law is presupposed by the word of judgement, but it is a new law, inscribed on our hearts, that the prophets of the return from exile proclaim, thereby bringing about a tension between an ethics based on prophecy and one based on the traditional prescriptions.

I shall not speak here of what the wisdom writings or even more the Psalms bring to this unfolding of the literary genres. I shall have an opportunity to do so in my next lecture under the rubric of the response of biblical humanity to the call that stems from the narratives of deliverance and settlement, the prophecies of misfortune and liberation, and the multifaceted legislation placed under the emblematic name of Moses. Here I want instead to place the accent on the polyphonic character that results from this interweaving of multiple literary genres. This completes, without contradicting, the kind of imaginative unity that typology assures to the incredible diversity of the writings that make the Bible a library rather than a simple, a relatively simple, poem, like the Iliad or the Odyssey, or something more simple like Greek tragedy. What makes this complex unity a polyphony is the unique naming of God that takes place from text to text and that circulates among all the forms of discourse whose most visible differences as regards literary structure I have pointed to.

God, we have to say, is named differently in the narration that recounts, the prophecy that speaks in his name, in the prescription that designates him as the source of the imperative, in the wisdom that seeks him as the meaning of meaning, and in the hymn that calls out to him in the second person. This is why the word God cannot be understood as a philosophical concept, even that of Being, whether we take this in the medieval sense or following Heidegger. The word God says more than the word Being because it presupposes the whole context of narratives, prophecies, laws, wisdom writings, psalms, and so on. What then does it signify that is of importance to the problematic of selfhood? Two things, it seems to me. On the one hand, the referent God is intended by convergence of all these partial discourses, inasmuch as it expresses the circulation of meaning among all those forms of discourse wherein God is named. On the other hand, the referent God is also the sign of the incompleteness of all the discourses of faith marked as they are by the finitude of human understanding. It is thus both the common aim of all these discourses and the vanishing point exterior to each and every one of them.

From the first perspective, a polyphony of figures of the self can respond to the polyphony of genres. For the second perspective, it is an always deferred unity that corresponds to the unnamable Name.

Let us follow the first of these paths to conclude the present step in our investigation centered on the polyphonic structure of the Bible based on an analysis in terms of literary genres.

The passage from the polyphony of literary genres to the eventual poly-semy of figures of selfhood is made easier if we shift the accent from the literary genres as such to the theologoumena that can be set forth by a biblical theology, which unlike systematic or dogmatic theology, stays closely atten-tive to the internal structures of the biblical text. What characterizes these theologoumena is that they all imply in their innermost signification a type of response on human beings' part Here we have a note-worthy difference from the earlier literary analysis, where the closure of the text on itself imposed a kind of extrinsic aspect to the mimetic relation that goes from the internal structures of the text to the dispositions of the audience. The theologoumena, on the contrary, present a dialogical structure in that they confront the words and acts of God with the response they demand from human beings. This dialogical structure is, ultimately, the only guiding thread for exegesis that rejects the idea of one theological center (and perhaps finds no attraction in the imaginative unity produced by a typological reading).

An example of this kind of approach can be found in Claus Westermann's little book *What Does the Old Testament Say About God?,* which attempts to group the various symbolic expressions relating to God around four major themes or schemata, each of which calls for a human counterpart, no longer outside the text, but implied in the very signification of what is said in this way about God.[9] Westermann describes four such themes. First, there is the God who saves, that is, who delivers from external danger. The theology of the Heilsgeschichte, which was so dominant in biblical theology earlier in this century, was constructed on the basis of this theme to the detriment of the other schemata. Second is the God who blesses, that is, who dispenses the gift of creation, of fertility, of the promised land, of an existence full of meaning. Third is the God who punishes, that is, who declares himself to be against those who have transgressed the commandments and the specific laws of the community of Israel. Finally, there is the merciful God who suf-fers because of his own anger, repents, and pardons. Each of these themes offers a dialogical scheme, as can be verified if we take as our guide the literary categories we have already distinguished. One or the other of these themes is predominant, but in each case balanced by a specific response on the human side, whether it be a question of an individual or the elect people, or of humanity as a whole.

For example, the great narratives centered on the exodus, which valorize the figure of the God who saves, correspond a confession of praise, as we can see in the central text of Deut. 26:5-11, which von Rad places at the center of the Hebraic *Heilsgeschichte*, and which ends with a sacrificial vow as a sign of this praise. What is more, at the very heart of the narrative of deliverance that this passage from Deuteronomy celebrates, it is said of God that he had seen the distress of his people and had heard their cries, and that it was to this lamentation that he replied with a series of liberating acts.

In the narratives of the conquest and settlement of the land, which follow chronologically, and in the prescriptions addressed to a people tied to the promised and given land, it is the figure of the God who blesses that predominates. To it corresponds a soul that itself blesses, in the twofold sense of the Hebrew *berak*, which means to give thanks for the creative generosity thanks to which the self knows itself forgiven. Within the overall narrative structure constituted by the Deuteronomic historiography, it is the figure of God the judge that dominates. What corresponds to him on the human side is a global attitude of repentance and penitence. As a result, the narration finds itself wholly impregnated by a condemnatory judgment, whose dialogical structure, however implicit it may be, is constantly taken for granted. The reading of this history works like a warning and an appeal.

As for those texts stemming from the prescriptive genre, they are either commandments, that is, simply prohibitions such as "you shall have no other god before me," "you shall not kill"—or complex laws of the form "if someone does this or that which is wrong, such and such a punishment is to be applied." In both cases, the meaning attached to the word that teaches, the Torah, is inseparable from the response of obedience or disobedience that goes along with it.

In turn, the condemnation pronounced by the prophets is God's response to the lack of human response that constitutes the apostasy, which is intermingled from the very beginning with the history of salvation, as we can see in the episode of the golden calf, which is so strongly denounced by the prophets of judgment and woe, from Amos and Hosea to Isaiah, Ezekiel, and Jeremiah. But this prophetic word itself calls for a response, whether it announces a judgment or makes a promise: a response of repentance to the judgment of condemnation, a response of confidence and hope turned toward the new future opening beyond all disaster through the promise of pardon and re-creation, a response that blesses a God who will again bless us after having saved and punished.

In this way, the human response to be found in the Hebrew Bible is surprisingly varied. The Psalms, in this regard, are the document where we find brought together, brought to language—to the language of prayer—and articulated according to canonical forms, innumerable nuances of this multiform response. The space of meaning thereby articulated unfolds between the poles of the lament and praise—the praise of one who has been delivered, pardoned, blessed with life, enjoying life in the community and the moments of joy that interrupt the bounds of a generally impoverished existence; the lament of one in peril who calls on a God who saves, the lament of the sinner faced with a God who judges, the lament of someone afflicted with misfortune who calls on God for deliverance and compassion. We should perhaps add memory to this pair of lament and praise, the well-known "remember" of Deuteronomy, which itself replies to a "forgetting" wherein the prophets discern both the cause and the effect of the great apostasy, that internal danger more harmful than any external danger, whether it be the captivity in Egypt or even exile in Babylon, to which responds the God who saves. Forgetting God expresses the dialogical structure of sin as such, which remains, even in its depths, an experience with God.

LIMIT EXPRESSIONS

As the last step in our exploration of the relations between the book and mirror, it remains to justify the second perspective opened by the polyphony of literary genres as naming God. The referent "God," I have said, is not only the index of the mutual belonging together of the originary forms of the discourse of faith, it is also the mark of their incompleteness.

What prevents our transforming the polyphonic naming of God into knowledge is that God is designated at the same time as the one who communicates and the one who withdraws. In this regard, the episode of the burning bush in Exod. 3:13-15 has a special importance. The tradition has rightly called this episode the revelation of the divine name. But this Name is precisely an unnamable name. Whereas outside of Israel, knowing the name of a god was to have power over him, the name confided to Moses is instead one that human beings cannot in fact pronounce, that is, submit to the mercy of their language. Moses asked, "'But if they [the children of Israel] ask what is his [the god of the ancestors] name, what shall I say to them?' God then said to Moses, 'I AM WHO I AM.' And he added, 'This is how you shall address the children of Israel, 'I AM' has sent me to you.'" The appellation Yahweh-He is-is not a name that defines but rather one that points to the gesture of deliverance. Indeed the text continues as follows. "God also said to Moses, 'Thus you shall say to the children of Israel: Yahweh, the God of your ancestors, the God of Abraham, the God of Isaac, and the God of Jacob, has sent me to you. This is the name I shall bear forever, with which all future generations shall call upon me.'" Far therefore from the declaration "I AM WHO I AM" authorizing a positive ontology capable of crowning the narrative naming along with all the other namings, it protects the secret of the for-itself of God. And this secret, in return, refers us to the narrative naming, signified by the names of Abraham, Isaac, and Jacob, and, by degrees, to the others as well.

The text of Exodus finds an echo in the New Testament. Northrop Frye would say that the declaration "I AM WHO I AM" is a type that finds its anti-type in an expression that the evangelists attach to Jesus' preaching, namely, the expression the kingdom of God. Here we have the limit expression of a reality that escapes all description. The kingdom is signified only by the kind of linguistic transgression that we see at work in the parables, in some proverbs, and in some of the paradoxes of eschatological discourse. This indirect character of naming God is particularly noticeable in the parables of Jesus. As tales, they are just small stories with a metaphorical import: The kingdom of God is like. . . . But it is not the parable that introduces into the plot an implausible, surprising, disproportionate, even scandalous aspect-a grain of wheat that produces a hundredfold, a mustard seed that grows into an immense tree, a worker hired at the last minute who is paid the same as the one who had worked all day, an invited guest who is thrown out because he was not wearing a wedding garment, and so on. Through this kind of extravagance, the literal sense is borne toward an ungraspable metaphorical meaning. The extraordinary breaks through the ordinary and points beyond the narrative.

The same transgression of meaning can be observed in the eschatological proclamations where Jesus makes use of forms of discourse common to his day regarding last things in order to subvert such calculations: "The coming of the Kingdom of God cannot be observed and no one can say, here it is, there, for the kingdom is among you." A similar transgression affects the ordinary sense of proverbs, which is to guide life in typical circumstances. Paradoxes and hyperbole dissuade the listener from forming a coherent project and from giving his existence some continuous totality. A paradox: whoever tries to save his life will lose it, and he who loses it will keep it. Hyperbole: if someone strikes you on the right cheek, turn your other to him as well. If someone wishes to bring you to trial and take your tunic, give him your cloak as well. If someone asks for one measure of grain, give him two. Just as the parable, submitted to the law of extravagance, makes the extraor-dinary stand forth within the ordinary, the proverb, submitted to a law of paradox and hyperbole, reorients by disorienting.

If now we bring together what has been called the unnamable Name indi-cated by the episode of the burning bush, and the kind of transgression of the usual forms in the parables through the concentrated use of extravagance, a new discursive category unfolds, that of limit expressions. This is not a supplementary form of discourse, even if the parable as such does constitute an autonomous mode of the expression of faith. It is rather a matter of an indication, a modification, that no doubt can affect all forms of discourse by a kind of passage to the limit. If the case of the parable is exemplary, it is because it brings together narrative structure, metaphoric process, and limit expression. In this way, it constitutes an abbreviated form of naming God. Through its narrative structure, it recalls the initial rootedness of the language of faith in narrative. Through its metaphoric process, it makes manifest the poetic character (in the sense already discussed) of the language of faith overall. Finally, in joining metaphor and limit expression, it provides the very matrix of theological language insofar as it conjoins analogy and negation in the way of eminence: God is like . . ., God is not . . .

This latter comment leads me to express a certain reserve regarding the use of the expression "Wholly Other" to designate God. It served as the emblem of what has been called "dialectical" theology. But, in one sense, it is not sufficiently dialectic, inasmuch as it does not take into account the pulsation among the manifestations of the Name by way of and through the polyphony of kinds of discourse (narratives, laws, prophecies, etc.) and the withdrawal of the Name beyond language, as is borne witness to by the episode of the burning bush and the extravagance of the parables. Yes, for Christians, this pulsation takes on different senses in the Old and the New Testaments, but without a real break between the two testaments. The Old Testament says one thing concerning God, that he is One. Nevertheless, this affirmation has two sides: that of the unnamable—I am the first and I am the last (Isa. 44:6), but also that of the polyphonic unity among all the names of God: God is the same, whether he saves, blesses, judges, takes pity, etc. The continuity between the two testaments is assured in this regard by the typological bond that holds them together. On the side of the manifestation of the name, the resurrection narrative echoes that of the exodus; on the side of the withdrawal of the name, the limit expression concerning the kingdom of God in the parables of Jesus responds and corresponds to what we can retrospectively call the limit expressions of the episode of the Burning Bush. The "newness" of the New Testament is, of course, undeniable. It is summed up in the function of the center that the poem of Christ confers on the poem of God. For the impulse toward the center is what, for a Christian reading of the Bible, is at work within the "imaginative unity" of the Bible. The New Testament identifies this center with the person of Christ.[10] Yet this identification in no way abolishes the dialectic of the manifestation and withdrawal of the name. Instead, it intensifies it, to the extent that the kingdom that Jesus preaches is the kingdom of God, the resurrection is an act of God, and the Jesus of history—as known by way of the Christ of faith—has been interpreted by the confessing community as "the man determined in his existence by the God that he proclaims," as Wolfhart Pannenberg has put it. It is this reference from Christ to God that intensifies without abolishing the dialectic of manifestation and withdrawal.

What results from this dialectic as regards the constitution of the responsive self? Readers of the Bible, I shall say again with Northrop Frye, are finally invited to identify themselves with the book that itself stems from the metaphorical identification between the Word of God and the person of Christ. Through this second-degree identification, readers are equally invited to "repeat"—in the Kierkegaardian sense of "repetition"—the pulsation between the withdrawal of the name and the quest for the center. What corresponds and conforms to the unity of God in the withdrawal of his name on the side of the self is the disappearance of the ego, the letting go of self: who seeks to save his life shall lose it and who loses it will keep it. As for the quest for a personal center, it can only reflect the always deferred "imaginative unity" conveyed by the withdrawal of the Name.

NOTES

1. "The Self in the Mirror of the Scriptures," in *The Whole and Divided Self: The Bible and Theological Anthropology*, ed. John McCarthy, trans. David Pellauer (New York: Crossroad, 1997), 201–20. Appearing by permission with the publisher.

2. See "The Summoned Subject in the School of the Narratives of the Prophetic Vocation," in Paul Ricoeur, *Figuring the Sacred: Religion, Narrative, and Imagination*, ed. Mark Wallace, trans. David Pellauer (Minneapolis: Fortress Press, 1995), 262–75.

3. I adopt the expression "responsive self" from H. Richard Niebuhr's *The Responsive Self* (New York: Harper & Row, 1963).

4. See Jean Greisch, *L'Age Hermeneutiquede la Raison* (Paris: Cerf, 1985).

5. See David Tracy, *The Analogical Imagination* (New York: Crossroad, 1981), esp. part 1, chaps. 3 and 4: "The Classic" and "Interpreting the Religious Classic."

6. Northrop Frye, *The Great Code: The Bible and Literature* (New York: Harcourt Brace Jovanovich, 1981).

7. In this respect, I believe that Frye is correct in pointing out that the Gospels themselves are more concerned about the correspondence of the events that they recount with this or that prophecy from the Old Testament than in showing the way to some verification of these events by methods external to the text. The Gospel writers seem to have taken particular care to cut off the referential points of their texts, to the point of sealing from within the testimony that they bear to the person of Jesus as the Christ (see Frye, *Great Code*, 4 2).

8. "Kerygma is a mode of rhetoric, though it is rhetoric of a special kind. It is like all rhetoric a mixture of the metaphorical and 'existential' or concerned but, unlike practically all other forms of rhetoric, it is not an argument disguised by figuration.

It is the vehicle of what is traditionally called revelation, a word I use because it is traditional and I can think of no better one" (ibid., 29).

9. Claus Westermann, *What Does the Old Testament Say About God?* (Atlanta: John Knox, 1979).

10. See Frye, *Great Code*, 76–77, 137–38.

Chapter 7

Fides Quaerens Intellectum

Biblical Antecedent?

Paul Ricoeur, Translated by David Pellauer

The Anselmian Argument can be seen as occupying a strategic position on the long trajectory that originates with the biblical scriptures, both Jewish and Christian, and continues through Kant's refutation of the "ontological proof" properly speaking, and, beyond Kant, to Nietzsche's proclamation of the "death of God."[1] According to this perspective, it is plausible to say that if we start from the endpoint we can gain not only an overarching view of the whole length of this trajectory but also we can grasp the dynamism that animated the kind of thinking produced along the way to its supposed exhaustion. On the other hand, it is perhaps by starting from this announced exhaustion that we may undertake a new thoughtful dialogue with the biblical sources situated before the argument itself. This is, in a broad sense, the working hypothesis that governs my inquiry.[2] This inquiry will not take up the second part of the trajectory I have referred to, the subsequent destiny of the Anselmian argument from Descartes to Kant, and from Kant to Nietzsche. Instead, I shall limit myself to the biblical sources of the Anselmian argument. However, I take it for granted that, in this very limited investigation, we shall never lose sight of the subsequent destiny of this argument, which, in bringing its descendants to ruin, may have opened the way to new interpretations buried in what had been their provenance.

THE NAMING OF GOD ACCORDING TO SAINT ANSELM

Three features of Anselm's argument refer us back to its Hebraic sources. The first one has to do with the dimension of invocation that frames his argument. We read in chapter II of the Proslogion:

And so, Lord, do thou, who dost give understanding to faith, give me, so far as thou knowest it to be profitable, to understand [ut. . .intelligam] that thou art as we believe; and that thou art that which we believe. And, indeed, we believe that thou art a being than which nothing greater can be conceived [credimus te esse aliquid quo nihil maius cogitari potest].[3]

Both the French and the English translations of this invocation have a "thou" five times where in the Latin text it only appears once explicitly, but where it is implied in the four verbs in the second person, as well as in the vocative domine. We may say without fear that the argument will become a proof when it will have broken its ties to this invocation that contains it. Yet it is also by way of this invocation that this argument remains attached to biblical faith, whose energy it prolongs. Indeed, the invocation consists in asking for an understanding of faith, which in advance recognizes itself to be placed under the sign of a gift.

Second feature: it is expected that this understanding will "recognize" if we follow the apt French translation of intelligere by Michel Corbin-what is already implicit in faith.[4] The sought for argument, despite the independence that will be claimed for it, thus remains bound to the contents of faith by a relation that we may call one of approximation. What is it a question of recognizing? This: "that thou art as we believe; and that thou art that which we believe." The recognition (or approximation) at issue here bears directly on being, but under the guise of a verb conjugated in the second person, and thus in harmony with the thou of the invocation. Hence, we can suspect a second time that the argument will become a proof when the verb "being," released from the second person, will be turned into a substantialized infinitive, wholly neutral as regards grammatical persons. In this way it will be prepared for all the reinterpretations inspired by Greek ontology, which is not aware of the "thou art."

Third feature: the understanding of faith, as recognition and approximation, becomes an argument, hence a movement of thinking aimed at the autonomy of a proof, once the equation is posited between the name called upon-God-bound to the invocation, and a predicated name, where the someone becomes something: "that thou art that which [aliquid], etc." Anselm suggests that this passage from someone to something is in some way already the object of faith ("we believe that. . .") and that the understanding of faith consists in unfolding this nexus of someone and something; in recognizing it, but in such a way that recognition becomes by itself a proof. Do we not read in the Preface:

I began to ask myself whether there might be found a single argument which would require no other for its proof [ad se probandum] than itself alone; and alone would suffice to demonstrate [et solum ad astruendum] that God truly exists [quia deus here est].[5]

It is in this sense that Anselm's argument constitutes a strategic point along the trajectory referred to earlier. On the one hand, as contained in the invocation, it remains dependent; on the other hand, as aiming at autonomy ("a single argument which would require no other for its proof"), it leaves the orbit of the invocation and undertakes a solitary course, which will be precisely that of "proofs for the existence of God" by reason alone. How are we to account for this over-determination of an argument that presents itself as both the recognition of a content of the faith that precedes it (and which in a way constitutes its preunderstanding) and as a proof sufficient to itself alone?

Two answers can be invoked here: the continuity presumed by the first status conferred on the argument is made possible by a prior conceptual reflection and analysis that means we are not dealing here with a bare faith, if I may put it this way, that reason undertakes to understand, to recognize, but with an already interpreted faith, already bearing rational significations. What then would understanding prove and demonstrate? Not just that "God truly exists," but also that he "is a supreme [summum] Good requiring nothing else, which all other things require for their existence and well-being; and whatever we believe regarding the divine Being."[6] What is "believed" has already to a significant degree been thought about, and this has happened following a certain conceptual tradition that is indicated by the four segments of what is predicated of God: supreme good, having need of no other, which all other things require for their being, and for their well-being. In short, Anselm's argument does not connect directly back to biblical faith. It draws upon a secular basis of thought, which had up to that time remained within the bounds of faith, but which, for the first time, seeks to be autonomous, without for all that denying its dependence on the invocation that asks to receive such understanding, therefore such autonomy, as a gift.[7]

Here is where the continuity between faith and the understanding of faith is compensated for by an interruptive effect produced by the fool who says in his heart "there is no God" (Ps. 14:1, 53:1, Rom. 3:10-12). This interruptive effect is so powerful that it motivates the dialogue of the believer with himself, when he asks whether, like every sinner, he has not "lost that for which he was made."[8]

Yet despite this irruption of someone who is a stranger to faith, a minimal understanding with him is presupposed, namely: "this very fool, when he hears of this being of which I speak—a being than which nothing greater can be conceived—understands [intelligit] what he hears, and what he understands is in his understanding; although he does not understand [intelligit] it to exist."[9] It is the discourse addressed to the fool that calls for the signification "a being than which nothing greater can be conceived" to be isolated twice over: from the invocation, on the one hand, and from the affirmation of existence, on the other. Hence it will be a question for Anselm if we return to a point before his argumentative apparatus we do not reach a point where invocation and affirmation of existence are inseparable. Yet the fool is there constraining him to carry to the noetic plane the predicative name that faith confesses, and which will henceforth be posited apart from any connection to the invoked Thou and the sought for actuality: "for, it is one thing for an object to be in the understanding, and another to understand that the object exists."[10] Here is the point from which the argument that God cannot be conceived not to exist (Chap. III) unfolds. This argument consists in demonstrating that this separating of the noetic sense from existence is not thinkable. It puts back together what the fool's discourse had claimed to set apart. This is what we read at the end of Proslogion IV: "For, God is that than which a greater cannot be conceived. And he who thoroughly understands this, assuredly understands that this being so truly exists, that not even in concept can it be non-existent. Therefore, he who understands that God so exists, cannot conceive that he does not exist." The predicative name (that than which nothing greater can be conceived) has again become a proper name. God, that is, the one who is invoked, and the subject and predicate are. once again fused. The argument consists, therefore, in reuniting what was already united for faith, and that the fool's discourse had claimed to dissociate, at the price of an absurdity. If faith had united invocation, noetic denomination, and existence, the argument would have nothing to "recognize." But it is the fool who, in dissociating the sequence, returns its plenitude of meaning to God's name. Thus, in his way, it is the fool who makes the argument necessary,[11] but within the limits of an argument by reductio ad absurdum that, unlike the ontological proof, lacks its own compelling force.

What follows, especially the end of the Proslogion, confirms this. Chapters V to XII enrich the quid and quad of the argument, in terms of the dimensions of a faith that has already been identified and interpreted. "What are thou, then, Lord God, than whom nothing greater can be conceived?" (Chap. V). The answer is to be found in chapter XII: "But undoubtedly, whatever thou art, thou art through nothing else than thyself. Therefore, thou art the very life whereby thou livest; and the wisdom wherewith thou art wise; and the very goodness whereby thou art good to the righteous and the wicked; and so of other like attributes." What is pronounced here is the identity of the subject (thou) and the predicates designating those goods, intended by human desire but apprehended in their supereminence. This identification of subject and predicate provides the sense of the proposition "whatever thou art, thou art through nothing else than thyself." At this stage, the understanding that sets into play the conceptual difference between "being through oneself" and "being through another thing" cannot be discerned from the invocation. It is in this sense that it is the recognition of the contents of faith. And it is from this enrichment that follows what Corbin calls the second name: "a being greater than· can be conceived." Now the naming of God implies the negation by transcendence of every desired good, which beings who are not God have only through some other thing

> "Hast thou found what thou didst seek, my soul? Thou has found him to be a being which is the highest of all beings [eum esse quiddam summum omnium], a being than which nothing better [quo nihil melius] can be conceived; that this being is life itself, light, wisdom, goodness, eternal blessedness and blessed eternity; and that it is everywhere and always."[12]

What does this second name add to the first name? Essentially, the relation to the desire that underlies the dynamic of seeking and finding. And this desire has as its goal the goods here enumerated (life, light, etc.). The second name designates what is excessive in relation to what is desirable, just as the first name designated what is excessive in relation to what is thinkable. However, to the extent that thinking is seeking, hence desire, the second name envelops the first name. And, with this, we understand retrospectively how the argument in chapters II and IV works. It is limited to denying that what faith takes as united can be dissociated: thou, the supereminent goods, existence. The argument creates nothing; it denies that the separation of the invoked God and the predicates that make up the predicative name, united to the divine thou, is thinkable.

Hence we must next seek the biblical source for this work of naming.

Two questions will govern what I shall call our step backward: (1) What, in the proclamation of the name, holds together (a) the invocation of the divine thou, (b) naming properly speaking (that is, the predicative assertion of those eminent qualities capable of being taken for the antecedent of the quo nihil majus of the first name and the quo nihil melius of the second name cogitari potest), and (c) the assertion of existence? (2) What, in human desire, in human thought, in short, in the quest that joins desire and thinking, provides an audience for the word of the fool who "says in his heart, there is no God"? In other words, what dynamism drives the invocation to the argument?

THE BIBLICAL SOURCE

God's Self-Presentation

In the faith of the Hebrew Bible, invocation, naming, and the assertion of existence are in principle inseparable. This is due to the fact that in the thought world and discourse of the Hebrew Bible, the invocation is itself preceded by what exegesis characterizes as God's self-presentation, to which the human invocation responds. A divine "I" announces himself, rendering unnecessary any invocation, naming, or assertion of existence.

From Self-Presentation to Invocation

Let us begin with the briefest of such instances of God's self-presentation, Leviticus 18:5 and 21: "I [am] Jahweh." According to Zimmerli, this formula expresses the full presence in person of Jahweh in his word.[13] In relation to the commandments that the repeated formula frames, it functions first as an authorization, then as a signature. This formula is the shortest one we can conceive. Yet, at the same time that its plenitude lies in its very brevity, it calls for, following another remark of Zimmerli, "development and a subsequent explication." Here is an initial development. In the same context we read: "I [am] Jahweh, your God" (or: "me Jahweh I [am] your God"). In presenting himself, Jahweh bears witness to himself at the same time as the object of a certain form of human recognition. The possessive form—your God, my God—recalls that Jahweh never presented himself to Israel in any other way than as the God of his people. The covenant, about which I shall have more to say below, is thereby associated with God's very name. And from this initial development comes the opening of our formula to a process of explication that is principally narrative and prescriptive in form. "It is me Jahweh, your God, who brought you out of the house of Egypt, out of the house of slavery. You shall have no other gods besides me" (Exod. 20:2-3). Then follows the Decalogue. The relative narrative "me . . . who brought you" followed by the primary commandment makes for a predicative assertion immediately joined to the self-presentation. As for the exclusive demand inscribed in the first commandment, it too goes as one with this initial development of the "I [am] Jahweh" in the clause "your God."[14] The relative narrative includes in the Name the whole narrative of the Exodus, at the same time that the great commandment links the whole Decalogue to this Name. Thus, on the basis of "I [am] Jahweh," the initiative belongs to the "I" who announces himself as the source of history and ethics. The invocation that responds to him comes second.

From Invocation to Naming

The narrative clause and what we can call the legislative clause, which unfold the "I [am] Jahweh," constitute in turn the core of the naming of God. Let us understand here by naming the attribution of a predicate having the value of a proper name. We will speak of predicative naming in order to distinguish it from what we can call appellative naming (El Shadda, YHWH). Anselm's naming follows from this predicative naming, proper to the Hebrew Bible. For him, as in the Bible, the predicative naming adheres at this point to the appellative naming, in that it calls upon the same object in its invocation: "Thou who . . . " Here then we have the seed for the Anselmian name—as name one or name two—in the biblical domain.

For the Hebrew Bible, the name/predicate is above all else the Unique One. The key text here is the one known, in Hebraic literature, under the name of the shema (shema means: Listen! in the imperative mode): "Hear, O Israel: Jahweh our God [is] the one Jahweh" (Deut. 6:4). In this text, the proclamation in the third person-Jahweh [is]-is equivalent to the self-presentation we have been discussing.[15] This declaration of oneness is immediately followed by the great commandment that, here again, is literally one with it: "You shall love Jahweh your God with all your heart, with all your soul, and with all your might." Throughout something exclusive is attested to: just as the one Jahweh excludes the other gods, a total love excludes any sharing with other objects of love.[16] We may disagree about whether existence is refused to other gods by this proclamation of oneness. In fact, the accent is not on the ontological status of idols, but on the undivided devotion due to Jahweh. Indeed, we need to take the entire sequence of Deuteronomy 6:4-19 as a whole: keep these words "engraved in your heart, "recite them to your children," remember the tradition of the Exodus ("take care that you do not forget. . ."), remain confident in the promise that has no guarantee. The whole counts as a (predicative) naming of God.[17] This naming, like God's self-presentation, is indivisibly ethical ("you shall love . . .") and narrative ("remember . . ."). In this sense, it unfolds predicatively the confession of the divine oneness that, itself, responds to the call "Hear, O Israel."

This then is the distant source of the Name according to Anselm: "than which nothing greater. . ." "than which nothing better . . . ." In effect, the ethical and narrative unfolding of the confession of oneness can be taken as the seed for the declaration of supereminence attested to by the Name according to Anselm. But this declaration remains without a guarantee. We shall ask below whether it leaves a place for something like an argument by means of which the understanding adds the surety of its "recognition." Before doing so, however, let us continue our investigation into the biblical sources.

From Naming to the Attestation of Existence

The third step is the one most filled with obstacles. It has to do with the existential import of invocation and of naming. Do we find on the biblical plane any indication that an ontological problematic, in our sense, as heirs of the Greeks, belongs to the development of the appellative and the predicative name? The texts we have so far considered " I [am] Jahweh" and "Hear, O Israel, your God [is] One" do not allow us to decide this question, inasmuch as Hebrew does not have a copula form for being, and therefore does not permit the shift from being as copula to being taken absolutely. At most, we can say that the self-presentation of God does not allow us to dissociate, as Anselm proposes to his antagonist, the fool, the noetic sense, included in the naming, from its existential sense, become extra-noetic. In this regard, we can risk saying that the self-presentation is equivalent to a self-monstration.

And the faithful respond to this by an invocation that, on its side, allows for no slippage between what would be merely thought and what is attested as truly existing. The question simply does not arise. Thus, we have seen the shema proclaiming the oneness of God unfolding in an ethical-narrative dimension. This unfolding stands for an attestation of existence in the applicable sense.

Indeed, the evocation of past deliverances, in Deuteronomy 6:4-19, gives rise to, on the side of the receiver of the message, an assumed, faultless belief in the past actuality of those events that the faithful are enjoined to remember. The ethical efficacy of the commandment, joined to the power of the injunction "Hear, O Israel," is no less than what we might call the narrative efficacy from which it is inseparable. Still, in the absence of any critical reflection on the truth of the past and on the authority of the supreme legislator, the ontological question simply does not arise as a critical question.

Someone may object to these reticent comments that the Hebrew Bible includes at least one assertion about the being of God that cannot be overlooked. This assertion, of course, is the one found in Exod. 3:14, which contains the verb being two times: eyer asher eyeh. The Septuagint translates this enigmatic formula by ego eimi ho on; the Vulgate has ego sum qui sum; and in French one would like to use je suis celui qui suis [I am the one who am], but the grammar imposes je suis celui qui est [I am the one who is]. To this affirmation of exclusive identity seems to be joined that of a plenitude of identity with an ontological overtone. Is not a bridge thereby set up between the language of faith and that of Greek philosophy, authorizing Etienne Gilson, for example, to speak in this regard of a "biblical metaphysics?"[18] That the verb being is obstinately used twice in the first person in 3:14, then a third time in the continuation of this text, which I shall consider below in terms of its literary unity, should place on guard against too rapid an assimilation of the Hebrew "I am" and the Greek *einai*. In this regard, Anselm still has one foot in the biblical camp, inasmuch as he preserves the second person in an affirmation that is also an invocation: "we believe that thou art a being than which nothing greater can be conceived." That, in Exodus 3:14, the verb is conjugated in the first person, to the exclusion of any slippage from the "I am" to a substantialized infinitive "being," invites us to ask if the verb being, extracted from the "I am," has the same sense as the one presupposed by the Anselmian argument and already filtered through a long onto-theological tradition, where the Hebrew origin had already been interpreted in terms of the Greek ontology of being.

In order to reply to this perplexity, it is important, following most Old Testament exegeses,[19] to replace the famous formula in the context from which it is too readily detached, namely, the narrative of the call of Moses (Exod. 3:1-4:7).[20]

This narrative is itself preceded by the vision of the burning bush from which comes God's call, "Moses, Moses, "to which Moses replies, "here I am." This response of Moses already stands as the recognition of a presence that is all the more imperious in that it is marked by the "great spectacle" (3:3) of the burning bush that is not consumed. The history of his call could end there. But this is not the case. Called, Moses objects to his calling five times. A first time: "who am I to. . . " And God replies, "I will be with you." Is not this reassurance sufficient? No. Moses again objects: "But if [the children of Israel] ask what is his name [the name of the God of the fathers who sends the prophet], what will I answer them?" It is to this objection that the famous *eyeh asher eyeh* replies. The place of the "I am the one who am" (or "who is") is therefore in no way immaterial if we are to make sense of this formula. It is important that the Revelation of the Name—which is the way this fragment is usually referred to—replies to an objection that itself is one segment in a call narrative.

In this regard, what follows is not less important than what had preceded it. Indeed, it is surprising to see that the "I am" becomes the subject of the verb that in fact utters the sending of Moses: "Thus you shall address yourself to the children of Israel: 'I am has sent me to you.'" The predicative name "I am" has become an appellative name. This is not all. A bit further on, the name Jahweh is placed in the same grammatical position as the third "I am": "you shall speak thus to the children of Israel: Jahweh, the God of your fathers . . . has sent me to you. This is the name I shall bear forever, by which you will call on me in future generations." Here two features cannot be neglected. First, the fact that the "I am the one who am" (or "who is") is part of the response to an objection on the part of the called prophet. Next, the fact that the third "I am," set in the subject position, hence as an appellative name, leads toward the ultimate appellation, the tetragrammon YHWH.[21]

Certainly, the narrative framing of the "I am the one who am" does not attenuate the force belonging to this formula, concerning which we can legitimately affirm that it exceeds the framework of the game of question and answer that serves in a way as the setting for this jewel. Yet this very excess suggests that the redoubled (even tripled) *eyeh* creates an exceptional hermeneutic situation, namely, the opening to a plurality of interpretations of the verb, being, itself. Precisely because the formula exceeds its context, its meaning becomes inseparable from its *Wirkungsgeschichte,* its history of effects, in the sense of effects of reading. In this regard, the Aristotelian-Thomistic interpretation is just one of these interpretations, which has determined Western metaphysics. And Anselm's argument can be seen as one marker along the way of this interpretation. But if, as I suggested in the introduction to this chapter, we consider the whole trajectory for which the ontological argument, from Descartes to Kant, is just one segment, and if we follow this trajectory up to the anti-kerygma of Nietzsche: "God is dead," then we can ask if other interpretive possibilities have not been covered over by the one that triumphed, beginning with the Septuagint translation, where the second *eyeh,* translated as *ho on,* is divested of the first person formulation that it has in common with the first *eyeh,* the redoubling of the "I am" engendering a kind of indeterminate proposition. This is why we may expect from a hermeneutics that stays closer to the text and to its framework, not some lost univocity which perhaps never existed, but precisely a plurivocity; namely, an indetermination that gives the formula the shock value of an enigma. In this regard, attempted alternative translations are especially interesting. I would like to recall that of Buber and Rosenzweig, which substitutes *Werden* (becoming) for *Sein* (being). But perhaps interpretation has to go beyond a simple word by word translation and needs to explore other semantic fields; that of efficacy, for example. (Thus, in German *Wirksamkeit* remains related to *Wirklichkeit,* which preserves the root *wirken,* to work, to operate, to be active. In this way, we take into account the active, operative aspect of the divine presence.) Or perhaps that of fidelity, implied in the structure of the covenant, which I shall discuss below. In any case, what was said earlier about the connection between the divine self-presentation and the memory of past liberations and a firm confidence in new, as yet unannounced deliverances suggests this connection between efficacy and fidelity.

What .is essential is: (1) not to base the Hebrew "I am" on a signification of *being* that would oppose it to mere thinking, to subjective cognition. There is no need to fuse essence and existence, for the distinction between them is foreign to Hebrew "thinking." (2) To preserve a plurivocity of the verb that we translate, for lack of anything better, by "is." (3) To hold in reserve the hypothesis that the response, concerning which we have said that it exceeds the question and the whole situation constituted by a call narrative, is not after all a response, but rather a way of *retreat* into the incognito, something that would exile the so-called response into something outside the text. Between the guarantee of the sending, which encloses the formula within the call narrative, and the dissimulation of the Name, which marks the excess of the response in relation to its narrative framework, we perhaps need not choose, but rather hold these two limit-interpretations as the two extremities of the space of variation offered to the hermeneutics of the divine Name.[22]

Another way of marking the divergence between the Hebrew "I am" and the Greek "being" would be to emphasize the ·more ethical than ontological function of the revelation of the Name. From this point of view, we must not lose sight of the quite specific function that the revelation of the Name exercises in the call narrative, namely, that of guaranteeing Moses's mission. Even if, once again, the formula goes beyond this function, which is still tributary to the narrative framework, it remains that this formula is a mandate that designates itself as existing, that is, as efficacious. It would then be the objection that provides the occasion for this response that holds the metaphysics of the Name within the ethical orbit of the mandate. It is fundamentally a question of removing the ambiguity that weighs on the mission (true or false prophet?) through a formula whose existential charge cannot be denied, but whose function as authenticating is even more obvious. The reality of God sets its seal of authenticity on Moses's mission. Even if we insist on the excess of meaning in this formula in relation to its function within the framework of the prophetic mission, we must say not only that the Greek "being" can be said in different ways, but also that there exists a non-Greek way of saying it, even several such ways that remain to be explored beyond any alleged "end of metaphysics." As Brevard Childs puts it, we must not break the connection between "self-disclosure" and a "call for commitment." Therefore we have to maintain the "I am who am" (or "who is") between two limits: a simple expansion of the formulas to authenticate the mandate in the call narratives, and the opening through the verb "being" of a space of plurivocity other than the one explored by the Greeks, culminating in the divine incognito that stands over against the authentifying function.[23]

What are we to conclude if not that the conjunction with Greek ontology is a part of the history of the reading of Exodus 3:14, and that it is the totality of the destiny of this reading that today is presented to our critical evaluation?

THE BIBLICAL SOURCE

Self-Presentation and Contestation

Now we come to the other side of the problem formulated at the end of my brief comments on the Anselmian argument. What, in biblical faith, might tilt the invocation toward an argument capable of claiming its autonomy in relation to this faith that it is supposed to "recognize," and thereby to set itself up as a proof that finds its demonstrative force within itself?

At first glance, the self-presentation of God seems to cut short any such claim to autonomy. That God only reveals himself *in* calling, in recalling his past accompanying of his people, in signing his commandments with his Name, would seem to leave no place for a slippage at the heart of the self-presentation that is in the same movement a self-attestation.

However, this is not the case if we consider the faith of the Old Testament. Paradoxically, it is the self-presentation as such that calls for a human complement capable of covering the whole range that runs from invocation to contestation.

A human complement: the Hebrew Bible knows nothing of a God in and for himself. It only knows a God encountering human beings and even creation as a whole. The biblical God, as many have emphasized, is a relational God, which will justify Luther's subsequent thesis that the object of theology is not God, but God and humanity. The inclusion of humanity in God's self-presentation was already apparent in the first formula we have considered: "I am Jahweh" is immediately developed as "I am Jahweh, your God" (or "me Jahweh am your God").[24] God allows himself to be apprehended only as the God of his people, and these people are known to God only as the people of God. The narrative clause and the ethical clause of what I have called the predicative naming of God bring the human component even closer to the God's self-presentation.

The expected response on the side of this human component is surely the invocation. The "thou" of invocation is the only response to the "I" of self-presentation, the "thou" in which we have recognized the *incipit* of the Anselmian argument. However this responsive invocation is just the limit form of a dramatic relation that the Hebrew Bible explores in all its potentialities. The narrative clause, which prolongs the "I am Jahweh, your God," sums up a history of deliverance that is not stripped of suffering, complaints, even of rebellion. In this regard, Robert Alter suggests that the biblical narrative as a whole proceeds from the confrontation between a divine, ineluctable plan and a human reluctance that paradoxically temporalizes it.[25] And what does the imperative clause say? Would there be any sense in proscribing false gods and false cults if the spontaneous movement of the heart and the will were not the idolatry that Amos and Hosea call "prostitution" and that the Deuteronomic chroniclers denounce as an "abomination?"

The Hebrews have an expression to convey the God/humanity relation into which the whole span of human replies, running from invocation to confrontation, is inscribed. This relation is the covenant, for which many exegetes find an antecedent, even a model, in the Hittite treaties between a suzerain and a vassal.[26] Two points here are important for our discussion. If the covenant stabilizes the bipolar relation constitutive of Israel's faith, it remains an asymmetric relation, in which the suzerain declares his sovereignty even while granting his protection' whereas the submissive, yet contracting party promises obedience. If it is true that the covenant, when compared to the unequal Hittite type of treaties, is far from an instance of simple capitulation, it is also true that it includes resources for protest, even for accusation, hence a power of reply inscribed in the very asymmetry of the relationship. These seeds of discordance are expressed in the theme of the trial that God holds of humanity, especially through the mouths of the prophets, but they are expressed as well in the trial humanity holds of God, a trial that culminates in the book of Job. Yes, God is on trial by his people and they are on trial by God. The questioning that will subsequently serve as the antecedents for the call for intelligibility inscribed in the Anselmian *fides quaerens intellectum* can be derived from this contestation implicitly in the covenantal relation.

The "Objection" to the Call

We can find a symptom of this quarrel with God already in the narrative of the call of Moses. This symptom is Moses's objection to his call, to which responds precisely the redoubled "I am." The narrative in Exodus 3–4 takes care to dramatize this objection in a five-stage crescendo, which cannot be reduced to the effects of the narrative art, however much this text constitutes an admirable example of the biblical art of narration.[27] Here we find all the ingredients for a dissociation in the relationship between the sender and the one sent and, in the background, between the self-presentation and the obedient response.

The Lamentation

The turning point in the curve outlined in the objection, ending in the words of the fool to which Anselm undertakes to reply, is constituted by the lament that in the psalms—a common treasure of the Jewish and Christian communities—constitutes the opposite pole of the song of praise.

We may see in this pair-lamentation/song of praise-the most basic dialecticalization of the invocation. For the lamentation is still, or also, an invocation: "how long O Lord!" An elementary logic might incline us to consider the song of praise as the only legitimate response called for by God's self-presentation. We might also be tempted to take recalcitrance, that is, sin, as the only dissonance in the bipolar relationship between God and humanity. However, the lament gives a voice to one who has undergone evil that is not reducible to the simple confession of evil committed, that is, to the language of penitence.

In fact, evil as undergone brings into play another dimension than that of the human historical condition, especially if this is reduced, wrongly, to just the "history of salvation" (the well-known *Heilsgeschichte* of exegesis and Old Testament theology). This other dimension is that of creation considered on a cosmic scale. The lament, in effect, is the cry that expresses the rending that affects every part of the creature as such, beyond the person of the covenant, beyond that of history, beyond even that of the *Heilsgeschichte*.

·What do we gain by referring at this point to the lament of the creature? This: I said above that the biblical God is a relational God. Now the first relation-at least the one that the biblical canon puts at the head of the scriptures-is that of creation: "In the beginning God created . . ." This relation is first to the extent that the Bible ignores everything that might apply to a time before creation and, to this extent, every assertion about God considered in isolation. (Given the interpretation we have considered so far, this comment even holds for the "I am the one who is.") The Bible knows God only as related to his people, to humanity, to the whole of creation.[28]

The relation of creation considered in itself includes a dissonant element in principle that we may sum up as the persistence of evil. A speculative theology, claiming to speak of God in himself, "before" or "apart" from creation, may delay the confrontation with the problem posed by the persistence of evil and turn it into a separated chapter from any consideration of the divine perfections. A relational approach, on the contrary, has to think together and at the same time of creation and the persistence of evil.[29]

We can quickly see the consequences of this state of affairs for our inquiry concerning the biblical antecedents of Anselm's argument. Anselm could focus his argument on the supereminent aspects of God taken as God. Biblical humanity, which can only be considered in terms of a relational schema, whether it is a question of the history of salvation or of the history of creation, cannot adjourn to some later stage its discourse on the problem of evil. Here the question of omnipotence finds itself posed simultaneously with the "I am the one who is."

It may be objected that the so-called priestly narrative of creation, which we read in Genesis 1, culminates in the contemplation of divine response, after God has set like a seal on creation the "yes" of approbation expressed in the admirable "God saw everything he had made and it was good" (Gen. 1:13). How, then, can there be any basis for complaint in creation, apart from humanity's "subsequent" sin? Is there anything other than evil committed? And is not evil undergone just retribution for evil committed? Far from being alien to our investigation, this question is related to whether the predicative name of God can be stated as "perfect being," as will be the case with Descartes, or as "greater than can be conceived," as in Anselm's second name. It is easy to see that it is the argument in its claim to the status of being a proof that is at issue, in its very starting point. The fragility of what will become the ontological argument does not lie perhaps only in the "deduction" of existence from essence, but in the equation between God and the highest good, which decides the divine nature, the predicative name of God. If it is true that the authors of the creation narratives are unaware of the concept of creation *ex nihilo.* Indeed, if they preserve, in their admiration for sovereignty, fear and trembling in the face of a drama, a combat, that not only has always had chaos as its enemy, but which is never done with its adverse forces, then the Old Testament discourse on creation throws up a positive obstacle to the idea of a perfect being, and even to that of a unique locus of highest goods.

That the lament of the creature is organically part of the relational God/ creature structure can be read even in the biblical creation narratives. Even in its mildest form, the one we read in the first chapter of Genesis (and that the scribes responsible for the establishment of the canon meant to honor by putting there), creation is a drama where the initial vulnerability to chaos allows us to anticipate the fragility of the created order. So the glory of creation and lamentation in the face of the persistence of evil go together throughout the Hebrew Bible.[30] It is easy to understand why. It is during periods of distress, principally during the time of the exile, that the hope for return and for restoration finds a foundation in creation *in illo tempora,* as a victory over adverse forces. The celebration of victory and the experience of the violence of history constitute the two sides of a single confession of faith. In this sense, the lamentation is the existential context for recalling the mythic victory. An abyss exists that will never be closed between the liturgical affirmation of the sovereignty of God and the everyday experience of the persistence of evil. The psalms bear witness to this, where the faithful one naively recalls God to remember his victories and his ancient promises (Ps. 74). The sovereignty of God is thus the immemorial recall of an "ancient" creation, when it is not reported as a future beyond human mastery, thanks to the eschatological representation of a final, complete victory (as can already be seen in the little Apocalypse in Isaiah 25, called the "messianic banquet"). Affliction can be taken to be transitory, nonetheless it occupies the whole field of "historical" experience. We cannot overemphasize therefore the unmediated juxtaposition, in the Hebrew Bible, of the liturgical and hymnic affirmation of the omnipotence of God and the confession of the persistence of evil, a confession that is itself raised to the lyrical plane of the lamentation. The relation of the full sovereignty of God to the end of time only underscores the dissonance between the proclamation of omnipotence and the confession of the "terror of history." It is this counterpoint, in the form of a dialectic without resolution, that prevents the establishment of the equation of the God of Abraham, Isaac, and Jacob with the idea of perfection assumed by the Anselmian argument, and, later, by the different variations of the ontological argument. To do so we would have to be able to think God in himself, hence to subtract him from the drama of creation, which continues to be confronted with the confession of the persistence of evil. The biblical God cannot be thought apart from the work by which he brings about a fragile order, centered on a habitable earth, itself submitted to human governance prey to malfeasance and unjust suffering. Everything happens as if God were not yet God.

Contestation

At the other extremity of the range of human replies that the structure of the covenant makes possible appears that contestation that adjoins without losing itself in the words of the fool who says in his heart: "no, there is no God."[31]

Contestation indicates the nonservile character of the consent of the human party in the great covenant between God, his people, humanity, and creation. It takes on several different guises in the Hebrew Bible. The prophet's objection to the call that convokes him is already an attenuated form. The lamentation, in turn, sometimes rises to the level of a reproach, as when the

complainant addresses himself to Jahweh as to a forgetful God, even a sleep-
ing God-a complaint that many of those deported to Babylon and many of the
conquered who remained during the time of the exile could not avoid joining
to their cries of distress: "How long Lord. . . wake up! Wake up, as in past
generations" (Isa. 51:9).

A further step along the pathway of contestation is taken when a figure
debates with God, even defies God, as we find illustrated in the supplication
that Abraham addresses to God who is about to destroy Sodom and Gomorrah: "Abraham stood again before Jahweh. He drew near and said, are you
really going to sweep away the righteous along with the sinner? Suppose
there are fifty righteous in the city. Are you really going to destroy them and
will you not pardon the city for the fifty righteous who are within it? Far be
it from you to do such a thing! To slay the righteous along with the sinner, so
that the righteous will be treated like the sinner. Far be it from you! Will the
judge of all the earth not do what is just?" (Gen. 18:23-25).[32] Everything takes
place as though Abraham challenges God to act according to the same model
of justice that God imposes on humans. We may even say that Abraham
argues with God, as if the future theological debate wherein the unlimited
freedom of God as regards every logical and ethical norm is opposed to the
identification of God and the norms he cannot transgress were already laid out
by this sequence. The Bible does not formulate this debate in abstract terms.
Instead, it takes its stand at the heart of a dramatic dialogue between God and
a human being where this human being questions God, to the point of calling
him into question.[33]

It is against this background that we can situate the book of Job, where
obedience, the independence of critical judgment, and the sovereignty of God
clash without any conceptual resolution. This is not the place to examine this
book in detail. I shall limit myself to the aspect of inconclusive dialectic that,
in my opinion, prevents us from thinking of God apart from his twofold relation with humanity and with the whole of creation. The framework for the
"testing," according to the terms of the prologue, is burst apart by the body
of the poem—chapters 3–37 are undoubtedly of a literary origin distinct from
the Prologue to which we find them attached. The controversy here is pushed
to the point of accusing an unjust and cruel God. In demolishing the ideology
of retribution, for which every evil undergone is the punishment for some
evil committed, Job lays bare the scandal of unjust suffering, without which
it is not possible to think about God, so long as we preserve the relational
structure that binds together God, humanity, and the world, as seems to be
the case throughout the Hebrew Bible. In this sense, it has been said that the
book of Job marks the extreme point of the crisis of the covenant. Hence it is
stupefying to hear Jahweh, in the prose epilogue to the book, declare that Job
alone has "spoken rightly" of God (Job 42:7). The difficulty for the exegete is

to perceive the unity of meaning that holds the text in its final state together. In chapters 38–41, God, speaking from the depths of the whirlwind, does not respond to the accusation of injustice, but instead sets the totality of human experience—including unjust suffering and no doubt the legitimate protest of the suffering righteous—within the vast framework of a repetition of the cosmogony. "Where were you when I laid the foundations of the world?" (38:23-7). God, it almost seems, is not responding here to the Job of the Prologue, but to a Prometheus who dissimulates his *hubris* in his accusation and his insolence of comparing himself to God.[34] God does not answer the man, he discomfits him. It is the Abraham of the binding of Isaac more than the Abraham who pleads for the remaining righteous of Sodom and Gomorrah who can be heard in the final words of the conquered hero:

> And Jahweh called to Job and said to him: Will the adversary of Shaddai yield? Is the one who censors God going to reply? and Job answered Jahweh: I have spoken thoughtlessly; what will I answer you? Instead I cover my mouth with my hand. I spoke once . . . I shall not do so again; twice . . . I shall add nothing. (50:1-5)[35]

To the withdrawal of God into the unfathomable secret of the creator in majesty corresponds the withdrawal of Job into the silence of the non-question: "Thus I take back my words, I repent with dust and ashes" (42:6). In this double withdrawal, the human being's complaint seems lost from view, even forgotten.

It was necessary no doubt to go so far as Job's contestation, and even more so up to its ambiguous denouement, to perceive the obstacle that a fundamentally relational approach, where not only is God never named in himself and for himself, but where he always appears as the *other* of a dramatic confrontation, constitutes in relation to a predicative naming of God, where the only things stated are the supereminent predicates. The main mediation that the Hebrew Bible proposes, then, is not to be sought on the side of Wisdom, which, through the mouth of Job, "confuses the counsels [of Jahweh] by meaningless proposals" (42:3), as if the point of wisdom were the word of the fool. This mediation appears instead to be that of a practical obedience, itself divided between mute submission and open disputation. The Anselmian argument may thus be interpreted as an attempt to reopen on a theoretical and speculative plane the debate that Wisdom—at least that expressed in the book of Job—seems to have led to a dead end. But the price to pay for this audacious enterprise seems to be the following. For the relational conception of God, with all its dramatic implications, is substituted an abstract concept in which the predicates of supereminence, which are alone retained from the predicative naming of God, find themselves dissociated from the counterpoint of a perhaps incomplete creation, or in any case from a creation marked by the persistence of evil. An inconclusive dialectic, scanned by the alternation of praise and lamentation, thus finds itself broken in the excess of the cry: "how long, Jahweh, will you forget me? To what end?" (Ps. 13:2) an excess that exceeds itself only in the words of the fool: "No more God!" (Ps. 14:1).

NOTES

1. *"Fides Quaerens Intellectum*: Biblical Antecedents?" in *The Honeycomb of the World: Interpreting the Primary Testament with André LaCocque*, ed. W. Dow Edgerton (Chicago: Exploration Press, 2001), 179–208. Reprinted with permission from the publisher.

2. My position is close to that of Eberhard Junge!, *God as the Mystery of the World: On the Foundation of the Theology of the Crucified One in the Dispute Between Theism and Atheism,* trans. Darrell L. Guder (Grand Rapids: Eerdmans, 1983).

3. *St. Anselm: Basic Writings,* trans. S. N. Deane (LaSalle, Illinois: Open Court, 1% 2), 7.

4. See Anselme de Canterbury, *Oeuvres,* vol. 1: *Monologion, Prosologion,* trans. Michel Corbin, S.J. (Paris: Cerf, 1986), 15.

5. St. Anselm: Basic Writings, p. 1.

6. Ibid.

7. Corbin indicates this work of the concept in what he designates as the second name: "thou concerning whom nothing better can be thought." See his introduction to his translation of the *Prosolgion* in *Anselme de Canterbury,* 209–24.

8. Corbin takes chapters *XN* and XV of the *Proslogion* to be "the geometrical center of this work" (Ibid., 209).

9. *St. Anselm: Basic Writings,* 7.

10. Ibid.

11. In the language of Boetius, which Anselm draws upon, an argument is a proposition "capable of deciding among the alternatives that are born from the diversity of human opinions" *(Anselme de Canterbury,* 210).

12. *St. Anselm: Basic Writings,* 20

13. Walter Zimmerli, "Ich bin Jahwe," in *Gottes Offenbarung,* edited by Walter Zimmerli (Munich: Kaiser, 1963), 11–40. See also Karl Elliger, "Ich bin der Herr— euer Gott," in *Theologie als Glabenswagnis* (Hamburg: Furche, 1954), 9–34. According to Zimmerli, "Des lch Jahwes wird aus dem Munde J. selber horbar gemacht." It does not matter for us that, from a historical point of view, the self-presentation, which we read in a written text, should take the place of an oral self-presentation, included in some regular ritual, where God would have taken the voice of a priest as his spokesperson, or where, to put it another way, the priest would have spoken in the name of Jahweh. For a canonical reading, such as that of Brevard Childs, *Introduction to the Old Testament as Scripture* (Philadelphia: Fortress Press, 1979), which I shall

return to below, all that matters are that the texts have been received into the canon, with the signification they receive from being located therein.

14. Another text, which exegesis attributes to the Priestly source (P) can be also be cited in this context, Exodus 6:2.: "God also spoke to Moses and said to him: 'I [am] Jahweh. I made my self manifest to Abraham, Isaac, and Jacob under the name El Shadda, but I did not make myself known to them under my name Jahweh.'"

15. From the point of view of the literary structure, someone is recounting what Moses said: "Hear, O Israel." The well-known "Jahweh is one" is pronounced, in the third person, as the content of this injunction. Next comes, in the imperative mode, the ethical tenor of this proclamation: "You shall love Jahweh, your God. . ."

16. This bipolarity (proclamation of oneness/ commandment to love) is strongly emphasized in Raymond Brown's commentary on the Exodus in The *Book of Deuteronomy: Introduction and Commentary* (Collegeville, Minnesota: The Liturgical Press, 1965), 41–43.

17. See also Deuteronomy 11:13–21, Numbers 15:37–41. We may refer here also to Rashi's commentary: "Hear, O Israel, the Lord is our God, the Lord is One." *Commentary:* The Lord who is our God now and not the God of *other* nations, will become the One Lord as it is said in Wisdom 3:9: "then I shall change the tongue of peoples into a pure tongue so that they call upon the Name of the Lord"; and as it is said in Zechariah 14:9: "in that day, the Lord will be One and his Name will be One." YOU SHALL LOVE. Accomplish his words through love. He who acts through love does not resemble the one who acts out of fear. He who serves his master out of fear, when this latter tyrannizes him, will leave his master and go away. *With all your heart:* with your two penchants. Another explanation: let not your heart be divided as regards God. *With all your soul:* even if he takes your life. *With all your might:* with all your money. There are those who love money more than themselves Another explanation: with all the measure by which he measures you, be this a good measure or one that chastises. And thus David said (Ps. 116:13 and 3): "I shall lift up the cup of salvation. If I suffer distress and anguish, I shall call on the name of the Lord." And what is this love? That *his words . . . be* By this means, you can know the Holy, Blessed be He, and take up his ways (from *Commentaire de Rachi au "Pentateuque,"* bad. du rabbinat francais (Paris: Fondation S. Levi, 1975).

18. Etienne Gilson, *L'Esprit de la Philosophie Medievale* (Paris: Vrin, 1954), 50–52. Regarding the philosophical and theological interpretations of Exodus 3:14, see Alain de Libera and Emilie Zurn Brunn, *Celui qui est: interpretations Juives et Chretinennes d'Exode III 14* (Paris: Cerf, 1986); *Dieu et l'Etre, Exegeses d'Exode III, 14 et de Coran* XX, *11–24* (Paris: Etudes Augustiniennes, n.d.). See also, D. Bourg et al., *L'Etre et Dieu,* Travaux du C.E.R.I.T. (Paris: Cerf, 1986).

19. Certain exegetes (Zimmerli, Habel, and others) have underscored the structural kinship between the narrative of the call of Moses and other narratives about the call of the prophets (e.g. Jeremiah 1; Judges 6; Isaiah 6). The schema is something like the following: confrontation (here, the burning bush), an introductory speech (here the call: "Moses, Moses" and the response "here I am"), the call properly speaking (here 3:10: "Now go"), then the objection, to which we shall return when we see the trace of a human recalcitrance in the great conversation between God and man. It is to one

of the objections that the "I am the one who am" replies. Finally, comes the word of reassurance (here repeated following the crescendo in Moses' objections).

20. See Brevard Childs, "The Call of Moses," in his *The Book of Exodus: A Critical, Theological Commentary* (Philadelphia: Westminster, 1974), 47–89.

21. Werner H. Schmidt, *Der Iawename und Ex. III 14,* places the accent of his exegesis on the progressive construction of the name Jahweh, which, we ought not to forget, becomes the *Rufnahme,* "the name I shall bear forever, by which you will call on me in future generations" (3:15). If we follow this exegetical line, 3:14 gives the meaning of the name Jahweh, by describing the third person in terms of the first person.

22. Enigmas are not lacking even in the immediate context. Why is this question about God's name lent to the people? Have they forgotten the God of the fathers, or is he nameless? Are they seeking a new Name or meaning? And, if this is the case, in what way does this validate Moses'' mission? What is more, we have emphasized the threefold "I am." But the third occurrence provides the occasion for a substitution, the Tetragrammaton taking the place of the "I am" previously placed in the position of the grammatical subject of the verb "to send." Ought we then to go so far as to say that the series of "I am" s is there in order to prepare for the announcement of the Tetragrammaton, thanks to the grammatical kinship between the "I am" and a "he is" implied in one of the attested etymologies for the term Jahweh, which would be the verb "being" in the third person of the "incomplete" singular?

23. That an ontology distinct from the function of authentification could have been grafted to Exodus 3:14 is easy to understand. But this is just one interpretive path among others. Do we not read in second Isaiah 43:12-13: "and I am God, from eternity I am"? Childs suggests that the "ontological overtones" (83) virtually present in the formula of Exodus 3:14 may have found an initial expansion (which I would call proto-ontological) in the formula of Revelation 1:8, "he is, he was, and he is to come," and that this declaration could serve in tum as a bridge toward the Septuagint translation, which was already an interpretation and a creation of meaning. Philo, *Vita Moses,* 1.75, could be placed along this trajectory: "Say to them that I am the one who is, and that they can learn the difference between what is and what is not and . . .furthermore that no name can be properly applied to me to whom alone belongs existence." Here it is existence, by a kind of recoil effect, that renders the Name ineffable.

24. Zimmerli observes that the exclusive character of the possessive relation "your God" is opened by Ezekiel among others to the other nations: "You will recognize that I am Jahweh. The peoples will recognize that I am your God" (Ezek. 38:23). As Zimmerli says, the brief *Selbsvorstellung* formula ("I am Yahweh"), through its very development, calls for an *Erkenntnisaussage* on the side of its human counterpart taken as a whole.

25. Robert Alter, *The Art of Biblical Narrative* (New York: Basic Books, 1983).

26. See Jon D. Levenson, *Creation and the Persistence of Evil: The Jewish Drama of Divine Omnipotence* (San Francisco: Harper and Row, 1985).

27. The first objection is still an objection of a lack of adequacy: who am I to undertake such a mission? The second, to which the "I am who am" responds, takes

an oblique tum: if the children of Israel ask what is his name, what shall I answer them? The third takes as its pretext the people's possible nonrecognition of the one sent: "if they refuse to believe me and to listen to me and if they say: did Jahweh appear to you?" In other words, if they take me for a false prophet? The great contest between the prophets of Jahweh and those of Baal in the book of Kings comes to mind. In Exodus, the miracle of the staff that becomes a serpent for a brief moment, and then that of the leprous hand that becomes healthy again do not end the argument. There comes a fourth objection: "I am slow of speech and slow of tongue." The response to this is an affirmation of sovereignty that brings to mind the answers given in the book of Job: "who gave man a mouth with which to speak?" Then a fifth objection: "send someone else for this mission," which anticipates the defection of Jonah, fleeing in the opposite direction. And what do we read here? "Then Jahweh was angry with Moses." *As* for the splitting of the role between Moses and Aaron, which seems to put an end to the argument, this is heavy with future threats if one knows the episode of the golden calf that will divide Moses and Aaron.

28. I shall leave aside here any discussion bearing on the chronological priority of the preaching of the savior God over that of the creator God. This question has returned to prominence recently with the overthrowing of the chronology based on the classical theory of four sources. The only fixed point, it seems, is the proclamation of second Isaiah: only a God who created all things can change the course of history to the benefit of his captive people and thereby set the history of salvation into motion once again.

29. What follows owes much to the work of Levenson cited above.

30. Levenson notes that the Hebrew Bible does not know the notion of *creatio ex nihilo,* in the sense that was subsequently applied by Jewish, Christian, and Muslim theologians. In the first place, the Bible bears the traces, principally in Psalms and in Job, of myths similar to those of Babylon and Ugarit, where God fights against uncreated primordial powers, principally sea monsters. God comes out the winner, but chaos subsists. In this respect, the flood narrative, as a narrative of de-creation and re-creation, constitutes a valuable testimony concerning, on the one hand, the vulnerability of order, and, on the other hand, the connection between this order and the covenant. God's faithfulness, in promising never to destroy his creation again, turns out to be the sole guarantee of order. Creation has become a corollary of the covenant. Psalm 104 gives an account of an intermediary stage between creation as combat and the creation with no opposition of Genesis 1. This is not a narrative, but rather the panorama of the splendors of creation. The abyss still appears as menacing, but Leviathan appears as a work that "you form for your laughter" (v. 26). Creation, as in Job 38, consists of containing chaos within assigned limits, according to calculated measures. As for the narrative in Genesis 1, if chaos seems to be docile concerning the order that is impressed upon it, following the mode of divisions and successive apportionings, nothing says that it is not primordial, as perhaps the shadows that the creative work makes alternate with the day convey. Levenson is perhaps correct to emphasize that the "rest" of the seventh day, in founding and sanctifying the sabbath, provides a human counterpart to the divine sabbath. And the sabbath itself is only a respite in the sequence of works and days, a liturgical pause where the contrast with

bad times is once again underscored. Levenson boldly places his exegesis of the creation narratives under the sign of the subsequent speculations of certain Talmudists and of the Kabbala (38). We might ask whether this idea of an incomplete creation and perhaps, by a kind of recoil effect, of a God who is not yet God does not find an unexpected echo in the philosophy of Alfred North Whitehead.

31. See Levenson, p. 38.

32. What follows, of course, is: "Abraham continued: 'I am a fool to speak to my Lord, I who am dust and ashes. But perhaps of the fifty righteous, five are lacking. Will you, for the lack of five, make the whole city perish?' He answered, No, if forty five righteous are to be found there." Abraham spoke up again and said: "Suppose there are only forty." And he answered: "I shall not do so, due to the forty." From forty, Abraham passes to thirty, then to twenty, then to ten: "Let my Lord not become angry and I shall speak one last time: suppose there are ten to be found" and he answered: "I shall not destroy them, due to the ten" (Gen. 18:27-32). Levenson underscores the paradox so well indicated by Abraham's embarrassment ("I am a fool to speak to my Lord, I who am dust and ashes")—the paradox of a situation where it becomes both necessary and absurd to tell God what he ought to do.

33. The paradox referred to in the previous note is redoubled if we oppose to this episode of Abraham's pleading that of the binding of Isaac, where Abraham urges submission to the divine command ("Here am I" is pronounced two times!) to the point of being ready to sacrifice his son as a burnt offering. Genesis in reporting this scene, so often interpreted in literature and in works of art, puts it under the theme of the "test" (22:1). The end of this episode confirms this: "I now know that you fear God; you have not refused me your son, your only son" (22:12). Bringing these two episodes which have to do with the same character together, Levenson sees in them the two poles of the Jewish attitude to God: one forbids judging the inscrutable God, the other is not afraid to argue with him. This spiritual dialectic, Levenson thinks, results from the nature of the covenental relation, where the consent of the contracting human being is both preserved and surpassed. It is this same spiritual dialectic that unfolds its variations in the narrative, legislative, and cosmogonic texts. Here is confirmed the idea put forth above that the myth of a combat at the origin of creation, in making room for the persistence of evil, indicates at the same time a space of obedience for human beings, where they express their collaboration in the creation.

34. See Levenson, p. 155.

35. After Jahweh's second discourse, which shows Behemoth and Leviathan as submissive to him, Job makes this answer to Jahweh: "I know that you are all powerful: what you conceive, you can realize. I was the one who confused your counsels, by my meaningless proposals. I spoke without understanding of marvels that surpass me and that I am unaware of (Listen, let me speak, I am going to question you and you will instruct me). I knew you only through hearsay, but now my eyes have seen you. I take back my words, I repent with dust and with ashes" (42:1-6). The book of Job seems to be a result of the fact that the Hebrew Bible leaves argumentation and obedience juxtaposed (Levenson, 148–56).

Afterword

Continuing Conversations with Paul Ricoeur

Joseph A. Edelheit and James F. Moore

We agreed that this volume would both contain the original title and go beyond in order to prompt the readers to sustain their engagement with Paul Ricoeur. *Refiguring the Sacred: Conversations with Paul Ricoeur* is intended to offer a generational "companion" to Mark Wallace's original collection *Figuring the Sacred: Religion, Narrative and Imagination*, 1995.

The three editors—Joseph Edelheit, James F. Moore, and Mark Wallace—all studied with Ricoeur at the Divinity School; each shared in personal conversations as well as learned from the many conversations they experienced in the courses from Ricoeur and others. Two of the participants, George Taylor and Steven Kepnes, also were students with Ricoeur at the Divinity School and each offered essays that continue their work, and the conversations anchored in their relationships with Ricoeur. Dan Stiver, a past president of the Society of Ricoeur Studies and co-editor of the Studies in the Thought of Paul Ricoeur from Lexington Press, of which this project will belong, has been translating his Baptist faith and role as a philosopher and seminary faculty through Paul Ricoeur most of his career. Stephanie Arel, a past president of the SRS and a feminist scholar who works in Trauma Studies, and Timo Helenius, a Finnish Lutheran Bishop and leader of European Ricoeur scholarship, represent the new generation whose conversations with Ricoeur's ideas, texts, and scholarship added new generational depth to the project.

Our subtitle, "Conversations with Paul Ricoeur," is the essential thread which sustains all of the generations who are engaged in the texts, ideas, and values of this unique thinker. These conversations are all anchored in the unique engagement of the Text, and as such the Introduction argues that the founding generation of "Rabbinic Sages" provide an interesting point of comparison to Ricoeur, because both share a commitment to the Sacred in their pursuit of meaning from the Text. The founding rabbinic generation of interpreters of biblical texts produced the laws, rituals, ethics, and theology which would become the "Oral Law," post-biblical Judaism. Again, Abraham Joshua Heschel's insights into Rabbi Akiba echo Paul Ricoeur's unique role as a religious thinker and continental philosopher.

> The assumption that the Oral Teaching is inherent in the Bible was Rabbi Akiba's seminal thought. Through the virtuosic artistry of his interpretations, he was able to discover the one inside the other. To a certain degree he altered the very texture of the Bible: the frozen words began to thaw, to flow, and alongside the explicit readings, unsuspected meanings and intuited traditions bubbled forth. He had a new relationship to the Bible. He sensed that its words are containers for undivulged teachings, that the Torah is full of signs and hints. His goal was to fathom these signs and to interpret them, revealing new layers of the Bible. The astonishing dimensions that were exposed by this powerful expansion excited the attention of his contemporaries.[1]

We find within the textual remnants *Dvar Acher*, a Rabbinic Hebrew idiom which illuminates the unique oral/aural realities of the dynamic institutions that produced both Midrash and Halacha between the second CE to the fifth CE. The rabbis studied, argued, interpreted, and studied more, and during their engagement of explanations and understandings of a text, all in the dynamic of the aural/oral, someone uses a previous statement, adding a new idea and continues the conversation, expanding upon the already developed interpretations. *Dvar Acher* is the idiom used in the written texts of those original ancient oral conversations; it means another commentary, another idea, or another interpretation. I use it to conclude our project, in order to both prompt and offer *another conversation.*

Mark Wallace concludes his essay with a reflection on Paul Ricoeur, Elie Wiesel, and Evil. This prompts my engagement: *Dvar Acher!* Paul Ricoeur's use of Elie Wiesel's understanding of Evil reminds me of when Paul Ricoeur came to Emanuel Congregation in May 1989 to offer a sermon, "The Memory of Suffering," an essay included in *Figuring the Sacred*. In the opening paragraph, Ricoeur teaches that the Holy is being present, being engaged in the conversation:

> Rabbi Joseph A. Edelheit invited me a few months ago to join your congregational memorial to "the six million" on this Shabbat evening. I am eager to express my deep gratitude for this very moving invitation. I take it as a testimony that, beyond authentic friendship, your rabbi knew quite well that I consider myself as one of the innumerable recipients of the promise bestowed upon Abraham: "I will bless those who bless you and him who curses you, I will curse; and by you all the families of the earth shall bless themselves."[2]

Paul Ricoeur came to the synagogue because of his relationship with the rabbi, his student, his friend, and most significantly with his conversation partner! He accepted the invitation because he understands himself to be "one of the innumerable recipients of the promise bestowed upon Abraham," a Protestant Christian who links themselves through Scripture to the blessings of the past and the not-yet-fulfilled blessings of Salvation. Paul Ricoeur's sermon is his participation in the Holy, his presence in multiple relationships each of which prompts and provokes conversations which each require reflection, readings, and then more reflection in response. He concludes with the continuation of these relationships and conversations already in mind:

> We wondered at the beginning whether the call of Moses to remembrance-which is related to the gift of the Torah and to the liberation from "the house of bondage"-and our pious commemoration of the victims of the Shoah were two radically different expressions of memory. The answer, it seems to me, is no. Lamentation needs memory as much as praise does. We remember "the six million" with all the more dedication.[3]

The sacred burden and responsibility of memory are not just for survivors and Jews but for persons like Paul Ricoeur, who embrace the Salvific promise of the biblical texts of liberation, praise, and lamentation. In order to model Ricoeur's values, we sustain our pursuit of meaning, our commitment to the conversations with reference to our contributors' insights.

Steve Kepnes continues his conversations with his teacher with "Paul Ricoeur's Biblical Theology and Jewish Theology."

> "for the text and its rhetoric and literary devices along with his appreciation of multiple and changing interpretations, Ricoeur's Biblical hermeneutics comes close to Jewish hermeneutics. And since his investigations into the Biblical text and its interpretations culminate in some rather surprising and perceptive theological insights, insights that are not necessarily dependent on the New Testament and Christianity, I believe he has much to teach those of us who are interested in Jewish theology and specifically in a Biblical Jewish Theology. . . . What Ricoeur takes away from the Bible and attending to the specifics and particularities of Biblical literature is a rich interchange between the Biblical text, the moral person and God. The Bible presents us with a triangular relationship which Franz Rosenzweig describe as God, World, Person. The Bible tells the stories of people who exist in rich relationship to others, to society, and to God. *(Kepnes from this volume)*

Kepnes is unequivocal in his affirmation that Ricoeur's relationship with Scripture is an affirmation of his lifelong engagement with Jewish life. Interfaith dialogue was not an additional aspect of Ricoeur's personal or academic life; rather, it is an essential religious value of his faith.

Before offering his sermon, "The Memory of Suffering," Paul Ricoeur shared the Sabbath meal at the rabbi's home with his longtime friend Andre LaCocque, with whom he would write the award-winning text *Thinking Biblically: Exegetical and Hermeneutical Studies.* LaCocque invokes his dialogue partner: "Paul Ricoeur, a man endowed with remarkable humility, acknowledged coming second to the people of Israel, and he was always grateful for this shared privilege."[4] The value of dialogue in Ricoeur's work is especially important today, so Steven Kepnes' work stimulates a renewal.

George Taylor illuminates Ricoeur's important work on religious imagination, referencing the essay, "Philosophy and Religious Language" in *Figuring the Sacred.* "I restrict myself to the wager that despite criticisms in the secondary literature that Ricoeur makes religious imagination too much subordinate to the poetic imagination, in fact understanding the religious imagination in relation to the poetic imagination deepens rather than reduces the meaning of the religious imagination." *(Taylor in this volume).*

> For Ricoeur, the interconnection between the imagination in biblical resources and the imagination of interpretation begins in the biblical text itself. Biblical meaning is inseparable from the forms in which it appears.[5] Ricoeur has been particularly acute in this assessment. We must comprehend that biblical language is composed of "speech acts"—"invocation, worship, lamentation, disputation"—rhetorical tropes—"metaphor, metonymy, synecdoche, irony"—and literary genres—"narrative, law, prophecy, hymn, wisdom sayings."[6] Attention to these forms returns us, at a deepened level, to the nature of the biblical text as poetic, with a productive imaginative capacity, a capacity that in turn calls for interpretation.[7] . . . Due to the nature of textual mediation, in Ricoeur's view, the world of the text, including the religious text, is the proposal of a world, a proposal that is *as if.* The text configures a meaning, and a reader or interpreter refigures it. *(Taylor in this volume)*

Taylor, an important interpreter of Ricoeur's work, emphasizes the ongoing essential engagement of every Ricoeur student and teacher. We are all "refiguring" the texts in our continual conversations. The clarity of this argument underlines the title of this project, *Refiguring the Sacred,* our collective participation for the purpose of continued conversations which in turn are meant to stimulate still more study, reflection, and further conversations.

Dan Stiver continues the conversation about Ricoeur's important work in "praxis" by reading the original essays in *Figuring the Sacred* through the lens of the past nearly thirty years.

> Ultimately, hermeneutical, holistic practical wisdom (phronetic thinking) is needed in a situation to bring all of the elements together. Building the bridge of judgment between the poetics of love and the prose of justice thus requires a high level of creativity, imagination, and wisdom. . . . One can add to the need

for practical wisdom the dynamics of Ricoeur's later emphasis on the self as both capable and limited, as faced with possibility and yet constraints, as creative but also suffering. . . . The practical wisdom that thus founds the development of a practical theology is a practical poetics but one also haunted by the specters of embodied ideology, trauma, and tragedy. This wisdom is a religious bridge between prose, poetics, and praxis, but one where repairs are often made while in traffic, swaying in the wind. In the end, it is a practical wisdom backed up by one's whole life of faith. No one can escape this. *(Stiver in this volume)*

Ricoeur's engagement with the Sacred is a significant illustration of his demand that we "act" not merely think about. Stiver's emphasis on the "religious bridge" reaffirms both the thought and public roles and responsibilities that Ricoeur accepted throughout his career.

Timo Helenius and Stephanie Arel represent a new generation of Ricoeur scholars, each adding their own unique role and identity in teaching Ricoeur through very different experiences. Timo's reading of Ricoeur's biblical thought is both significantly academic and intentionally accessible for the community:

Both an individual and a community, Ricoeur argues, gain an understanding of their respective identities by taking a detour through culture in which their identities are manifested and objectified in such a way that a person's or a community's existence can be appropriated in reflecting upon those cultural works that narrate the mute but experienced life. The self, both individual and communal, is formed "in front of the text" or by the cultural means that allow for their "reading" in such manner that the self can be identified in the very act and process of reading. This also means that Ricoeur's hermeneutics is not purely a personalist kind and his commentary on the canon is an exemplary for the very point that could well be made of any other literary composition that in some manner has served and serves some human community: "The biblical world has aspects that are cosmic (it is a creation), communal (it involves a people), historicocultural (in concerns Israel, the kingdom of God), as well as personal." . . . A reader is one who responds . . . "to a call in the sense of conforming to the conception of existence it proposes." As Ricoeur explains it, "this call does not come from philosophy but from the Word, harbored in scripture and transmitted by the tradition and interpretive traditions issuing from these writings." *(Helenius from this volume)*

Timo Helenius sustains Ricoeur's inherent commitment to Scripture as the primary text through which all of his thought began and was sustained. This is a conversation that must continue if the presence of Paul Ricoeur is truly to be honored and cultivated.

Stephanie Arel's most recent work, *Bearing Witness: The Wounds of Mass Trauma at Memorial Museums*, is an example of her Ricoeur scholarship being translated through one of the newest multidisciplinary disciplines.

Her contribution on hope is a significant example of twenty-first -century Ricoeurian engagement.

> Hope is practical engagement on the path toward the good "which is not some-thing to be grasped intellectually, nor is it a static goal or achievement" but manifests in one's temporal existence. Ricoeur further draws on Kierkegaard: "hope makes of freedom the passion for the possible against the sad mediation of the irrevocable." The passion for the possible serves as a synonym for hope. Hope implies no illusion; life is not the contrary of death, but its denial, super-abundance or the excess of sense exceeds non-sense. In this latter construction, Ricoeur unites, "the logical, the ethical, the existential, and the religious aspects of meaning and meaninglessness in life." *(Arel from this volume)*

Arel's analysis of Ricoeur scholarship leads her to challenge the past from within the immediate reality of today's traumatic universe.

> I want to pause here and note that my concern is the ability to access hope in the face of despair, and in the face of trauma. Ricoeur's theory sits useless before a child who watches horror before her or endures wounding daily, not statistically an exceptional situation. These words are for the survivor who car-ries a sense of worthlessness as a result of human betrayal, a worthlessness that emerges from the double edge sword of trauma which inspires both terror and helplessness. If trauma of human betrayal can be framed as evil, then, it adds the important element of "The theme of radical evil plays here the same role as that of transcendental illusion in the speculative philosophy; it adds a practical despair to theoretical despair. This twofold despair is the reverse side of hope." *(Arel from this volume)*

Refiguring the Sacred: Conversations with Paul Ricoeur offers its readers and the community at large a diverse platform of new ideas all deeply rooted in the ideas, texts, and model of Paul Ricoeur. Each participant in this vol-ume brings their personal and professional gratitude for the conversations they have had both in person and in textual presence; this volume now con-cludes with the solemn urging that Paul Ricoeur's life of thought was Sacred because the conversation never ended.

Thus, we offer two additional essays from Ricoeur as an indication not that this finishes the conversation but rather that this indicates how the pos-sibilities for further thinking and interaction are never-ending. Of course, the essays previously published are only part of Ricoeur's reflections on the themes found in the essays. His comment on Anselm connects with the essay in *Figuring the Sacred* on "Naming God." In addition, the essay *"Fides Quaerens Intellectum"* clearly connects with the whole tradition of "faith seeking understanding." The essay "The Self in the Mirror of the

Scripture" is obviously linked to his ongoing reflections on the self. What this means is that these two essays only open up still more conversations and beg for others to offer comments on the meaning of Ricoeur's thought for today. The point is not to focus on Ricoeur but rather to take his lead in forming new directions of thought and new partners in conversation with Paul Ricoeur.

NOTES

1. Heschel, Abraham Joshua. *In This Hour: Heschel's Writings in Nazi Germany and London Exile* (p. xxvii). The Jewish Publication Society. Kindle Edition.

2. Paul Ricoeur. "The Memory of Suffering" *Figuring the Sacred: Religion, Narrative and Imagination* (Kindle Locations 4209–4212). Kindle Edition.

3. Ibid. Kindle Locations (4209–4212). Kindle Edition.

4. Andre LaCocque, "Reading Scripture with Paul Ricoeur: Homage," *Reading Scripture with Paul Ricoeur*, Joseph Edelheit and James Moore, ed. (Lanham, MD: Lexington Books, 2021), p. 17.

5. Paul Ricoeur, "Philosophical Hermeneutics and Biblical Hermeneutics," in *From Text to Action*, 90.

6. Paul Ricoeur, "From One Testament to the Other," trans. Barnabas Aspray, *Modern Theology* 33, no. 2 (April 2017): 240–41. Ricoeur also attends to these dimensions of religious discourses in the opening pages of "Philosophy and Religious Language," which we have not previously referenced. Ricoeur, "Philosophy and Religious Language," 35–36.

7. Ricoeur, "Biblical Hermeneutics," *Semeia* 4 (1975): 32.

BIBLIOGRAPHY

Heschel, Abraham Joshua. *In This Hour: Heschel's Writings in Nazi Germany and London Exile* (p. xxvii). The Jewish Publication Society. Kindle Edition.

LaCocque, Andre. "Reading Scripture with Paul Ricoeur: Homage," *Reading Scripture with Paul Ricoeur*, Joseph Edelheit and James Moore, ed. (Lanham, MD: Lexington Books, 2021).

Ricoeur, Paul. "Biblical Hermeneutics," *Semeia* 4 (1975): 32.

Paul Ricoeur, "From One Testament to the Other," trans. Barnabas Aspray, *Modern Theology* 33, no. 2 (April 2017).

Ricoeur, Paul. "The Memory of Suffering" *Figuring the Sacred: Religion, Narrative and Imagination* (Kindle Locations 4209–4212). Kindle Edition.

Ricoeur, Paul, "Philosophical Hermeneutics and Biblical Hermeneutics," in *From Text to Action*, 90.

Ricoeur, Paul. "Philosophy and Religious Language," *Figuring the Sacred*, Mark Wallace, ed. (Minneapolis: Fortress Press, 1995).

Index

narrative clause, 184
narrative figuration, 94
narrative identities, 99
narrative temporality, 85
narrative theology, 82
narrative theory, 113
narrativization, 81; kerygmatic, 87
Naturwissenschaften, 30
Neh. 8:8, 5
Neo-Thomists, 21
Nicomachean Ethics (Aristotle), 15
Nietzsche, Friedrich, 10, 107, 179, 188
noumenal world, 206
numinous: sacred as, 13; word and, 28

Ogden, Shubert, 21
The Old Testament: Canon, Literature and Theology (Barton), 89
Oneself as Another (Ricoeur), 126, 131, 146–48, 161, 164
ontological argument, 188, 192–93; about God's existence, 150–52; Kant and, 179
onto-theology, 24
opening, 110–11
Oral Law, 4, 202
Oral Torah, 26
Osiander, Andreas, 90
Otto, Rudolf, 13, 15–16, 28

Pannenberg, Wolfhart, 176
parables, 86, 175–76
"The Paradigm of Translation" (Ricoeur), 9
paradoxes, 175
A Passion for the Possible (Treanor and Venema), 47
Peirce, C. S., 31
Pellauer, David, 146
phenomenology, 23, 131
Philosophical Anthropology, 116
"Philosophical Hermeneutics and Biblical Hermeneutics" (Ricoeur), 98
philosophy: faith relation to, 162; of limits, 110

"Philosophy and Religious Language" (Ricoeur), 43–46, 49, 54–56, 204
phronetic judgment, 130
poetic hermeneutics, 44, 46
poetic imagination, 43–46, 61–62
poetics, 204–5; biblical, 169; of imagination, 59; practical theology and, 125–33; reorientation and, 128; of will, 105
Poétique du possible (Kearney), 82
polyphonic unity, 169, 176
polysemy, 169, 172
power: imagination and, 43, 50; interpretation and, 7–8
practical theology, 125–26, 128, 131–32; imagination and, 129; justice and, 130; love and, 130
practical wisdom, 130–32
praxis, 204
priestly narrative of creation, 192
problem of evil, 142–45, 152
proclamation, 23, 27–29
productive imagination, 45–47, 58, 62, 86; types of, 43
prophecy, 170–71
Proslogion, 179–80, 182
protest theology, 156
psycholinguistic, 60–61
PTSD, 115

question and answer schema, 162–63
"Quest of Hope" (Stewart), 111

rabbinic hermeneutics, 4
Rabbinic Judaism, 26
Rawls, John, 125
reader: interpretation and, 31; text in dialogue with, 97–99
reader-response criticism, 97
reconciliation approach, 90
reconfiguration, 95, 99
redescription, 52
refiguration, 95, 164
reflection, 13; as rupture, 112
Reformation, 111, 129

About the Contributors

Stephanie Arel teaches at Fordham University. She was previously an Andrew W. Mellon Fellow at the 9/11 Memorial & Museum and a visiting researcher at New York University. She is the author of *Affect Theory, Shame, and Christian Formation* (2016) and *Bearing Witness: The Wounds of Trauma at Memorial Museums* (2023). She is co-editor of *Post-Traumatic Public Theology* (2016), *Ideology and Utopia in the 21ˢᵗ Century: The Surplus of Meaning in Ricoeur's Conception of the Dialectical Relationship of Ideology and Utopia* (2018), and *Probing Human Dignity: Exploring Thresholds from an Interdisciplinary Perspective* (2024). She has written extensively on Paul Ricoeur and is the past president of the Society for Ricoeur studies (2018–2020).

Joseph A. Edelheit is Emeritus Professor of Religious and Jewish Studies at St. Cloud State University, Minnesota. He has also served as a Reform Rabbi for more than fifty years. He studied with Paul Ricoeur and David Tracy at the Divinity School of the University of Chicago in the 1980s. At that time, he was the Senior Rabbi of Emanuel Congregation in Chicago and invited Paul Ricoeur to give the sermon during the Holocaust Memorial Service. Ricoeur's text, "The Memory of Suffering," was included in *Figuring the Sacred: Religion, Narrative, and Imagination* (1995). Since the beginning of the Society for Ricoeur Studies, he and James F. Moore have offered their Jewish/Christian dialogues. He authored *What Am I Missing? Questions About Being Human* (2020) and the Brazilian Portuguese translation *"O Que Me Esta' Faltando? Questoes Sobre Ser Humano,"* translated by Paulo Geiger, Jaguatirica. He co-edited with James F. Moore, "Reading Scripture with Paul Ricoeur." Recently an article also co-written with James F. Moore, "An Interfaith Dialogue on Paul Ricoeur's Challenge of Tolerance in Our Day," was published in Portugal after this paper was presented in an international

Ricoeur conference. Edelheit was honored as Alumnus of the Year (2021) by the Divinity School of the University of Chicago for his career in Interfaith Dialogue; he was the first Rabbi to be honored by the Divinity School.

Timo Helenius is Permanently Affiliated Associate Professor (Docent) in Philosophy at the University of Turku, Finland. Helenius has taught philosophy and ethics at Boston College, Mount Ida College, the University of New Brunswick Saint John, University of Helsinki, and the University of the Arts Helsinki. Helenius received his PhD in philosophy from Boston College, and he has conducted research at the Department of Religious Studies at Brown University and the Science, Religion, Culture Program at Harvard Divinity School. His many publications in continental philosophy and systematic theology include *Ricoeur, Culture, and Recognition: A Hermeneutic of Cultural Subjectivity.*

Steven Kepnes is Professor of World Religions and Jewish Studies at Colgate University, Hamilton, New York He is the author of eight books including *The Future of Jewish Theology* (2013). He is editor of the *Cambridge Companion to Jewish Theology* (2020).

James F. Moore is Senior Research Professor of Theology at Valparaiso University. He is author of *Sexuality and Marriage* (1987), *Christian Theology After the Shoah: a Re-interpretation of the Passion Narratives* (1993, 2004), *Post Shoah Dialogues* (2004), and *Toward a Dialogical Community* (2004). His essay "Cosmology and Theology: The Re-Emergence of Patriarchy" in *Zygon*, won the 1996 Templeton award for best essay in theology and science. He has also written numerous articles on Christian theology and the Holocaust, and on science and religion, including "The Amazing Mr. Jesus." He has also published essays on teaching about Judaism, the Holocaust, and antisemitism. He is on the editorial board of the Studies in the Shoah series of the University Press of America and the advisory board of the Wyman Institute. He is also on the board of the Center for Advanced Study in Religion and Science and the Executive Board of the Annual Scholars' Conference on the Holocaust the Churches. He also contributed the article on HIV/Aids for *Religion for Religion Past and Present: An Encyclopedia of Theology, Bible and Religious Studies* and contributed an article on Christianity and violence for the *Encyclopedia of Religion and Violence* published in 2011. He has also more recently published "Self-inflicted Wounds: The Fate of the African American Community," co-authored with Prof. Nova Smith. He co-edited with Joseph Edelheit "Reading Scripture with Paul Ricoeur." Recently an article, also co-written with Joseph Edelheit, "An Interfaith Dialogue on Paul Ricoeur's Challenge of Tolerance in Our Day," was published in Portugal after this paper was presented at an international Ricoeur conference.

Dan R. Stiver is Professor of Theology at the Jesse B. Fletcher Seminary, San Antonio, Texas; Cook-Derrick Professor of Theology in the Logsdon School of Theology of Hardin-Simmons University, Abilene, TX (1998–2019); Professor of Christian Philosophy at Southern Baptist Seminary, 1984–1998). His publications include *The Philosophy of Religious Language: Sign, Symbol, and Story* (1996), *Theology after Ricoeur: New Directions in Hermeneutical Theology* (2001), *Life Together in the Way of Jesus Christ: An Introduction to Christian Theology* (2009), and *Ricoeur and Theology* (2012). He was President of the Society for Ricoeur Studies from 2010 to 2012 and is co-editor with Greg Johnson of the Series on the Thought of Paul Ricoeur. He co-edited with Greg Johnson the first book in the series, *Paul Ricoeur and the Task of Political Philosophy*, and with Stephanie Arel, *Ideology and Utopia in the Twenty-First Century: The Surplus of Meaning in Ricoeur's Conception of the Dialectical Relationship of Ideology and Utopia.*

George H. Taylor is Emeritus Professor of Law at the University of Pittsburgh. He specializes in legal hermeneutics and hermeneutics more generally. He studied as a graduate student under Paul Ricoeur, and he is the co-editor of Ricoeur's *Lectures on Imagination* and editor of Ricoeur's *Lectures on Ideology and Utopia*. He has written on Ricoeur extensively.

Mark I. Wallace is James Hormel Professor of Social Justice in the Department of Religion at Swarthmore College. At Swarthmore, he directs the Chester Semester Fellowship, in which college students work alongside Chester, Pennsylvania, city partners in high-value internships focused on education and environmental justice. He has been a visiting professor at the University of Pennsylvania, Princeton Theological Seminary, and Japan International Christian University, and is core faculty for the U.S. State Department's Institutes on Religious Pluralism at Temple University. His books include *When God Was a Bird: Christianity, Animism, and the Re-Enchantment of the World* (2019), awarded the 2019 Nautilus Gold Award for the best book in Western religious thought; *Green Christianity: Five Ways to a Sustainable Future* (2010); *Finding God in the Singing River: Christianity, Spirit, Nature* (2005); *Fragments of the Spirit: Nature, Violence, and the Renewal of Creation* (1996, 2002); and *The Second Naïveté: Barth, Ricoeur, and the New Yale Theology* (1990, 1995). He is also the editor of Paul Ricoeur's *Figuring the Sacred: Religion, Narrative, and Imagination* (1995) and co-editor of *Curing Violence: Essays on René Girard* (1994). His research has been supported by the American Council of Learned Societies, the Andrew W. Mellon Foundation, the Eugene M. Lang Foundation, the American Academy of Religion, and the National Endowment for the Humanities.

Milton Keynes UK
Ingram Content Group UK Ltd.
UKHW011001050724
445177UK00003B/28